W/O
Be a ch...

pop. 310-313 strengths & weaknesses of Buddhism & Christianity
p. 227 - FAQ's
p. 299 - only one way

Buddha and Jesus

Buddha and Jesus:
Could Solomon Be the Missing Link?

R. E. Sherman

First printing: July 2011

ISBN: 978–1461086543
Library of Congress Control Number: 2011910224

Cover Design by Katrina Johanson

Printed in the United States of America

Please visit our website www.buddha-christ.info
For information regarding author interviews, please call 541-821-4238

Table of Contents

Acknowledgments

This book would not have been possible without the love and encouragement of my wife Ann, the support of my research assistant Diane H. Abdo, the insights of my book editor Katherine H. Streckfus and the helpfulness of a Buddhist lama, who shall remain anonymous. I am very grateful to all of them.

R. E. Sherman
July 2011

How many people have provoked this question: not "Who are you?" with respect to name, origin, or ancestry, but "What are you?—what order of being do you belong to, what species do you represent?" Not Caesar, certainly. Not Napoleon, nor even Socrates. Only two, Jesus and Buddha.

—Huston Smith, *The Religions of Man* (1965)

Invitation to the Reader

In the West, I do not think it advisable to follow Buddhism. Changing religions is not like changing professions. Excitement lessens over the years, and soon you are not excited, and then where are you? Homeless inside yourself.

—The Dalai Lama[1]

Why did the Dalai Lama say such startling things? This book offers plausible explanations of interest to anyone who has ever been curious about Buddhism.

Many spiritually hungry people have turned to Buddhism. Most were previously disappointed with Christianity or Judaism. They are drawn by media stories about the Dalai Lama and by accounts of people who have truly found some calm in this hectic world by practicing meditation. Elements in Buddhism that are very similar to Judeo-Christian teachings resonate with them. They think, *Here is a wise, practical path to follow—without the constraint of submitting to an exacting God.*

They desire world peace and compassion for all people, and they want to take an open stand for nonviolence. Buddhism is exotic and inviting. It shuns the violent, materialistic culture of the West. It offers the opportunity to tailor a unique path to becoming a better person, and, ultimately, to attaining enlightenment. Beginning is easy. You choose the kind of meditation that feels good to you, and you select what you will meditate on.

Many begin this way and then become more serious about Buddhism. To their surprise, some things do not feel comfortable. Most likely, these are some of the distinctively Eastern elements of Buddhism. That is why Patrick French, the author of *Tibet, Tibet,* noted: "I was . . . cautioned by the Dalai Lama's own refusal to proselytize. After long observation, he had decided that conversion usually led to confusion, and that without the support of the prevailing culture, it was hard to maintain your spiritual practice."[2] The Dalai Lama has said that "westerners who proceed too quickly to deep meditation should learn more about Eastern traditions and get better training than they usually do. Otherwise, certain physical or mental difficulties appear."[3]

Buddhism has two strongly contrasting sides. One feels Western, or common to all people, and the other, quite Eastern. This book offers a plausible explanation for this: When Buddha was formulating his new religion, he blended the wisdom of the West (from Solomon, who preceded him by four hundred years) with many ways of the East (from Indian detractors to Hinduism). The result was a new "Middle Way."

It is the Western (or common) elements of Buddhism that attract people in the West. After delving more deeply into their adopted religion, they encounter its Eastern elements. Many beginning Buddhists balk at these and begin to pick and choose the aspects of Buddhism they will practice. Yet this cafeteria-style approach to spirituality usually doesn't work very well. So Western Buddha-seekers end up homeless—as the Dalai Lama put it in the quotation above—alienated from the Western traditions in which they were raised, and yet unwilling to adopt the Eastern ways of Buddhism fully.

Patrick French, whose book (*Tibet, Tibet*) includes the first two quotations above, provided this glimpse into his own story of how he came to be "homeless within himself":

> As time passed, some aspects of Tibetan Buddhist teaching remained with me, becoming part of my life, while others faded. I did not anticipate liberation from the cycle of existence, or an end to the experience of desire, however illusory I might know its satisfactions to be. When I had passed through the various stages of learning, inquiry and rejection, I was left with tech-niques of meditation and the philosophy of Buddhism; a way of looking. I felt no need to go through a process of declarative conversion, as you would when joining a revealed religion like Islam or Christianity. Instead I slipped into something near it, avoiding classification, borrowing and incorporating bits of another culture to make my own life easier.[4]

What is missing here is any sense of what Mr. French's choices imply for his future, both here on earth or in whatever hereafter awaits him. He is skeptically living in the now, watching out for self above all else. He became "homeless within himself." He has a lot of company.

You may doubt that the Dalai Lama said the things quoted above. After all, hasn't he spent decades traveling the globe as the world's most visible Buddhist? While this is certainly true, what is not often appreciated is that one of the Dalai Lama's chief objectives has been to serve as a rallying point for the cause of the liberation of Tibet. Portraying Buddhism in the most positive light possible aids him in furthering the cause of the autonomy and welfare of the Tibetan people, for whom he has served as "the temporal and the spiritual leader" for more than half a century.[5]

What if Jesus had given a warning to present-day Christians similar to the Dalai Lama's precautions? He might begin with similar words, such as, "I do not think it advisable to blend my teachings with Western culture." He might then continue with the following warning, which is an excerpt from the Bible:

> Because you say, "I am rich, and have become wealthy, and have need of nothing," and you do not know that you are wretched and miserable and poor and blind and naked, I advise you to buy from Me gold refined by fire so that you may become rich, and white garments so that you may clothe yourself, and that the shame of your nakedness will not be revealed; and eye salve to anoint your eyes so that you may see. Those whom I love, I reprove and discipline; therefore be zealous and repent.[6]

Where to Begin

This book is really two books in one. The first book is Part One, the second, Part Two. The first, entitled "Buddha and Solomon," is summarized in the book's subtitle, "Could Solomon Be the Missing Link?" The second is aptly named, "Buddha and Jesus." To decide where to begin, ask yourself which of these statements better describes your real interests:

"I am more interested in comparing Buddha and Jesus."	"I am more interested in how Buddha and Solomon might be related."
Read Part Two first, starting at Chapter Eleven.	Read Part One first, starting at Chapter One.

If you start with Part One and don't want to work your way through the large number of comparisons of proverbs in Chapters Three through Nine, try jumping ahead to Part Two.

If you are at all acquainted with the wisdom of the Old Testament, as a Jew, as a Christian, or as someone reasonably knowledgeable about these religions, you will find in this book a fascinating and helpful gateway from the wisdom of Solomon to the Western aspects of the path of Buddha.

If you are well acquainted with the Jesus of the New Testament, you will learn much by comparing Buddha and Jesus, side by side, in dozens of key ways. You will also a gain thorough appreciation for the similarities and differences between Buddhism and Christianity.

Let us begin . . .

---

[1] Patrick French, *Tibet, Tibet* (New York: Alfred A. Knopf, 2003), 27.

[2] Ibid., 27.

[3] Mary Garden, "Can Meditation Be Bad for You?" Humanist, September/October 2007, www.thehumanist.org/humanist/MaryGarden.html, retrieved Nov. 22, 2010.

[4] French, *Tibet, Tibet*, 27.

[5] "His Holiness the 14th Dalai Lama of Tibet," www.dalailama.com/, retrieved April 11, 2011.

[6] Revelation 3:17-19, New American Standard Bible (NASB).

Part One: Buddha and Solomon

Chapter One
Buddha: The Solomon of India

Who Buddha was, and how Buddhism came to be, are deep mysteries to most westerners. We have images from Indian legends about Siddhartha Gautama, or "the Buddha" (the "Awakened" or "Enlightened" one), who was born in what is now Nepal in about the sixth century B.C.:

> He was born as a prince in a royal family and, despite being protected from seeing the sufferings of the world, came in the course of his life to see the ravages of old age, sickness, and death. These drove him to investigate whether there was a technique for being liberated from such sufferings, and if there was, how it could be implemented. At age 29 he escaped from the palace, relinquishing the princely robes of his royal line, left the householder life, cut his hair, practiced asceticism for six years to achieve concentrated meditation, and ultimately became enlightened under the Bodhi tree at Bodh Gaya. For 49 days Buddha did not immediately speak about what he had realized but considered who might be suitable to hear about it, and finally decided to teach five disciples the four noble truths. Then, after 45 years of teaching, he displayed the signs of passing away into nirvana at age 81.[1]

Buddha shut out all outside voices and only looked deep within. There, it is said, he found the way to enlightenment. Through his teachings and that of his followers, he became the essential source of truth to hundreds of millions of devotees. That is what statues of Buddha, big and small, symbolize.

This book takes a Western approach to comprehending who Buddha was and what he taught. Rather than seeing Buddha as someone who devoted himself entirely to looking within, it portrays him as a great man who synthesized the ideas of his Indian contemporaries and those of a well-known Western philosopher who predated him by four centuries.

Is it possible that much of the strength and vitality of Buddhism was derived from the ethical foundation and path of spiritual formation detailed by this Western sage? This is a disturbing notion to followers of most Eastern religions and New Agers. It casts uncertainty over a central tenet of most Eastern religions—that the most reliable source of truth lies deep within each person. It was by tapping into that source that Buddha is said to have attained enlightenment and the whole substance of his new religion. To suggest that Buddha may also have drawn on outside sources of greater antiquity may be as troubling to easterners as nontraditional views of Jesus (that deny his divinity) have been to practicing Christians.

What is this surprisingly different portrait of Buddha like? It is very respectful, and yet it sees him very much as a product of his day and of prior wisdom. He was exceptionally brilliant, sensitive, and perceptive. And yet, by four simple steps offered in this book, the reader can start from what is Western and transition to this Buddha. That this is so suggests that Buddhism may have come into being that way. Whether or not this is how it happened, this four-step bridge can be a substantive aid to cross-cultural understanding.

Buddha very ably sized up the great agonies of his day. He lived at a time when India was in enormous turmoil spiritually. Hinduism and its teeming galaxy of gods and priests were being challenged by brave skeptics and independent thinkers with sharply divergent points of view. These spiritual rebels were eager to seize upon a wealth of heretical ideas to undermine India's ruling religious establishment. Buddha was one of their leaders. Historian Will Durant offered this depiction:

> When Buddha grew to manhood he found the halls, the streets, the very woods of northern India ringing with philosophic disputation, mostly of an atheistic and materialistic trend. The later Upanishads and the oldest Buddhist books are full of references to these heretics. A large class of traveling Sophists— the Paribbajaka, or Wanderers—spent the better part of every

year in passing from locality to locality, seeking pupils, or antagonists, in philosophy. . . . Large audiences gathered to hear such lectures and debates; great halls were built to accommodate them; and sometimes princes offered rewards for those who should emerge victorious from these intellectual jousts. It was an age of amazingly free thought, and of a thousand experiments in philosophy.[2]

In contrast to these cynical antagonists, Buddha advocated a constructive way of life that offered liberation from the corruptions, abuses, and onerous caste system of Hinduism. By so doing, he succeeded where many others failed. Buddha attracted a small band of devoted men who gave up everything to follow him. He traveled extensively for forty-five years, teaching and drawing more followers. He remained faithful, through all those years, to his teachings, staying focused on a tight set of essentials. He successfully led a spiritual revolt against a Hinduism that, according to Huston Smith, a preeminent religious studies scholar, "had become a technique for cajoling or coercing innumerable cosmic bellhops to do what you wanted them to do" . . . "Onto this religious scene, bleak, corrupt, defeatist, and irrelevant, matted with superstition and burdened with worn-out rituals," Smith wrote, "Buddha came determined to clear the ground that truth might find purchase and spring again in freshness, strength, and vitality."[3]

To be sure, Buddha was intensely disciplined in his inward-focused meditative practices. Yet this alternative Buddha was open-minded and curious enough to assess and heed the voices of other seekers and great thinkers from foreign cultures. He welcomed wisdom from distant lands and blended it with the best ideas of his fellow heretics. By being teachable and perceptive, he gained an appreciation for what had to be done to avoid the moral pitfalls of other great wise men who had preceded him.

For six years Buddha was part of the predominant resistance movement against the Hinduism of his day. Then he changed and espoused a "Middle Way" between Hinduism and its opponents. This Middle Way strongly corresponded with the wisdom and ethics of a world-famous, non-Indian philosopher who lived four hundred years earlier. Was he a significant source of Buddha's inspiration? There is much to suggest this possibility. This ancient sage was known the world over as a man of peace, tolerance, and wisdom. His pithy sayings were renowned for their great insight and inspiration. He taught his followers to live by his sayings, meditate, and try to lead righteous lives as the path to enlightenment. Though he had become a great king, he grew to despise power, wealth, and all the things of this world. He was not Asian, but was one of the greatest kings of the Middle East. His name was Solomon.

Was it Solomon's ethics and path of spiritual formation that Buddha imported as an antidote to the excesses of Hinduism? Was that infusion of new thought a major contributor to Buddhism's emergence as a major world religion? The addition of Eastern ideas and practices to this Western foundation did not weaken its ethical and spiritual base. In some ways, Eastern practices actually strengthened the Western foundation. Perhaps Buddha saw that the ideas of his fellow rebels could help prevent the moral corruption that characterized Solomon's later years. If only Solomon had embraced the Eastern imperative of renouncing the world's attractions, instead of hoarding women, gold, and horses, he might well have completed his reign with the same exhilarating righteousness he had when he first became king of Israel.

It is very unlikely we will ever know whether Solomon influenced Buddha. However, if we consider that possibility as part of our exploration, we find that it enables us to grasp the thrust of Buddhism much more quickly—to the extent that we are already familiar with Solomon's Proverbs and book of Ecclesiastes. It could also explain why there are so many similarities between Buddha's teachings and those of Jesus: They each had Solomon, and Judaism, as predecessors. Chronology certainly underscores the feasibility of the idea, as the following chart makes clear.

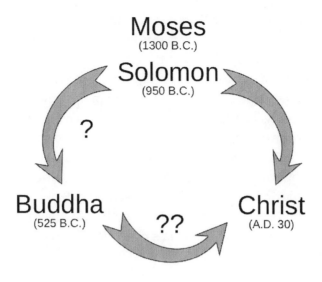

(Illustration notes: Moses[4] and Solomon[5])

The single question mark next to the arrow connecting Solomon to Buddha represents the hypothesis we will investigate in this book. Jesus was a Jewish rabbi who was thoroughly knowledgeable about the Old Testament. There is no reason for a question mark next to the arrow on the right. Buddha was much more similar to Solomon than Jesus was to Buddha. Hence, the twin question marks above the arrow from Buddha to Christ represent the uncertainty about claims of Buddhism influencing Jesus.

In considering whether the Solomon-to-Buddha arrow is reasonable, we have chosen to focus *almost exclusively* on Buddha's earliest sayings as contained in the Dhammapada, a collection of his proverbs compiled by his followers after his death. Later, roughly forty other books appeared that were said to contain his teachings. Examining all of them for Solomon's influence would be a daunting task, even for someone who committed a lifetime to the work. Fortunately, there is no need to search all forty books. If Solomon influenced Buddha, it would be natural for this to be evident in the earliest record of his sayings and teachings. The Dhammapada will therefore be our main source on Buddha's ideas.

Taking the Dhammapada in hand along with Proverbs and Ecclesiastes of the Old Testament, this book will guide the reader through an illuminating tour of the sayings of two of the wisest men in history, laid side by side each step of the way. This comparative excursion will be enriching and stimulating, helping the reader to delve more deeply into each of these gold mines of wisdom.

Spiritually, Buddha was exceptionally advanced for his time, and, many would say, for any time. And yet, virtually all of his ethical teachings are the same as Solomon's. Surprisingly, the proverbs of Buddha are less comprehensive than Solomon's. The topics of women, family, government, and borrowing and lending are virtually untouched in Buddha's proverbs, but well covered in Solomon's. That these voids would exist is predictable, given Buddha's intentional renunciation of his royal position, his wife, his child, and all money. In fact, if you graft Solomon's teachings onto the Jain religion (a resistance movement against Hinduism that arose three hundred years before Buddha), the result is virtually indistinguishable from Buddhism.

Some scholars[6] have tried to substantiate the Buddha-to-Christ arrow, citing important similarities between the religions these two leaders inspired and noting many parallel sets of sayings, such as the following:

Buddha (~ 525 B.C.)	Christ (~ A.D. 30)
Hard it is to understand: By giving away our food, we get more strength; by bestowing clothing on others, we gain more beauty.[7]	Give, and it will be given to you. A good measure, pressed down, shaken together and running over, will be poured into your lap. For with the measure you use, it will be measured to you.[8]

Some Eastern commentators[9] have speculated that Jesus may have journeyed to India before he began his public ministry. Since New Testament accounts provide no information about Jesus' life between the ages of twelve and thirty, similarities such as the one in the example above give this notion some plausibility. Buddhist missionaries lived in Greece at the time of King Ashoka (260–218

B.C.)[10] and in Alexandria, Egypt, during the life of Christ.[11] These are some of the better-known proposed missing links between Buddha and Christ. In spite of many such parallels, Christians often assert that Buddhism is quite different from Christianity. Later in this book, extensive, objective comparisons of a broad range of the beliefs and practices of these two great religions will be presented.

More than centuries would have been needed for the arrows in the figure to represent likely influence if Palestine and India had been truly isolated from one another. In Chapter Two, we will see that a high level of interchange between these lands took place prior to Solomon as well as in the years between Solomon and Buddha. That extensive interchange occurred between the times of Buddha and Christ is well known and undisputed.

Similarities in Sayings

Close parallels of thought and phraseology between Solomon and the young Buddha are pervasive, leaving one to wonder if Solomon's writings influenced Buddha as he formulated his new religion. Consider the following saying of Solomon:

> The path of the righteous is like the first gleam of dawn, shining ever brighter till the full light of day.[12]

Following a path of righteousness in pursuit of enlightenment. . . . Isn't that what Buddhism is about? In hundreds of proverbs, Solomon detailed what was involved in pursuing "the path of the righteous," the same path that is so central to Buddhism. In doing so, Solomon covered virtually every aspect of the essentials of Buddhism, except for a few presumptions of Hindu India (e.g., reincarnation and vegetarianism) that were contrary to Judaism. Solomon also presumed the principle of karma in over two dozen proverbs[13] decades before the Law of Karma became a cornerstone of Hinduism[14] and later of Buddhism. It seems possible that the Hindus adopted this concept from Solomon and modified it by blending in the implications of repeated reincarnation for the inexorable operation of karma.

Undoubtedly, Solomon was influenced by wise sayings from neighboring cultures. He made peace with neighboring empires, marrying hundreds of their women.[15] This gave Solomon's Ecclesiastes a different spiritual flavor from the rest of the Hebrew Bible. He was well acquainted with the beliefs of peoples of nearby countries:

> There is nothing new under the sun. Is there anything of which it may be said, "See, this is new? It has already been in ancient times before us."[16]

In contrast, Buddhists believe something radically new occurred when Buddha became enlightened. From that spiritual plateau came forty-five years of teaching that would forever change much of Asia and impact many in the modern world. If Buddhists are right, then Solomon was wrong. Similarly, Christians tend to view Jesus' teachings as new, even though many of them have strong precedents in Judaism.

Buddha did not derive all of his proverbs from prolonged meditation. One of them is prefaced, "This is *an old saying*, O Atula, this is not only of to-day: "[17] Obviously, this is just one instance. However, in this book I will present more than one hundred close parallels between the proverbs of Buddha and Solomon. Perhaps these pervasive similarities could be simply due to the common struggles of all human beings. Shouldn't any comprehensive set of ethics and philosophy naturally address comparable situations with similar insights and responses? Ultimately, readers will decide for themselves.

The Dhammapada contains 423 of Buddha's proverbs. Many of them seem to be echoes of Solomon's writings in Proverbs and Ecclesiastes. Did Solomon's ideas influence Buddha? In the remainder of this chapter, we will explore seven aspects of spiritual and textual similarities that support this notion.

1. Most of the key emphases of Buddhists are prominent themes in Solomon's writings.

When westerners think of Buddhism, many words come to mind: peace, tolerance, meditation, enlightenment, monks, and secular ethics. The effort to overcome ignorance with wisdom and understanding also comes to mind. All of these were key parts of Solomon's life and writings. Let's look at each of these in turn along with some other recurring themes in Buddha and Solomon.

Peace

Buddhists greatly value peace. The word "Solomon" means peace in Hebrew. Solomon's entire twenty-nine-year reign as king of Israel was an uninterrupted time of peace, in contrast to the frequent wars and internal conflicts that characterized the forty-year reign of Solomon's father, David. How important was this distinction to the God of the Jews? The prophet Nathan told David that God wouldn't let him build a temple because he was a man of blood, but that God's temple would be built by his son, Solomon, a man of peace.[18]

Solomon greatly valued peace. He wrote, "Better one handful with tranquility than two handfuls with toil and chasing after the wind."[19] And he believed that a person could find peace through self-directed mental discipline:

> So then, banish anxiety from your heart and cast off the troubles of your body.[20]

To Buddha, peace was one of the greatest treasures:

> His thought is quiet, quiet are his word and deed, when he has obtained freedom by true knowledge, when he has thus become a quiet man.[21]

Tolerance

Buddhists greatly value tolerance. Solomon was known for stretching tolerance to an extreme. He honored the gods and goddesses worshipped by his seven hundred wives and three hundred concubines,[22] many of whom were not Jewish, often as gestures of peace to surrounding peoples. Each of these practices were in clear violation of the laws of the Torah:[23]

> As Solomon grew old, his wives turned his heart after other gods, and his heart was not fully devoted to the LORD his God, as the heart of David his father had been. He followed Ashtoreth the goddess of the Sidonians, and Molech the detestable god of the Ammonites. So Solomon did evil in the eyes of the LORD; he did not follow the LORD completely, as David his father had done. On a hill east of Jerusalem, Solomon built a high place for Chemosh the detestable god of Moab, and for Molech the detestable god of the Ammonites. *He did the same for all his foreign wives, who burned incense and offered sacrifices to their gods.*[24]

This World as an Illusion

Buddha viewed this world as an illusion. Solomon expressed the same view centuries before him:

> Vapor of vapors and futility of futilities, says the Preacher. Vapor of vapors and futility of futilities! All is vanity (emptiness, falsity, and vainglory).[25]

Suffering

Solomon stressed the pervasive nature of suffering in this life, a central theme of Buddha's proverbs. The following three quotations are from Solomon:

As he came from his mother's womb, naked shall he return, to go as he came; and he shall take nothing from his labor which he may carry away in his hand. And this also is a severe evil—just exactly as he came, so shall he go. And what profit has he who has labored for the wind? All his days he also eats in darkness, and he has much sorrow and sickness and anger.[26]

Again I looked and saw all the oppression that was taking place under the sun: I saw the tears of the oppressed—and they have no comforter; power was on the side of their oppressors—and they have no comforter. And I declared that the dead, who had already died, are happier than the living, who are still alive.[27]

All things are weary with toil and all words are feeble; man cannot utter it. The eye is not satisfied with seeing, nor the ear filled with hearing.[28]

Meditation

Buddhists practice meditation extensively. In Chapter Eight, within the discussion of the eighth step of the Noble Eightfold Path, I cite over a dozen verses referring to meditation that were written prior to Solomon's reign. Meditation was a key part of the practice of Judaism in Solomon's day. In its intended practice, the person who was meditating would become completely fixated on a proverb or a verse of the Torah. This is illustrated in the following:

Let your heart hold fast my words; keep my commandments and live.[29]

My son, keep your father's command, and do not forsake the law of your mother. *Bind them continually upon your heart*; tie them around your neck. When you roam, they will lead you; when you sleep, they will keep you; and when you awake, they will speak with you. For the commandment is a lamp, and the law a light; reproofs of instruction are the way of life.[30]

My son, keep my words and store up my commands within you. Keep my commands and you will live; guard my teachings as the apple of your eye. Bind them on your fingers; write them on the tablet of your heart.[31]

Proverbs were meant to serve as objects of meditation, as is intimated in the following proverb of Solomon:

Eat honey, my son, for it is good; honey from the comb is sweet to your taste. Know also that wisdom is sweet to your soul; if you find it, there is a future hope for you, and your hope will not be cut off.[32]

Overcoming Ignorance with Wisdom

Escaping the woes of ignorance is a goal of utmost importance to Buddhists. Buddha said:

But there is a taint worse than all taints, —ignorance is the greatest taint. O mendicants! throw off that taint, and become taintless![33]

Buddha espoused a way of escaping from ignorance by first gaining wisdom and understanding and then pursuing an intensive regimen of self-effort to progress toward enlightenment. Overcoming ignorance by seeking wisdom and understanding was also critical to Solomon:

Get wisdom! Get understanding! Do not forget, nor turn away from the words of my mouth. Do not forsake her, and she will preserve you; Love her, and she will keep you. Wisdom *is* the principal thing; *Therefore* get wisdom. And in all your getting, get understanding.[34]

Enlightenment

Solomon pursued a path leading to enlightenment:

> The path of the righteous is like the light of dawn, that shines brighter and brighter until the full day.[35]

He advocated a comprehensive range of practices under the general heading of "being righteous." Buddha taught the importance of following eight noble steps of right behavior and motivation. To Solomon, "the prospect of the righteous is joy."[36] For Buddha, "Nirvana [is] the highest happiness."[37]

Monks

Buddhists are known for their gatherings of monks in orange robes. During Solomon's reign, the order of priests (Levites) established by David was very active in maintaining ongoing temple worship and ceremonies. The Bible dictates that priests are to wear special garments ("a breastpiece and an ephod and a robe and a tunic of checkered work, a turban and a sash").[38]

Secular Ethics

A hallmark of Buddhism is its secular ethics. Likewise, God is mentioned in only a small percentage of the verses of Solomon's writings. This is in radical contrast to the writings of Solomon's father, David, where reference to God, either explicitly or implicitly, exists in *nearly every verse* of the seventy-five psalms he wrote. The contrast is very striking. The vast majority of Solomon's proverbs have a very earthly flavor, giving no explicit recognition of the presence or involvement of God in human affairs. Instead, Solomon leaves the reader with the sense that there is some kind of inexorable, universal force, like karma, that causes every person to receive the due consequences of their previous actions.

2. *Every one of the twelve key elements of Buddhism was also expressed, in great detail, in Solomon's writings.*

The twelve key elements of Buddhism are found in the Four Noble Truths and the steps of the Noble Eightfold Path. The content of a high percentage of Buddha's proverbs is very similar, and sometimes almost identical, to specific proverbs of Solomon. By and large, those proverbs that are exceptions to this rule are expressions of Hindu beliefs that clearly differ from Judaism.

In Chapters Three through Nine of this book we will review over one hundred instances where the essence and flavor of a proverb of Buddha is very similar to that of a proverb of Solomon. Below is an example:

Moses (1300 B.C.)	Solomon (950 B.C.)	Buddha (525 B.C.)
The stranger who dwells among you shall be to you as one born among you, and you shall love him as yourself; for you were strangers in the land of Egypt: I am the Lord your God.[39]	If your enemy is hungry, give him bread to eat; and if he is thirsty, give him water to drink.[40]	Hatred does not ever cease in this world by hating, but by love; this is an eternal truth . . . overcome anger by love, overcome evil by good, overcome the miser by giving, overcome the liar by truth.[41]

Often, as in the above comparison, the proverb of Solomon that is similar to one of Buddha's also has a precursor in earlier Old Testament writings. We will see that much of the wisdom of Buddha is much more ancient than he was.

3. Solomon's ways of the "righteous" coincide with Buddha's "right" ways of thinking and acting.

Every one of the steps of Buddha's Noble Eightfold Path consists of "right" ways of thinking and acting—each of which have very close parallels in Solomon's depiction of the ways of the "righteous" and the "upright." This is covered in detail in the Appendix. The following table provides some notable examples.

Right . . .	Precursor in a Proverb of Solomon
View	He who *trusts* in his riches will fall, but the righteous will flourish like the green leaf.[42]
Intention	The *desire* of the [consistently] righteous brings only good, but the expectation of the wicked brings wrath.[43]
Speech	The *lips* of the righteous nourish many, but fools die for lack of judgment.[44]
Action	The sluggard's *craving* will be the death of him, because his hands refuse to work. All day long he craves for more, but the righteous *give* without sparing.[45]
Livelihood	A righteous man cares for the needs of his *animal*, but the kindest acts of the wicked are cruel.[46]
Effort	He who *pursues* righteousness and love finds life, prosperity and honor.[47]
Mindful-ness	. . . an upright man *gives thought* to his ways.[48]
Concen-tration	. . . Guard my teachings as the apple of your eye. Bind them on your fingers; write them on *the tablet of your heart*.[49]

4. Buddha's Five Moral Precepts closely parallel the last five of the Ten Commandments of Moses, a prominent foundation of Judaism.

The first four moral precepts of Buddhism are very close to the sixth through ninth of the Ten Commandments. These precepts are presented in two proverbs of Buddha:

He who destroys life, who speaks untruth, who in this world takes what is not given him, who goes to another man's wife; And the man who gives himself to drinking intoxicating liquors, he, even in this world, digs up his own root.[50]

The Ten Commandments[51]	The Five Moral Precepts of Buddha[52]
6. You shall not murder.	1. Do not kill.
7. You shall not commit adultery.	3. Do not indulge in sexual misconduct.
8. You shall not steal.	2. Do not steal.
9. You shall not give false testimony against your neighbor.	4. Do not make false speech.
10. You shall not covet your neighbor's house. You shall not covet your neighbor's wife, or his manservant or maidservant, his ox or donkey, or anything that belongs to your neighbor.	5. Do not take intoxicants.

The First Precept (do not kill) is much broader than the Sixth Commandment (do not murder). Killing includes taking the life of any sentient (i.e., conscious) being, including animals. The Tenth Commandment (do not covet) is covered in Buddha's Second and Third Noble Truths (desire is the cause of suffering, and to eliminate suffering, one must eliminate desire). The Fifth Precept is covered in some of Solomon's proverbs ("Wine is a mocker and beer a brawler; whoever is led astray by them is not wise"[53]), although other Old Testament references permit moderate drinking that does not involve becoming intoxicated.

5. An ideal that Solomon fulfilled during the earlier part of his reign is clearly described in one of Buddha's proverbs, even though that ideal was highly undesirable according to Buddha's own teachings.

The legend of Solomon is described in general terms in Buddha's 303rd proverb:

> Whatever place a faithful, virtuous, celebrated, and wealthy man chooses, there he is respected.[54]

Why would this proverb be in Buddha's collection? It is much too "establishment" in its message. If its content were true to Buddha's teachings, a person "celebrated and wealthy" would be viewed as someone who has delighted in the illusory pleasures and activities of this world. Even if a wealthy, famous person had managed to be a model of faithfulness and virtue, Buddha would not have revered this person because he or she had not renounced wealth and the status that comes from worldly success and position. This proverb contradicts the core of Buddha's teachings.

On the other hand, this proverb expresses the distilled essence of the legend of Solomon during the early part of his reign. God appeared to Solomon in a dream and told him to ask for whatever he wanted. Solomon very humbly asked only for "a discerning heart to govern your people and to distinguish between right and wrong." He added: "For who is able to govern this great people of yours?" The text continues:

> The Lord was pleased that Solomon had asked for this. So God said to him, "Since you have asked for this and not for long life or wealth for yourself, nor have asked for the death of your enemies but for discernment in administering justice, I will do what you have asked. I will give you a wise and discerning heart, so that there will never have been anyone like you, nor will there ever be. Moreover, I will give you what you have not

asked for—both riches and honor—so that in your lifetime you will have no equal among kings."[55]

Solomon displayed great humility, devotion, and virtue, and God rewarded him with wealth and fame. He was greatly respected during his reign:

> God gave Solomon wisdom and very great insight, and a breadth of understanding as measureless as the sand on the seashore. *Solomon's wisdom was greater than the wisdom of all the men of the East*, and greater than all the wisdom of Egypt. He was wiser than any other man. . . . And his fame spread to all the surrounding nations. *He spoke three thousand proverbs* and his songs numbered a thousand and five. . . . *Men of all nations* came to listen to Solomon's wisdom, sent by *all the kings of the world*, who had heard of his wisdom.[56]

Did Buddha have Solomon in mind when he spoke his 303rd proverb? We can also wonder about two of Buddha's proverbs that advocate hard work and the accumulation of wealth, which are very Solomon-like aspirations,[57] but which totally conflict with Buddha's teachings about the necessity of fulfilling vows of poverty:

> Men who have not observed proper discipline, and have not gained treasure in their youth, perish like old herons in a lake without fish. Men who have not observed proper discipline, and have not gained treasure in their youth, lie, like broken bows, sighing after the past.[58]

Proverbs of Buddha like those quoted above suggest that he was a collector of wise sayings from prior sources and incorporated them into his teachings, even when his other teachings contradicted them.

6. The core and bulk of Buddhism can be nearly replicated by following a four-step process.

The four-step process is as follows: (1) begin with Solomon's writings, excluding references to God; (2) assume reincarnation; (3) renounce the world; and (4) retreat within to insulate yourself from suffering. That this is true may not be a coincidence. It may be a summary of what actually took place in Buddha's mind as he developed his new religion. However, it is not clear proof.

7. Today, a high percentage of Western Buddhist leaders have a Jewish background.

A striking phenomenon today is that a disproportionate percentage of Western Buddhist leaders were once, or still are, Jews. According to one Jewish author:

> A large number of Jews currently practice Buddhism. Rodger Kamenetz, the author of *The Jew in the Lotus*, says, "A third of all Western Buddhist leaders come from Jewish roots." Half of the participants in the Vipassana meditation retreat near Dharamsala, India, are Israelis. According to one estimate, three out of four Western visitors to the spiritual center of Tibetan Buddhism and the seat of the Dalai Lama are Jewish. Most of the street signs in Dharamsala sport Hebrew letters.
>
> A recent cover story of the *Jerusalem Report* profiles three Jews who have been living in Dharamsala for years. . . . In describing his 253 monastic vows, such as dressing modestly and not sharing private space with women, Tenzin Josh remarks, "It's not much different from being an Orthodox Jew."[59]

That Jesus was influenced by Solomon is almost self-evident, for he was a Jewish rabbi well versed in the Old Testament. In fact, Jesus compared himself to Solomon:

25

> The Queen of the South . . . came from the ends of the earth to listen to Solomon's wisdom, and now one greater than Solomon is here.[60]

That Buddha was influenced by Solomon cannot be proven, so it is left to the reader to decide this question. Buddha's words were not committed to writing until 252 B.C., more than 225 years after he died. Instead, his teachings were passed orally from one monk to another. These monks had an enormous devotion to Buddha. Any evidence that some of his insights might have come from some prior sage would have been scorned. If a substantial portion of Buddha's teachings might be attributable to Solomon, we must sketch a very different profile of who he was. This Buddha would be more human and approachable than the Buddha we are used to hearing about. Whether or not he drew from Jewish sources, by noticing the resemblance of Buddha's teachings to prominent sections of the Old Testament, those who are familiar with Solomon's writings will be able to more readily appreciate Buddha's teachings and his historical contribution.

---

[1] His Holiness the Dalai Lama, *Becoming Enlightened*, translated by Jeffrey Hopkins (New York: Simon and Schuster, Atria Books, 2009), 216.

[2] Will Durant, *The Story of Civilization, Part I: Our Oriental Heritage* (New York: Simon and Schuster, 1963), 417–418.

[3] Huston Smith, *The Religions of Man* (New York: Harper and Row, 1965), 104.

[4] Walter A Elwell, ed., *Baker Encyclopedia of the Bible* (Grand Rapids, MI: Baker Book House, 1988), 1:737. A range of dates for the time of the exodus is cited, from 1440 to 1290 b.c.

[5] Ibid., 2:1975. Solomon reigned from 970 to 930 B.C.

[6] E. Washburn Hopkins, *History of Religions* (New York: Macmillan, 1918), 552, 556.

[7] "Buddha and Christ: Two Gods on the Path to Humanity," November 2003, Exotic India, www.exoticindiaart.com/article/buddhaandchrist/, retrieved April 12, 2010.

[8] Luke 6:38, New International Version (NIV).

[9] Swami Abhedananda, *Journey into Kashmir and Tibet*, translated by Kashmiri 0. Tibbate (Calcutta: Ramakrishna Vivekananda Math, 1987).

[10] Burjor Avari, *India: The Ancient Past* (London: Routledge, 2007), 113.

[11] John Brockman, "The Politics of Christianity: A Talk with Elaine Pagels," The Third Culture, July 17, 2003, Edge Foundation, www.edge.org/3rd_culture/pagels03/pagels_index.html, retrieved April 27, 2010.

[12] Proverbs 4:18 (NIV). To save space, line breaks in quotations from the Bible have not been retained.

[13] A typical example is Proverbs 14:11, "The house of the wicked will be destroyed, but the tent of the upright will flourish." (NASB).

[14] Ernest Valea, *The Buddha and the Christ: Reciprocal Views* (Seattle: BookSurge, 2009), 23: "The *Brahmana* writings, which are the first to mention a primitive idea of karma and reincarnation . . . were composed from the 9th century bc (Schumann 2004, p. 29) until about 500 bc (Dasgupta 1975, p. 14)."

[15] 1 Kings 11:3.

[16] Ecclesiastes 1:9–10, New King James Version (NKJV).

[17] Friedrich Max Muller, trans., *The Dhammapada: A Collection of Verses, Being One of the Canonical Works of the Buddhists,* in vol. 10, Part 1, *The Sacred Books of the East,* translated by Various Oriental Scholars, edited by F. Max Muller, available at "Dhammapada (Muller)," Wikisource, http://en.wikisource.org/wiki/Dhammapada_(Muller). This work is cited as "Dhammapada" hereafter. To save space, line breaks in quotations from the Dhammapada have not been retained.

[18] 1 Chronicles 22:7–8.

[19] Ecclesiastes 4:6 (NIV).

[20] Ecclesiastes 11:10a (NIV).

[21] Dhammapada 96.

[22] 1 Kings 11:3.

[23] 1 Kings 11:2.

[24] 1 Kings 11:4–8 (NIV) (emphasis added).

[25] Ecclesiastes 1:2, Amplified (AMP).

[26] Ecclesiastes 5:15–17 (NKJV).

[27] Ecclesiastes 4:1–2 (NIV).

[28] Ecclesiastes 1:8 (AMP).

[29] Proverbs 4:4b (NASB).

[30] Proverbs 6:20–23 (NKJV) (emphasis added).

[31] Proverbs 7:1–3 (NIV) (emphasis added).

[32] Proverbs 24:13–14 (NIV).

[33] Dhammapada 243.

[34] Proverbs 4:5–7 (NKJV).

[35] Proverbs 4:18 (NASB).

[36] Proverbs 10:28a (NIV).

[37] Dhammapada 204b.

[38] Exodus 28:4 (NASB). Additional details appear in Exodus 28:31–43.

[39] Leviticus 19:34 (NKJV).

[40] Proverbs 25:21 (NKJV).

[41] "Buddha and Christ: Two Gods on the Path to Humanity."

[42] Proverbs 11:28 (NASB) (emphasis added).

[43] Proverbs 11:23 (AMP) (emphasis added).

[44] Proverbs 10:21 (NIV) (emphasis added).

[45] Proverbs 21:25–26 (NIV) (emphasis added).

[46] Proverbs 12:10 (NIV) (emphasis added).

[47] Proverbs 21:21 (NIV) (emphasis added).

[48] Proverbs 21:29b (NIV) (emphasis added).

[49] Proverbs 7:2b–3 (NIV) (emphasis added).

[50] Dhammapada 246–247.

[51] Exodus 20:13–17 (NIV).

[52] Alan Khoo, "Leading a Buddhist Life and the Five Precepts," Buddhism Fundamentals, http://web.singnet.com.sg/~alankhoo/Precepts.htm, retrieved April 12, 2010.

[53] Proverbs 20:1 (NIV). See also Proverbs 21:17, 23:20–21 and 23:31–34.

[54] Dhammapada 303.

[55] 1 Kings 3:9b–13 (NIV).

[56] 1 Kings 4:29–34 (NIV) (emphasis added).

[57] For example, see Proverbs 6:6–11, 24:30–34, and 28:19 ("He who tills his land will have plenty of bread, but he who follows frivolity will have poverty enough!") (NKJV).

[58] Dhammapada 155–156.

[59] Sara Yoheved Rigler, "Difference Between Judaism and Buddhism," SimpleToRemember.com: Judaism Online, www.simpletoremember.com/articles/a/buddhismjudaism/, retrieved July 27, 2010.

[60] Matthew 12:42 (NIV).

Chapter Two
The Middle Way

Do not be excessively righteous and do not be overly wise. Why should you ruin yourself? Do not be excessively wicked and do not be a fool. Why should you die before your time?

—Solomon[1]

From the beginning Buddha's new religion was called "the Middle Way" because it avoided two extremes:

- A Hinduism that enabled those with means to obtain whatever they wanted by offering sacrifices to whichever god would condone or encourage it.
- A Jainism that required its ascetic practitioners to live in abject poverty, begging for every meal, owning nothing but a robe and sandals, and facing starvation and overexposure to the elements while they meditated continually in a search for inner truth.

Buddha was repelled by Hinduism's galaxy of deities, and he became disillusioned with extreme self-denial after practicing Jainism for six years. His new path would be secular. It must be reasonable, not fanatical, in taming the self. Given this frame of mind, the thorough system of secular ethics Solomon laid out in his proverbs would have been a solid foundation upon which Buddha could construct key facets of his new religion.

Importing the system of secular ethics of a well-known, respected sage from a foreign land far from India could have been an appealing choice for Buddha. The Shramana movement of Jainism was too focused on negatives—on passive rebellion against the predominant belief system—rather than on embracing something different as a positive alternative. Secular Judaism was an available alternative, and it would have been very natural for Buddha to have used it as a source of inspiration for his "Middle

Way" between ethically free-wheeling Hinduism and the radical asceticism of the Jains.

Hinduism and Jainism were diametrically opposed in numerous ways. Consider an extreme contrast: Hindu tantric sexuality versus Jain celibacy. Some Hindus engaged in tantric rituals involving intense, promiscuous sexuality, which they regarded as sacred.[2] As an utter opposite, most Jains were total ascetics, vowing lifetime chastity[3] as part of their withdrawal from the world in search of purity and truth. Buddha would have seen Judaic ethics about sex as a realistic middle ground between these two extremes. Get married; enjoy sex with your spouse; and be committed to only having sex with your spouse. That sort of sound approach is the stuff that could serve as the foundation of an ordered, flourishing society. Yes, there were many Hindu gods that honored traditional marriage, but there were also a large number of other Hindu gods to whom an Indian could turn for alternatives to conventional sexual mores. Judaism, on the other hand, offered just one true god and one consistent set of ethics. Buddhism stakes out a Middle Way between these two extremes by viewing marriage as a secular arrangement and not a sacrament.[4]

So we get down to the question of whether Buddha was aware of Solomon and Judaism. How likely would that have been?

Ancient East-West Traffic

There is much evidence of considerable traffic, not just of trade but also of travel and migration, between the Middle East and India during the centuries surrounding the lives of Solomon (950 B.C.), Buddha (525 B.C.), and Christ (A.D. 30).

1. Stories about Solomon were well known in India during his lifetime, four centuries before Buddha lived.

The possibility that Solomon's teachings could have influenced India long before Buddha lived finds direct support in the Old Testament:

> King Solomon was greater in riches and wisdom than all the other kings of the earth. *The whole world* sought audience with Solomon to hear the wisdom God had put in his heart. Year after year, everyone who came brought a gift—articles of silver and gold, robes, weapons and spices, and horses and mules.[5]

Here is a picture of the world around 950 B.C. People everywhere were eagerly seeking wisdom from credible spokesmen long before Buddha lived. The question, however, is: When the Bible uses the expression "the whole world," would this include India? Was the author of 1 Kings 10 even aware of India? Verse 22 of this same chapter provides a revealing clue:

> For the king had at sea a navy of Tharshish with the navy of Hiram: once in three years came the navy of Tharshish, bringing gold, and silver, ivory, and apes, and *peacocks*.[6]

Peacocks are native to India, Burma, and Java.[7] In contrast, ivory (from elephants) and apes could have come from either Africa or India. In any case, through these many visits from people far and wide, the Bible says, Solomon's fame and proverbs spread throughout the world:

> God gave Solomon wisdom and very great insight, and a breadth of understanding as measureless as the sand on the seashore. Solomon's wisdom was greater than the wisdom of all the men of the East, and greater than all the wisdom of Egypt. He was wiser than any other man. . . . *Men of all nations* came to listen to Solomon's wisdom, sent by *all the kings of the world*, who had heard of his wisdom.[8]

These three passages portray a world where Solomon was at the center of an exchange of proverbs among every nation in the known world. So, in a very real sense, when comparing the core tenets of Buddhism with Solomon's writings, we are surveying them side by side with the substance of the *collective* wisdom of the Near East some four hundred years before Buddha lived. Chief among Israel's neighbors during Solomon's reign were Egypt and Assyria. Some Egyptian kings and sages collected proverbs, not just a few of which were similar to Solomon's writings. Most notable among them were Ptah-hotep (c. 2500–2350 B.C.), Merikone (c. 2106–2010 B.C.)[9] and Amenemope, who lived sometime during the late New Kingdom (1300–1075 B.C.).[10]

Various historians have commented on the Middle East–India connection. Historian Will Durant offered this assessment of the antiquity of East-West trade: "The foreign trade of India is as old as her history; objects found in Sumeria and Egypt indicate a traffic between these countries and India as far back as 3000 B.C. Commerce between India and Babylon by the Persian Gulf flourished from 700 to 480 B.C.; and perhaps the 'ivory, apes and peacocks' of Solomon came by the same route from the same source."[11] And according to English archaeologist John A. Thompson, "there are some Hebrew legends and traditions that there were Jews in India in the days of King Solomon."[12] *The Legends of the Jews*, a collection of tales from rabbinic writings compiled by Jewish scholar Louis Ginzberg, contains an intriguing occult reference saying that Solomon "could grow tropical plants in Palestine, because his ministering spirits secured water for him from *India*."[13]

In 1568, Spanish explorer Alvaro Mendana discovered the Solomon Islands and gave them that name, believing them to be the land of Ophir mentioned several times in the Bible.[14] In several passages the Bible calls Ophir a destination of trade ships dispatched from Israel by King Solomon to embark on a three-year voyage of trade.[15] Many modern scholars believe that Ophir was located either on the coast of Pakistan or India, or somewhere in Yemen.

2. Some trade and travel between India and the Middle East occurred centuries prior to Solomon's reign.

In 1916, H. G. Rawlinson, the author of several historical studies on India, noted that "an axe head of white jade, which could only have come from China, has been found in the second city of Troy."[16] Troy II existed from 2350 to 2250 B.C. on the western shore of modern-day Turkey, far to the northwest of Israel.[17] Rawlinson also observed, "Trade between the Indus valley and the Euphrates is . . . very ancient. The earliest trace of this is . . . to be found in the cuneiform inscriptions of the Hittite kings . . . belonging to the fourteenth or fifteenth century B.C."[18] The Hittites were mentioned as immediate neighbors with the Israelites in numerous books throughout Old Testament history.[19]

The Jewish Virtual Library offered these observations: "Interactions between India and ancient Israel were overlaid upon older cultural patterns between India's Indus Valley Civilization (IVC, third to second millennium B.C.E.) and Sumer. Legendary accounts of the great wealth of India entered West Asian consciousness during antiquity and found their way into the Jewish imagination. Ancient tablets discovered at Ur, the city of Abraham, describe this flourishing trade."[20]

The city of Ur flourished from 2600 B.C. to 550 B.C. but was "no longer inhabited after about 500 B.C., perhaps owing to drought, changing river patterns, and the silting of the outlet to the Persian Gulf."[21] In other words, almost the entire 2,100-year existence of Ur as a notable city pre-dated the life of Buddha. Further, "Philologists have identified several Sanskrit and Tamil loan words in the Hebrew Bible, dating from as early as the Book of Exodus through the Books of Kings and Chronicles, indicating direct or indirect trade between India and ancient Israel."[22] The Book of Exodus, attributed to Moses, dates from around 1300 B.C.[23] Most of this ancient trade was made possible by large ships plying the sea lanes from the Persian Gulf to India. Numerous references to such trade appear in the Rig Veda,[24] a text that dates to 1500 B.C. or earlier.[25]

3. Trade and travel between India and the Middle East was quite extensive during the four centuries between Solomon and Buddha.

Evidence of travel and trade to and from India and the Middle East in the centuries between Solomon's death (930 B.C.)[26] and Buddha's birth is plentiful. Rawlinson observed that, "on the obelisk of Shalmaneser III, 860 B.C., are apes, [and] *Indian* elephants."[27] Shalmaneser III[28] was the King of Assyria to whom Jehu[29] of Israel sent tribute in 841 B.C., soon after Assyria had devastated the territories around Damascus.

Rawlinson also noted that Babylon overthrew the Assyrian empire in 606 B.C. and, "in the crowded marketplaces of that great city met the races of the world—Ionian traders, Jewish captives, Phoenician merchants from distant Tarshish, and *Indians from the Panjab*, who came to sell their wares."[30] Around 550 B.C., there were "Chinese silks known in Athens."[31] In addition: "The carrying of goods along the Silk Road [from China] to the Mediterranean began in the 6th century B.C. . . . At the same time traders began to take advantage of the monsoons for sea-borne trade with India and beyond."[32]

Trade clearly involves an exchange of goods, yet it inevitably creates opportunities for the exchange of ideas and culture. Regarding the extent of contact between the cultures of the world around the time of Buddha, Durant offered these comments: "It has often been remarked that this period was distinguished by a shower of stars in the history of genius: Mahavira and Buddha in India, Lao-tzu and Confucius in China, Jeremiah and the Second Isaiah in Judea, the pre-Socratic philosophers in Greece, and perhaps Zarathustra in Persia. Such a simultaneity of genius suggests more intercommunication and mutual influence among these ancient cultures than it is possible to trace definitely today."[33]

4. A colony of Jews settled in India around the time of Buddha's birth.

Prior to the birth of Buddha, the Jewish people suffered greatly under two expulsions from their homeland:

- Assyria conquered the northern tribes (excluding Judah and Benjamin) in 722 B.C. These tribes became known as the Ten Lost Tribes of Israel. Many settled in eastern Iran and western Afghanistan.
- Babylon conquered Judah in 588 B.C., expelling Jews who had returned to their land after the Assyrian conquest. Jews migrated to many countries around the world, including India.

The first settlement of Jews in India was established in Cochin in 562 B.C.,[34] a year after the birth of Buddha. This colony would have been at least thirty-four years old at the time that Buddha became enlightened. So we have this chronology.

Dates	Events
970–930 B.C.	King Solomon reigns in Israel. Writes Proverbs and Ecclesiastes.
722 B.C.	Assyria conquers northern Israel. Jewish refugees flee to eastern Iran and western Afghanistan.
588 B.C.	Babylon conquers Judah. Jewish refugees immigrate to countries around the world.
562 B.C.	The first colony of Jews settles in India.
563–483 B.C.	The life of Buddha.

Given this timetable, it is no stretch of imagination to suppose that Buddha could have actually met one or more Jews who had settled in India. (A "Postscript" to this book provides a fictional portrayal of such contact.)

Proverbs 25:1 states that chapters 25 through 29 of Solomon's Book of Proverbs were *copied* by the men of Hezekiah, who reigned as king from 715 to 686 B.C. In other words, there were written copies of parts of Solomon's proverbs in existence long before Buddha's day. Hezekiah "witnessed the forced resettlement of the northern kingdom of Israel by the Assyrians in 720 BC and was king of Judah during the invasion and siege of Jerusalem by Sennacherib in 701 BC."[35] So it is quite likely that the Jews expelled during the first and second diasporas took sacred scrolls to Jewish colonies scattered around the world. Their sacred writings—in the Torah (the first five books of the Bible) and the rest of the Old Testament, including Solomon's writings—enabled the Jews to retain their identity.

How would Jews have fared in northeastern India near where Buddha lived? As we saw from the first quotation by Will Durant in Chapter One, given an environment of free speech and wide-spread interest in disputation of spiritual matters, the likelihood that people in northern India were aware of the teachings of Judaism and the writings of Solomon would have been quite high. The existence of this society of tolerance and debate made north-eastern India a favorable place for a colony of Jews to settle. They may have participated in such public debates, being welcomed as a people offering a viable alternative to Hinduism.

Buddha's Counterculture Contemporaries

There were two prominent religious groups in India at the time of Buddha. Theologian Ernest Valea wrote:

> There was Brahmanism, in which gods ruled the universe and human affairs, and priests interceded on behalf of humans through the performance of sacrifices. It was the religion grounded on the ancient holy scriptures called the Vedas. . . . The other pattern was the Shramana tradition, inaugurated by the wandering ascetics who rejected Brahmanism. They left the priest-dominated society and withdrew to the wilderness to attain deeper spiritual knowledge by practicing asceticism and meditative techniques.[36]

A number of Shramana movements date to the pre-sixth-century B.C. Indus Valley civilization.[37] That civilization was very ancient: One of its major cities, Harappa, flourished from 2600 to 1700 B.C.[38] Buddha himself was part of this long-established resistance movement against the ruling priests of India.[39] He was immediately preceded by Mahavira[40] (599–527 B.C.), whose teachings are very similar to Buddha's. And yet, it is known that "Jainism existed before Mahavira, and his teachings were based on those of his predecessors. Thus Mahavira was a reformer and propagator of an existing religion, rather than the founder of a new faith. He followed the well established creed of his predecessor Tirthankar Parshvanath (877–777 BC)."[41]

The precepts of Jainism,[42] which can be traced to Parshvanath[43] (877–777 B.C.) or earlier, parallel those of Buddha in most respects. For the same reasons noted earlier in this chapter, it is quite possible that the Jains were influenced in their tenets by the wisdom of Solomon, who died in 938 B.C., sixty-one years before Parshvanath was born.

Counterculture movements are naturally attracted to foreign cultures that espouse beliefs and practices that clash with the establishment. We know this from the events of our own day. The Beatles, for example, in general,[44] and George Harrison,[45] in particular, embraced Hinduism as a way of protesting Western culture in the 1970s. The leading foreign cultures Buddha may have been aware of were those of the Middle East and of China. The writings of Solomon could have been prominent among documents from the Middle East accessible to Buddha and his contemporaries and his Shramana and Jain predecessors.

Sudden Synthesis

The fundamentals of Buddha's philosophy were clearly evident at the start of his forty-five years of teaching and changed little during his lifetime. "Unlike Hinduism," wrote Huston Smith, "which emerged by slow, largely imperceptible spiritual accretion out of an invisible past, the religion of the Buddha appeared overnight, full formed."[46]

Buddha came up with the whole framework of his new religion quite suddenly—according to legend, as a result of becoming enlightened beneath a bodhi tree.[47] To skeptical westerners, this legend suggests that many of his early tenets may have come from other sources, and that his genius lay more in synthesizing the practices and ideas of others into a compelling whole than in developing new practices and ideas. Part of his genius also lay in living a pure life by sheer act of will and mental discipline and in expounding these tenets effectively to a group of highly dedicated followers over a period of more than four decades.

Very early on, Buddha offered the Four Noble Truths and the Noble Eightfold Path as a Middle Way, "a path of moderation between the extremes of sensual indulgence and self-mortification," as the route to wisdom.[48] Given the suddenness of Buddha's formulation of a new religion, his radical departure from Hinduism could well have been inspired, at least in part, by one of the other great religions of his day. He may have found in Solomon's writings the essence of what he believed was so lacking in Hinduism: a solid foundation of clear-cut ethics. That Buddha's earliest work was a collection of 423 proverbs, the Dhammapada, suggests that he was using a familiar literary form—one that other religious thinkers had used. And the most famous collection of such proverbs, written by Solomon, had quite likely been brought to India via trade-route exchanges and by Jews in the diaspora.

Summary Timeline

Since this chapter mentions some two dozen events of historical significance, discussed topically, there is value in rearranging these in chronological order. They are divided into three different eras. The reader is encouraged to work through this chronology to gain more historical perspective.

Date(s)	Events
3000 B.C.	"Objects found in Sumeria and Egypt indicate a traffic between these countries and India."
2600–2250 B.C.	"An axe head of white jade, which could only have come from China, has been found in the second city of Troy."
1700–1100 B.C.	Rig Veda text refers to trade from the Persian Gulf to India in large ships.
1500–1300 B.C.	"Trade between the Indus valley and the Euphrates is . . . very ancient. The earliest trace of this is . . . to be found in the cuneiform inscriptions of the Hittite kings."
1271 B.C.	Death of Moses, author of the Torah (first five books of the Bible).
930 B.C.	**Death of King Solomon (author of Proverbs and Ecclesiastes).**

Events Between the Death of Solomon and Buddha's Enlightenment

860 B.C.	Obelisk of Shalmaneser III, King of Assyria, shows Indian elephants.
841 B.C.	Jehu of Israel sends tribute to Shalmaneser III, king of Assyria.
877–777 B.C.	Life of Tirthankar Parshvanath, founder of Jainism.
722 B.C.	Jews are expelled from northern Israel by the Assyrians and migrate to many foreign lands.
686 B.C.	Death of Hezekiah, king of Israel. Proverbs 25:1 states that Chapters 25–29 of Proverbs were copied by the men of Hezekiah.
700–480 B.C.	"Commerce between India and Babylon by the Persian Gulf flourished."
606 B.C.	Crowded marketplaces of Babylon sell the wares of Indians from the Panjab.
588 B.C.	Jews are expelled from Judea by the Babylonians and migrate to many countries.
563 B.C.	**Birth of Buddha.**
562 B.C.	First colony of Jews settles in India.

550 B.C.	Chinese silks are known in Athens.
599–527 B.C.	Life of Mahavira, an Indian sage who established the central tenets of Jainism.
528 B.C.	**Buddha attains enlightenment, begins public teaching ministry.**

Events After Buddha's Enlightenment

528–483 B.C.	Public ministry of Buddha.
484–425 B.C.	Life of Herodotus, who described a sect in India like the Buddhists.
252 B.C.	Dhammapada (Buddha's proverbs) published.
4 B.C.	**Birth of Jesus of Nazareth.**
A.D. 27–30	Public ministry of Jesus of Nazareth.

In the first two chapters we have looked at a broad range of reasons why Buddha may have been influenced by Solomon. In Chapters Three through Nine, we will review proverbs (and other writings) of Solomon that are precursors of every key facet of Buddha's Four Noble Truths and Noble Eightfold Path. These will appear adjacent to similar proverbs of Buddha. Later in this book, we will also make thorough comparisons of Buddha and Christ, in topically arranged sections, and consider the possibility that the similarities between them may be due to Solomon and Judaism as common predecessors.

The evidence presented in the first two chapters generally supports the feasibility of the inquisitive young Buddha encountering a learned man from a nearby Jewish settlement. To survive in India, some Jews had become quite fluent in Pali or Sanskrit. Most likely they had scrolls of the Torah and of other sacred writings, such as the Psalms and Solomon's writings. Perhaps portions of these had been translated into Pali or Sanskrit and copied onto scrolls. The people of northeastern India at the time of the young Buddha had a strong interest in viable alternatives to Hinduism. In that same spirit, Buddha may have obtained copies of these translations and studied them.

---

[1] Ecclesiastes 7:16–17 (NASB).

[2] According to the "Sexual Rites" article of Wikipedia, http://en.wikipedia.org/wiki/Tantra (retrieved January 27, 2011):
Sexual rites of Vamamarga may have emerged from early Hindu Tantra as a practical means of catalyzing biochemical transformations in the body to facilitate heightened states of awareness. These constitute a vital offering to Tantric deities. Sexual rites may have also evolved from clan initiation ceremonies involving transactions of sexual fluids. Here the male initiate is inseminated with the sexual emissions of the female consort, sometimes admixed with the semen of the guru. . . . The sexual act itself balances energies coursing within the *pranic ida* and *pingala* channels in the subtle bodies of both participants. The *sushumna nadi* is awakened and *kundalini* rises upwards within it. This eventually culminates in *samadhi*, wherein the respective individual personalities and identities of each of the participants are completely dissolved in a unity of cosmic consciousness. Tantrics understand these acts on multiple levels. The male and female participants are conjoined physically."

[3] "Jainism," Jainism Global Resource Center, www.jainworld.com/jainbooks/Books/Jainism.htm, retrieved April 12, 2010.

[4] "Buddhist Ceremonies. Personal Ceremonies: Marriage / Funeral Rites," Buddha Dharma Education Association, www.buddhanet.net/funeral.htm, retrieved March 28, 2011.

[5] 1 Kings 10:23–25 (NIV) (emphasis added).

[6] 1 Kings 10:22 (NIV) (emphasis added). The King James Version (KJV) differs from the NIV ("baboons" appears instead of "peacocks").

[7] "Peacock," Encyclopedia Britannica Online, www.britannica.com/EBchecked/topic/447818/peacock, retrieved April 12, 2010.

[8] 1 Kings 4:29–34 (NIV) (emphasis added).

[9] *NIV Archaeological Study Bible: An Illustrated Walk Through Biblical History and Culture* (Grand Rapids, MI: Zondervan, 2005), 960.

[10] "Amenemope," Encyclopedia Britannica Online, http://www.britannica.com/EBchecked/topic/19165/Amenemope, retrieved May 17, 2011.

[11] Will Durant, *The Story of Civilization, Part I: Our Oriental Heritage* (New York: Simon and Schuster, 1963), 479.

[12] John A. Thompson, "India," *Baker Encyclopedia of the Bible*, edited by Walter A. Elwell (Grand Rapids, MI: Baker, 1988), 1:1,030.

[13] Louis Ginzberg, *The Legends of the Jews*, vol. 4, *Bible Times and Characters from Joshua to Esther*, translated by Henrietta Szold, Philologos Religious Online Books, http://philologos.org/__eb-lotj/vol4/p05.htm#SOLOMON%20MASTER%20OF%20 THE%20DEMONS, retrieved April 12, 2010. *The Legends of the Jews* was originally published in 1909–1938. On Solomon, Ginzberg wrote:
Never has there lived a man privileged, like Solomon, to make the demons amenable to his will. God endowed him with the ability to turn the vicious power of demons into a power working to the advantage of men. He invented formulas of incantation by which diseases were alleviated, and others by which demons were exorcised so that they were banished forever. As his personal attendants he had spirits and demons whom he could send hither and thither on the instant. He could grow tropical plants in Palestine, because his ministering spirits secured water for him from *India*.

[14] 1 Kings 9:28; 10:11; 22:49; 1 Chronicles 29:4; 2 Chronicles 8:18; Job 22:24; 28:16; Psalms 45:9; Isaiah 13:12.

[15] "Alvaro de Mendana de Neira," www.britannica.com/EBchecked/topic/374724/ Alvaro-de-Mendana-de-Neira, retrieved April 12, 2010.

[16] H. G. Rawlinson, Intercourse Between India and the Western World (London: Cambridge University Press, 1916), 8, found at Columbia University Library Digital Collections, www.columbia.edu/cu/lweb/digital/collections/cul/texts/ ldpd_5949061_000/index.html, retrieved April 12, 2010.

[17] "Troy / Wilusa / Ilium," www.livius.org/to-ts/troy/troy_I-V.html, retrieved April 12, 2010.

[18] Rawlinson, *Intercourse Between India and the Western World*, 2.

[19] Walter A. Elwell, ed., *Baker Encyclopedia of the Bible* (Grand Rapids, MI: Baker, 1988), 982. Specific biblical references to Hittites appear in Genesis 26:34; 27:46; 49:29–32; 50:13; Exodus 33:2; Numbers 13:29; Deuteronomy 7:1; 20:17; Joshua 11:3; 12:8; 1 Samuel 26:6; 2 Samuel 11,12; 1 Kings 9:20; 10:29; 11:1 (wives of Solomon); Ezra 9:1, and Ezekiel 16:3,45.

[20] "India," Jewish Virtual Library, A Division of the American-Israeli Cooperative Enterprise, www.jewishvirtuallibrary.org/jsource/judaica/ejud_0002_0009_0_ 09525.html, retrieved May 12, 2010.

[21] "Ur" Wikipedia, http://en.wikipedia.org/wiki/Ur, retrieved May 12, 2010.

[22] "India," Jewish Virtual Library.

[23] Elwell, *Baker Encyclopedia of the Bible*, 1:737.

[24] Rawlinson, *Intercourse Between India and the Western World*, 4. From footnote: Rig Veda, I.116.3.

[25] "Rig Veda," Hindu Universe, www.hindunet.org/vedas/rigveda/, retrieved February 22, 2011.

[26] Elwell, *Baker Encyclopedia of the Bible*, 1:975.

[27] Rawlinson, *Intercourse Between India and the Western World*, 3 (emphasis added). Rawlinson commented, "Evidently from early days the Indian seamen built ships larger than those usually employed even at a much later date in the Mediterranean. . . . In the story of the invasion of Ceylon, probably in the sixth century bc . . . we hear of a ship large enough to hold over 700 people."

[28] "Shalmaneser III, King of Assyria (858–824 bc), British Museum, www.britishmuseum.org/explore/highlights/article_index/s/shalmaneser_iii,_assyr ian_king.aspx, retrieved April 12, 2010.

[29] Ibid.

[30] Rawlinson, *Intercourse Between India and the Western World*, 7 (emphasis added).

[31] Richard Overy and Geoffrey Barraclough, eds., *The Times Complete History of the World*, 7th ed. (New York: Metro Books, 2008), 78.

[32] Ibid.

[33] Durant, *The Story of Civilization*, 422.

[34] "History of the Jews in India," Wikipedia, http://en.wikipedia.org/wiki/ Indian_Jews, retrieved April 12, 2010.

[35] "Hezekiah," Encyclopedia Britannica Online, www.britannica.com/EBchecked/ topic/264743/Hezekiah, retrieved April 12, 2010.

[36] Ernest Valea, *The Buddha and the Christ: Reciprocal Views* (Seattle: BookSurge, 2008), 19.

[37] "Shramana," Wikipedia, http://en.wikipedia.org/wiki/Shramana, retrieved April 12, 2010.

[38] "The Ancient Indus Civilization," Harappa, www.harappa.com/har/indus-saraswati.html, retrieved February 22, 2011.

[39] Rupert Gethin, *The Foundations of Buddhism* (Oxford: Oxford University Press, 1998), 11.

[40] Keith Crim, ed. *The Perennial Dictionary of World Religions* (New York: Harper and Row 1989), 451.

[41] Mary Pat Fisher, *Living Religions: An Encyclopaedia of the World's Faiths* (London: I. B.Tauris, 1997), 115.

[42] "Jainism," New World Encyclopedia, www.newworldencyclopedia.org/entry/ Jainism, retrieved February 22, 2011.

[43] John Bowker, ed., "Parsva," in *The Concise Oxford Dictionary of World Religions* (Oxford: University Press, 2000), www.oxfordreference.com/views/ ENTRY.html?subview=Main&entry=t101.e5504, retrieved October 22, 2009.

[44] Richard Salva, "The Gurus of Sergeant Pepper," http://hinduism.about.com/od/ gurussaints/a/beatlesgurus.htm, retrieved April 12, 2010.

[45] Subhamoy Das, "Harrison and Hinduism: The Spiritual Quest of George Harrison," http://hinduism.about.com/od/artculture/a/harrison.htm, retrieved April 12, 2010.

[46] Huston Smith, *The Religions of Man* (New York: Harper and Row, 1965), 108.

[47] His Holiness the Dalai Lama, *Becoming Enlightened*, translated by Jeffrey Hopkins (New York: Atria Books, 2009), 216.

[48] Bhikkhu Bodhi, ed., *In the Buddha's Words: An Anthology of Discourses from the Pali Canon* (Boston: Wisdom Publications, 2005), 48.

Chapter Three
Precursors to Buddha's Four Noble Truths

Merriam Webster's Collegiate Dictionary defines a precursor as "one that precedes and indicates the approach of another." Most of the fundamentals of Buddhism have clear and extensive precursors in Solomon's writings in the biblical books of Ecclesiastes and Proverbs.[1]

In this chapter, we will be making comparisons between the Four Noble Truths (from Buddha's proverbs) and excerpts from Solomon's writings. In the ensuing five chapters, we will be examining parallels between each of the steps in the Noble Eightfold Path (also from Buddha's proverbs) and Solomon's writings. The Dhammapada is the earliest work purporting to contain the sayings of Buddha, and as such would be more likely to show marks of influence from outside sources than later collections.

First Noble Truth: Life Is Suffering

Even though Solomon was the richest and most famous king of his day, in his later years he developed a very negative view of the fundamental nature of life. Several parts of his Book of Ecclesiastes make this very clear. This same idea is the first of Buddha's noble truths. We will look at four aspects of the "truth" that life is suffering, as expressed by Solomon and Buddha.

Life Is Suffering and Is Full of Sorrow

Solomon gave a very bleak picture of the nature of life:

> And what profit has he who has labored for the wind? All his days he also eats in darkness, and he has much sorrow and sickness and anger.[2]

Similarly, Buddha saw life in this world as inherently involving suffering and sorrow:

> "All created things are grief and pain," he who knows and sees this becomes passive in pain; this is the way that leads to purity.[3]

Suffering Is Pervasive in This World

As Buddha noted in the proverb quoted above, a world full of suffering is pervasive. Solomon shared this view:

> Again I looked and saw all the oppression that was taking place under the sun: I saw the tears of the oppressed—and they have no comforter; power was on the side of their oppressors—and they have no comforter. And I declared that the dead, who had already died, are happier than the living, who are still alive.[4]

Life Is Fleeting

Solomon was painfully aware of the brevity of life and of his future death:

> As he came from his mother's womb, naked shall he return, to go as he came; and he shall take nothing from his labor which he may carry away in his hand. And this also is a severe evil—just exactly as he came, so shall he go.[5]

Buddha put it this way in the Dhammapada, in a proverb that appears just before the one quoted earlier:

> "All created things perish," he who knows and sees this becomes passive in pain; this is the way to purity.[6]

It Is Difficult to Be Happy

Both Solomon and Buddha said that happiness is very elusive. We are worn out from work, and neither words, nor what we see and hear, can bring true satisfaction. This is a common theme of Ecclesiastes, as exemplified in this verse:

> All things are weary with toil and all words are feeble; man cannot utter it. The eye is not satisfied with seeing, nor the ear filled with hearing.[7]

Similarly, Buddha noted that finding happiness as an ordinary person in society is difficult, much as it is in a monastery:

> It is hard to leave the world (to become a friar), it is hard to enjoy the world; hard is the monastery, painful are the houses.[8]

Second Noble Truth: Desire Is the Cause of Suffering

A number of Solomon's proverbs focus on specific types of people for whom desire is clearly the cause of suffering. Here is a dramatic example:

> The *desire* of the lazy [slothful] man kills him, For his hands refuse to labor. He covets greedily all day long, But the righteous gives and does not spare.[9]

Desire, in this case, leads to death. Likewise, Buddha foresaw death awaiting the pleasure seeker:

> Death carries off a man who is gathering flowers and whose mind is distracted, as a flood carries off a sleeping village.[10]

> Death subdues a man who is gathering flowers, and whose mind is distracted, before he is satiated in his pleasures.[11]

Solomon presented coveting as one of the worst forms of desire, for it is a longing to have what someone else has. It is a violation of the

Tenth Commandment. Coveting involves envy and jealousy, against which Solomon gave specific warnings about ensuing suffering:

Envy is rottenness to the bones.[12]

An anxious heart weighs a man down.[13]

I have seen that every labor and every skill which is done is the result of rivalry between a man and his neighbor. This too is vanity and striving after wind.[14]

The types of desire Solomon described in these proverbs do not necessarily involve wanting things that are blatantly sinful. Rather, they are entanglements in the things of this world—hankerings for what others have and urges to compete selfishly with others to gain worldly status and even potentially "wholesome" things. However, Solomon also warned that those who are devious will suffer because they will become ensnared by their wicked desires:

The righteousness of the upright delivers them, but the unfaithful are trapped by evil desires.[15]

In four proverbs, Buddha wrote about similar pursuits and the suffering that ensues:

Whomsoever this fierce thirst overcomes, full of poison, in this world, his sufferings increase like the abounding Birana grass.[16]

As a tree, even though it has been cut down, is firm so long as its root is safe, and grows again, thus, unless the feeders of thirst are destroyed, the pain (of life) will return again and again.[17]

A creature's pleasures are extravagant and luxurious; sunk in lust and looking for pleasure, men undergo (again and again) birth and decay.[18]

Men, driven on by thirst, run about like a snared hare; held in fetters and bonds, they undergo pain for a long time, again and again.[19]

Here, Buddha's references to undergoing "birth and decay" repeatedly have to do with the Eastern notion of reincarnation. Reincarnation was not a hopeful concept; instead, being in the cycle of death and rebirth was seen as continued suffering. When one reached enlightenment, Hindus and Buddhists believed, one was freed from this cycle.

Though Solomon did not subscribe to the idea of reincarnation, he did focus on the specific types of suffering that afflict those who have been successful and have accumulated wealth:

The abundance of a rich man permits him no sleep.[20]

Whoever loves money never has money enough; whoever loves wealth is never satisfied with his income. This too is meaningless. As goods increase, so do those who consume them. And what benefit are they to the owner except to feast his eyes on them?[21]

Will you set your eyes on that which is not? For riches certainly make themselves wings; They fly away like an eagle toward heaven.[22]

Solomon also described another kind of suffering, which is much like the Rolling Stones song, "I Can't Get No Satisfaction":

All things are weary with toil and all words are feeble; man cannot utter it. The eye is not satisfied with seeing, nor the ear filled with hearing.[23]

Solomon does offer a refuge, though, which he calls "wisdom," that involves a reining in and refocusing of one's emotions. Rather than seeking pleasures, one should seek to be wise and righteous:

A discerning man keeps wisdom in view, but a fool's eyes wander to the ends of the earth.[24]

For Buddha, too, there is a path of wisdom, and, as in Solomon's writings, it involves renunciation of desire.

Third Noble Truth: The Path to Liberation from Suffering Is to Renounce All Desire

The four-step process is as follows: (1) begin with Solomon's writings, excluding references to God; (2) assume reincarnation; (3) renounce the world; and (4) retreat within to insulate yourself from suffering.

Steps	Steps from Solomon to Buddha
Begin with a saying of Solomon's.	Banish anxiety from your heart and cast off the troubles of your body.[25]
Remove all references to God.	Him I call indeed a Brahmana who, after leaving all bondage to men, has risen above all bondage to the gods, and is free from all and every bondage.[26]
Possibly add some element of Indian belief or practice (e.g., reincarnation and the existence of many "worlds").	Him I call indeed a Brahmana who has left what gives pleasure and what gives pain, who is cold, and free from all germs (of renewed life), the hero who has conquered *all the worlds.*[27]
Renounce all desires.	The Third Noble Truth: The path of liberation from suffering is to renounce all desire.

To Solomon, banishing anxiety was an act of the will. The Buddhist action of renouncing all worldly desires is similar: You take each thing that you were desiring or worrying about and choose to treat it as not worth seeking in any way. Next, Buddha, as a radical existentialist, severs all human and "celestial" ties, both now and in the worlds to come (during future reincarnations). The fourth step, renunciation of every kind of desire, is a radical departure from

Judaism and Solomon's views and practices. And it is a critical part of Buddha's path to liberation.

At the very end of the Dhammapada are Buddha's sayings about the many requirements for becoming a "Brahman," one who is approaching enlightenment. Many of these focus on the renunciation of all desire. They are an extreme, radical application of the root idea present in Solomon's citations:

> Him I call indeed a Brahmana who fosters no desires for this world or for the next, has no inclinations, and is unshackled.[28]

> Him I call indeed a Brahmana who has no interests, and when he has understood (the truth), does not say How, how? and who has reached the depth of the Immortal.[29]

> Him I call indeed a Brahmana who in this world is above good and evil, above the bondage of both, free from grief from sin, and from impurity.[30]

> Him I call indeed a Brahmana who is bright like the moon, pure, serene, undisturbed, and in whom all gaiety is extinct.[31]

> Him I call indeed a Brahmana who has traversed this miry road, the impassable world and its vanity, who has gone through, and reached the other shore, is thoughtful, guileless, free from doubts, free from attachment, and content.[32]

Some of his Brahman proverbs portray the extreme to which Buddha went in pursuing renunciation:

> Him I call indeed a Brahmana who in this world, leaving all desires, travels about without a home, and in whom all concupiscence [sensual longing] is extinct.[33]

> Him I call indeed a Brahmana who, leaving all longings, travels about without a home, and in whom all covetousness is extinct.[34]

The notion that renunciation, right living and being are keys to escaping from the consequences of desiring (cited above) is implicit in Proverbs 21:25–26:

> The desire of the lazy [slothful] man kills him, For his hands refuse to labor. He covets greedily all day long, But the righteous gives and does not spare.[35]

When "the righteous" person "gives and does not spare," he or she is engaging in an act of renunciation. The implication of the contrast to the lazy man, who dies, is that the opposite type of person ("the righteous") will live.

The root idea, that renunciation of desires is key to being liberated from suffering, is clearly present in the above excerpts. Buddha sounded a similar theme in the following proverb:

> If by leaving a small pleasure one sees a great pleasure, let a wise man leave the small pleasure, and look to the great.[36]

This idea is also implicit in the next two proverbs of Solomon:

> A heart at peace gives life to the body, but envy rots the bones.[37]

> Better one handful with tranquility than two handfuls with toil and chasing after the wind.[38]

In the first verse, peace is presumably achieved by renouncing claims to whatever you have been seeking. The alternative is tenaciously desiring something someone else has, which "rots the bones." In other words, envy is bad for one's health. The second verse implies that one is better off with less if striving after more is causing stress.

Fourth Noble Truth: The Way Leading to the Cessation of Suffering Is the Noble Eightfold Path

The Noble Eightfold Path consists of a series of right perspectives, intentions, and actions that Buddhists believe will enable them to approach enlightenment and an end to all suffering. To the follower of Solomon, the dedicated practice of the set of commands about right intentions and actions that make up "wisdom" will free them from the pitfalls and snares of this life and reward them in important ways. While Solomon did not argue that all earthly desires should be eliminated, he did clearly indicate that a righteous person's determination to obtain wisdom should far exceed all other desires:

> Take my instruction and not silver, and knowledge rather than choicest gold. For wisdom is better than jewels; and all desirable things cannot compare with her.[39]

As we will next see in the next five chapters, the steps of the righteous person that Solomon advocated are virtually identical to those espoused by Buddha. The dedication that Solomon advised in following his path was substantial, though not as radical as Buddha advocated. Solomon said:

> My son, keep my words and store up my commands within you. Keep my commands and you will live; guard my teachings as the apple of your eye. Bind them on your fingers; write them on the tablet of your heart.[40]

How might someone write a set of commands "on the tablet" of his or her heart? Would it not be through memorization and meditation? Since meditation was a well-known practice in Judaism during Solomon's life (as detailed at the end of Chapter Eight), this would naturally be a reference to such practices.

In a parallel way, Buddha gave this teaching:

> And what, monks, is that middle way awakened to by the Tathagata? It is this Noble Eightfold Path; that is, right view, right intention, right speech, right action, right livelihood, right effort, right mindfulness, right concentration. This, monks, is that middle way awakened to by the Tathagata, which gives rise to vision, which gives rise to knowledge, and leads to peace, to direct knowledge, to enlightenment, to Nibbana.[41]

dha also offered this proverb:

> Cut out the love of self, like an autumn lotus, with thy hand!
> Cherish the road of peace. Nirvana has been shown by Sugata
> (Buddha).[42]

The Three Jewels

The core of Buddhism is summarized in the following proverbs of
Buddha:

> He who takes refuge with Buddha, the Law, and the Church; he
> who, with clear understanding, sees the four holy truths: — [43]

> Viz. pain, the origin of pain, the destruction of pain, and the
> eightfold holy way that leads to the quieting of pain; — [44]

> That is the safe refuge, that is the best refuge; having gone to
> that refuge, a man is delivered from all pain.[45]

The 190th proverb in the Dhammapada presents the Three Jewels of
Buddhism. Each of these Jewels has a distinct counterpart in
orthodox as well as secular Judaism.

The Three Jewels of Buddhism	Parallels in Orthodox Judaism	Parallels in Secular Judaism
Buddha	Moses	Solomon
The Dhamma (Buddha's writings)	The Torah (Moses' writings)	Proverbs and Ecclesiastes
Community of monks (sangha)	The Levites (priests)	Jewish philosophers

As we saw in the first two chapters, it is quite possible that Buddha
was well aware of both of these parallel systems within Judaism. In

developing his Three Jewels, he may have been inspired by what he believed was the best of each segment of Judaism in designing his new religion. Buddhism would be secular, and yet his followers would be much more attached to him than secular Jews were to Solomon. Moreover, Solomon's followers were not organized into a religious order, whereas in the law of Moses there was a priestly class, the Levites who served at the temple. Buddhist monks find a parallel in the Levitical priests rather than in the ordinary Jews who considered themselves students of Solomon's wisdom in secular Judaism. Buddha collected many proverbs (423 in the Dhammapada), much like Solomon's, intended for the average person, but there would also be many laws addressed specifically to the monks and nuns who had given up everything to follow him. There are 227 laws for monks[46] and 311 for nuns. Likewise, a portion of the 613 laws of Moses presented in the Torah prescribe Levitical duties and the operation of temple sacrifices.

What is strikingly different between Buddhism and Solomonic thought is Buddha's radical commitment to renouncing the pleasures and possessions of this world, both wholesome and otherwise.

---

[1] In this book I cite only proverbs attributed to Solomon when referring to the Bible's Book of Proverbs, unless noted otherwise in the text. A few chapters of Proverbs (i.e., chapters 29–31) are attributed to other authors.

[2] Ecclesiastes 5:16–17 (NKJV).

[3] Dhammapada 278.

[4] Ecclesiastes 4:1–2 (NIV).

[5] Ecclesiastes 5:15–16a (NKJV).

[6] Dhammapada 277.

[7] Ecclesiastes 1:8 (AMP).

[8] Dhammapada 302a.

[9] Proverbs 21:25–26 (NKJV) (emphasis added).

[10] Dhammapada 47.

[11] Ibid., 48.

[12] Proverbs14:30b (NKJV).

[13] Proverbs 12:25a (NIV).

[14] Ecclesiastes 4:4b (NASB).

[15] Proverbs 11:6 (NIV).

[16] Dhammapada 335.

[17] Ibid., 338.

[18] Ibid., 341.

[19] Ibid., 342.

[20] Ecclesiastes 5:12b (NIV).

[21] Ecclesiastes 5:10–11 (NIV).

[22] Proverbs 23:5 (NKJV).

[23] Ecclesiastes 1:8 (AMP).

[24] Proverbs 17:24 (NIV).

[25] Ecclesiastes 11:10b (NIV).

[26] Dhammapada 417.

[27] Ibid., 418, (emphasis added).

[28] Ibid., 410.

[29] Ibid., 411.

[30] Ibid., 412.

[31] Ibid., 413.

[32] Ibid., 414.

[33] Ibid., 415.

[34] Ibid., 416.

[35] Proverbs 21:25–26 (NKJV).

[36] Dhammapada 290.

[37] Proverbs 14:30 (NIV).

[38] Ecclesiastes 4:6 (NIV).

[39] Proverbs 8:10–11 (NASB).

[40] Proverbs 7:1–3 (NIV).

[41] Bhikkhu Bodhi, ed., *In the Buddha's Words: An Anthology of Discourses from the Pali Canon* (Boston: Wisdom Publications, 2005), 75–76 (SN 56:11: Dhammacakkappavattana Sutta; V 420–424).

[42] Dhammapada 285.

[43] Ibid., 190.

[44] Ibid., 191.

[45] Ibid., 192.

[46] "List of the 227 Rules of Patimokkha," http://en.dhammadana.org/sangha/vinaya/227.htm, retrieved April 16, 2010.

Chapter Four
Precursors to Buddha's Right View and Intention

The eight steps of the Noble Path seem to come in pairs, so we will review them that way in successive chapters:

- Right View and Intention (Chapter Four)
- Right Speech and Action (Chapter Five)
- Right Livelihood and Effort (Chapter Six)
- Right Mindfulness and Concentration (Chapters Seven and Eight)

This pairing makes a great deal of sense, in that:

(1) One's view of the world has a big impact on (2) one's intentions about how to live.

(3) One's words reflect what is inside and precede (4) one's actions.

(5) One's livelihood is the training ground for learning how to direct (6) one's efforts.

(7) Learning to be mindful and focused is key to (8) practicing meditation (concentration).

As part of the beginning of each step in the Noble Eightfold Path, a quotation from a popular Buddhist website[1] describing that step introduces our discussion of it in the text.

Right View

"To grasp **the impermanent and imperfect nature of worldly objects** and ideas, and to understand **the law of karma and karmic conditioning.**"[2]

Solomon believed it was absolutely critical that a person have a right view of this world and this life:

> Get wisdom! Get understanding![3]

The theme of pursuing wisdom is central throughout his Book of Proverbs, especially in the opening chapters that set the stage for the book. Buddha had the same sense that becoming freed from ignorance was a critical priority for the seeker of enlightenment:

> But there is a taint worse than all taints,—ignorance is the greatest taint. O mendicants! throw off that taint, and become taintless![4]

Why is ignorance the greatest impurity? Shouldn't it be intentional wickedness? Perhaps the reason is that what causes a person to become wicked is immersion and attachment to this world. Those attached to the world are ignorant of its delusions and prone to fall into wickedness; to renounce the world and be pure, one must dispel ignorance. That notion is implied in the following series of Buddha's proverbs:

> Come, look at this glittering world, like unto a royal chariot; the foolish are immersed in it, but the wise do not touch it.[5]

> O man, know this, that the unrestrained are in a bad state; take care that greediness and vice do not bring thee to grief for a long time![6]

> There is no fire like passion, there is no shark like hatred, there is no snare like folly, there is no torrent like greed.[7]

To Solomon, ignorance and error come upon a person not because of innocence, but because they fall for the invitations of "the adulteress," who symbolizes the false allures of this world:

> Say to wisdom, "You are my sister," and call understanding your kinsman; they will keep you from the adulteress, from the

wayward wife with her seductive words. At the window of my house I looked out through the lattice. I saw among the simple, I noticed among the young men, a youth who lacked judgment. He was going down the street near her corner, walking along in the direction of her house at twilight, as the day was fading, as the dark of night set in. Then out came a woman to meet him, dressed like a prostitute and with crafty intent. (She is loud and defiant, her feet never stay at home; now in the street, now in the squares, at every corner she lurks.) She took hold of him and kissed him and with a brazen face she said: "I have fellowship offerings at home; today I fulfilled my vows. So I came out to meet you; I looked for you and have found you! I have covered my bed with colored linens from Egypt. I have perfumed my bed with myrrh, aloes and cinnamon. Come, let's drink deep of love till morning; let's enjoy ourselves with love! My husband is not at home; he has gone on a long journey. He took his purse filled with money and will not be home till full moon." With persuasive words she led him astray; she seduced him with her smooth talk. All at once he followed her like an ox going to the slaughter, like a deer stepping into a noose till an arrow pierces his liver, like a bird darting into a snare, little knowing it will cost him his life.[8]

In this passage, much as in the proverbs of Buddha, the young man is portrayed as foolishly chasing worldly pleasures that will lead to his own ruin. Comparing him to an animal about to be slaughtered or trapped, Solomon makes it clear that the young man is ignorant of what his true situation is and the danger he is in. As in Buddha's proverbs, the world is a delusion, and the wise person will realize this and renounce its false attractions.

In any event, ignorance and error will not excuse a person from the suffering that will result from them. This is certainly true for Solomon's foolish young man, and it is also true for Buddha. The Dhammapada puts it this way:

They who fear when they ought not to fear, and fear not when they ought to fear, such men, embracing false doctrines, enter the evil path.[9]

They who forbid when there is nothing to be forbidden, and forbid not when there is something to be forbidden, such men, embracing false doctrines, enter the evil path.[10]

Buddha also placed great importance on having a "Right View" of this world and of life. To him, this was the most important starting point in the path toward nirvana:

They who know what is forbidden as forbidden, and what is not forbidden as not forbidden, such men, embracing the true doctrine, enter the good path.[11]

There are several aspects to the Right View that Buddha espoused, and for which we find parallels in Solomon. Each is covered in a separate section below.

The Irreality of Existence

Solomon decried all of existence as being futile and absent of reality and substance:

"Meaningless! Meaningless!" says the Teacher. "Utterly meaningless! Everything is meaningless."[12]

The Hebrew word translated as "meaningless" in the New International Version appears differently in other Bible translations. In the New American Standard Bible, Young's Literal, and Darby versions, it is translated as "vanity." Vanity is defined as a "lack of real value; hollowness; worthlessness." In the Amplified Bible, Ecclesiastes 1:2 is translated, "Vapor of vapors and futility of futilities, says the Preacher. Vapor of vapors and futility of futilities! All is vanity (emptiness, falsity, and vainglory)." In The Message, this verse reads, "Smoke, nothing but smoke. [That's what the Quester says.] There's nothing to anything—it's all smoke."

Buddha used very similar imagery:

Look upon the world as a bubble, look upon it as a mirage.[13]

This world is dark, few only can see here; a few only go to heaven, like birds escaped from the net.[14]

There is no path through the air, a man is not a Samana by outward acts. The world delights in vanity, the Tathagatas (the Buddhas) are free from vanity.[15]

Solomon lamented the tedious nature of all things and of life:

All things are wearisome, more than one can say. The eye never has enough of seeing, nor the ear its fill of hearing.[16]

Buddha struck a similar theme in the following three proverbs. To him, all objects in the physical world were "created," or "composite" things, that is, made up of different elements. They were not permanent because they would always eventually decompose, or "fall apart." They were not eternal:[17]

"All created things perish," he who knows and sees this becomes passive in pain; this is the way to purity.[18]

"All created things are grief and pain," he who knows and sees this becomes passive in pain; this is the way that leads to purity.[19]

"All forms are unreal," he who knows and sees this becomes passive in pain; this is the way that leads to purity.[20]

Buddha's "created" things, sometimes translated "compounded" or "composite" things, are very much like the smoke and vanity Solomon found in everyday life. In response to this insight, Solomon focused on the great value of right states of *being* as opposed to *having*, as wealth is illusory:

He who trusts in his riches will fall, but the righteous will flourish like the green leaf.[21]

This proverb claims that the direct consequence of trusting in the path of righteousness is that a person will thrive like a flourishing plant. In other words, wisdom does not reside in gaining wealth, but in being righteous. The theme is a recurring one in Solomon. For example:

Better is a little with righteousness, than vast revenues without justice.[22]

Wealth is worthless in the day of wrath, but righteousness delivers from death.[23]

Buddha noted:

There is no fire like passion, there is no shark like hatred, there is no snare like folly, there is no torrent like greed.[24]

So the path to purity is open to those who realize that the attractions of this world are very hazardous.

The Cyclical Nature of Life

Unlike the authors of nearly all of the rest of the Old Testament, Solomon viewed all of life as being cyclical and repetitive:

That which has been is that which will be, and that which has been done is that which will be done. So there is nothing new under the sun.[25]

Whatever is has already been, and what will be has been before; and God will call the past to account.[26]

Buddha also had a cyclical view of life, as was very common in India. He saw life as a wearisome series of repetitive beginnings and endings:

Looking for the maker of this tabernacle, I shall have to run through a course of many births, so long as I do not find (him); and painful is birth again and again. But now, maker of the tabernacle, thou hast been seen; thou shalt not make up this tabernacle again. All thy rafters are broken, thy ridge-pole is sundered; the mind, approaching the Eternal (visankhara, nirvana), has attained to the extinction of all desires.[27]

Long is the night to him who is awake; long is a mile to him who is tired; long is life to the foolish who do not know the true law.[28]

Although Buddha believed in reincarnation and Solomon did not, their ideas about the weariness and unending toils of life were very similar. What Buddha saw as a cycle that manifested in repeated lifetimes, Solomon simply saw as patterns repeating throughout the generations.

Men Are Like Animals

Again, unlike nearly all the other authors of the Old Testament, Solomon's views on the similarities between people and animals were very much in line with Hinduism:

I also thought, "As for men, God tests them so that they may see that they are like the animals. Man's fate is like that of the animals; the same fate awaits them both: As one dies, so dies the other. All have the same breath; man has no advantage over the animal. Everything is meaningless. All go to the same place; all come from dust, and to dust all return. Who knows if the spirit of man rises upward and if the spirit of the animal goes down into the earth?"[29]

Durant, commenting on Hinduism's views on the same topic, wrote: "To the Hindu mind there was no real gap between animals and men; animals as well as men had souls, and souls were perpetually passing from men into animals, and back again; all these species were woven into one infinite web of Karma and reincarnation."[30] Oddly, however, none of Buddha's proverbs touch on this point. One current Buddhist source on this issue says that "there is no clear distinction between non-humans and humans in Buddhist philosophy. Eons of transmigration have had a predict-able result: today's duck and dog are yesterday's human sisters and brothers. Each cow and chicken was at some point one's parent, and to harm one's parent is a particularly base act for Buddhists. All species are also subject to the same karmic process."[31] So we can assume that this concept was so widely accepted by Buddha and his followers that he felt no need to discuss it.

The Law of Karma

Karma is "that universal law by which every act of good or of evil will be rewarded or punished in this life, or in some later incarna-tion of the soul."[32] A number of Solomon's proverbs affirm the power of karma in dictating people's lives:

> The integrity of the upright will guide them,
> But the perversity of the unfaithful will destroy them.

> Riches do not profit in the day of wrath,
> But righteousness delivers from death.

> The righteousness of the blameless will direct his way aright,
> But the wicked will fall by his own wickedness.

> The righteousness of the upright will deliver them,
> But the unfaithful will be caught by their lust.

> When a wicked man dies, his expectation will perish,
> And the hope of the unjust perishes.

> The righteous is delivered from trouble,
> And it comes to the wicked instead.[33]

This set of six continuous proverbs repeatedly asserts the Law of Karma. We also see it clearly in two verses in Ecclesiastes:

> Cast your bread upon the waters, for after many days you will find it again. Give portions to seven, yes to eight, for you do not know what disaster may come upon the land.[34]

The *InterVarsity Press Bible Background Commentary* on these two verses offers these comments:

> **Bread on waters.** This proverb has been found in the Egyptian source the *Instruction of Ankhsheshonqy* ("do a good deed and throw it in the river; when it dries up you shall find it") and in Arabic proverbs. If Ecclesiastes follows the route of *Ankhsheshonqy*, it suggests that a spontaneous good deed carries no guarantees of reciprocity but that "what goes around, comes around."
>
> **Giving of portions.** The giving of portions generally assumes a situation in which goods or assets are being distributed (not just invested). This could be in the context of inheritance or generosity.[35]

In other words, Solomon subscribed to the concept that, as a general rule, one is ultimately rewarded when one is generous to others and does what is right, but bad things are in store for those who hoard wealth or act wickedly. The Buddhist idea of karma is almost identical, except that Buddhism allows for the consequences, whether good or bad, to occur in later lifetimes, whereas for Solomon the results are more immediate.

Like Solomon, Buddha touched on both the positive and negative effects of karma in his proverbs. As for good karma, he said:

> He who always greets and constantly reveres the aged, four things will increase to him, viz. life, beauty, happiness, power.[36]

The following series of successive proverbs offers the most dramatic portrayal in the Dhammapada of negative karma:

> He who inflicts pain on innocent and harmless persons, will soon come to one of these ten states: He will have cruel suffering, loss, injury of the body, heavy affliction, or loss of mind, or a misfortune coming from the king, or a fearful accusation, or loss of relations, or destruction of treasures, or lightning-fire will burn his houses; and when his body is destroyed, the fool will go to hell.[37]

So extensive are Solomon's and Buddha's proverbs that provide various expressions of the Law of Karma that Chapter Nine of this book is devoted entirely to this subject. Neither sage ever used the specific word "karma" in any of his proverbs, however.

Facing Death

Though it should be expected that any philosopher who contemplates his own death, and that of others, will have negative thoughts about it, it is intriguing that both Solomon and Buddha expressed similar styles of such views. There are three main points each of them made about the subject.

1. The Universality of Death

Solomon was painfully aware that all people must die, and he believed that awareness of this fact was necessary. It was a sobering influence and should cause people to act with greater wisdom and compassion:

> It is better to go to a house of mourning than to go to a house of feasting, because that is the end of every man, and the living takes it to heart.[38]

The wise man's eyes are in his head, but the fool walks in darkness. Yet I myself perceived that the same event happens to them all.[39]

Buddha stressed the same things:

The world does not know that we must all come to an end here;—but those who know it, their quarrels cease at once.[40]

Not in the sky, not in the midst of the sea, not if we enter into the clefts of the mountains, is there known a spot in the whole world where death could not overcome (the mortal).[41]

As a cowherd with his staff drives his cows into the stable, so do Age and Death drive the life of men.[42]

2. The Abject Fate of Dying

Solomon emphasized the fact that we will all die stripped of our dignity and utterly exposed to the elements:

Naked a man comes from his mother's womb, and as he comes, so he departs. He takes nothing from his labor that he can carry in his hand.[43]

Buddha stressed this same theme while adding some graphic descriptions of the horrible fate of our fleshly bodies when we die:

Before long, alas! this body will lie on the earth, despised, without understanding, like a useless log.[44]

This body is wasted, full of sickness, and frail; this heap of corruption breaks to pieces, life indeed ends in death.[45]

This world is dark, few only can see here; a few only go to heaven, like birds escaped from the net.[46]

3. Death and One's Children

Given that Solomon had seven hundred wives and three hundred concubines, he undoubtedly had "a hundred children," and may have been thinking of himself when he wrote the following section of Ecclesiastes:

> If a man fathers a hundred children and lives many years, however many they be, but his soul is not satisfied with good things and he does not even have a proper burial, then I say, "Better the miscarriage than he, for it comes in futility and goes into obscurity; and its name is covered in obscurity. It never sees the sun and it never knows anything; it is better off than he. Even if the other man lives a thousand years twice and does not enjoy good things—do not all go to one place?"[47]

Solomon realized that finding contentment and happiness in this life had real value. Without it, one is worse off than the miscarried fetus. In contrast, Buddha gave no value to possible wholesome satisfaction in this life, but instead urged people to seek the ultimate contentment attained in nirvana:

> Death comes and carries off that man, praised for his children and flocks, his mind distracted, as a flood carries off a sleeping village.[48]

> Sons are no help, nor a father, nor relations; there is no help from kinsfolk for one whom death has seized.[49]

> A wise and good man who knows the meaning of this, should quickly clear the way that leads to Nirvana.[50]

For both Buddha and Solomon, life was just as fleeting for the child as for the parent. The child's life could be very fleeting indeed, in Solomon's view, as even the fetus could be taken in death. Buddha also makes clear that, regardless of age, no one is protected from being "assailed by death." For both thinkers, awareness of the brevity of life is part of the right view of things and highlights the need to live wisely.

Immortality

Solomon affirmed a belief in life after death, at least for righteous people:

> When the storm has swept by, the wicked are gone. The righteous will stand firm forever.[51]

Buddha declared a similar belief in immortality—for people who are vigilant:

> Earnestness is the path of immortality (Nirvana), thoughtlessness the path of death. Those who are in earnest do not die, those who are thoughtless are as if dead already.[52]

We have reviewed several different aspects of Right View, and have seen how close Buddha's views were to Solomon's on the issues of wisdom, existence, the cyclical nature of life, the relationship between humans and animals, the Law of Karma, death, and immortality. Now we will turn to the concept of Right Intention.

Right Intention

"**The kind of mental energy that controls our actions**. Right intention can be described best as *commitment* **to ethical and mental self-improvement**. Buddha distinguishes three types of right intentions: 1. the intention of **renunciation**, which means resistance to the pull of desire, 2. the intention of **good will**, meaning resistance to feelings of anger and aversion, and 3. the intention of **harmlessness**, meaning not to think or act cruelly, violently, or aggressively, and to develop **compassion**."[53]

Solomon repeatedly set forth exhortations about the critical importance of Right Intention, urging one of his sons to have an intense "commitment to ethical and mental self-improvement". The italicized synonyms below highlight this level of devotion:

> When I was my father's son, tender and the only one in the sight of my mother, he also taught me, and said to me: *"Let your heart retain my words; keep* my commands, and live. *Get* wisdom! *Get* understanding! *Do not forget, nor turn away* from the words of my mouth. Do not forsake her, and she will preserve you; *Love her*, and she will keep you. Wisdom is the principal thing; therefore get wisdom. And in all your getting, get understanding. *Exalt* her, and she will promote you; she will bring you honor, when you *embrace her*.[54]

> My son, *keep* your father's commands and *do not forsake* your mother's teaching. *Bind them upon your heart forever; fasten them around your neck.* When you walk, they will guide you; when you sleep, they will watch over you; when you awake, they will speak to you. For these commands are a lamp, this teaching is a light, and the corrections of discipline are the way to life, keeping you from the immoral woman, from the smooth tongue of the wayward wife.[55]

> *Choose* my instruction instead of silver, knowledge rather than choice gold, for wisdom is more precious than rubies, and nothing you desire can compare with her.[56]

We see this same concept succinctly stated by Buddha:

> Through zeal knowledge is gotten, through lack of zeal knowledge is lost; let a man who knows this double path of gain and loss thus place himself that knowledge may grow.[57]

Both sages strongly emphasized how essential it was to have an intense commitment to valuing and seeking more wisdom.

Each of the four types of Right Intention Buddha enumerated have clear precursors in one or more proverbs of Solomon. We will look at each in turn.

The Right Intention of Renunciation

Although Solomon did not espouse the sweeping practice of renunciation that Buddha did, he clearly advocated renunciation of any desires to indulge in immoral pleasures:

> For these commands are a lamp, this teaching is a light, and the corrections of discipline are the way to life, *keeping you from the immoral woman*, from the smooth tongue of the wayward wife.[58]

One of the hallmark differences between Solomon and Buddha is in the extent of the practice of renunciation. Buddha's extreme version of the practice is well illustrated in the following proverbs:

> Let a man leave anger, let him forsake pride, let him overcome all bondage! No sufferings befall the man who is not attached to name and form, and who calls nothing his own.[59]

> Give up what is before, give up what is behind, give up what is in the middle, when thou goest to the other shore of existence; if thy mind is altogether free, thou wilt not again enter into birth and decay.[60]

> Let us live happily then, free from greed among the greedy! Among men who are greedy let us dwell free from greed![61]

> The world gives according to their faith or according to their pleasure: if a man frets about the food and the drink given to others, he will find no rest either by day or by night.[62]

Buddha sought to shun every kind of craving, even if it was for something seemingly harmless. Solomon's downfall was the increasing degree to which he sought wealth, power, and pleasure as he grew older. Nevertheless, in his proverbs he advocated denying cravings for these things and pursuing wisdom and contentment with little instead.

The Right Intention of Goodwill

Having a sincere wish for the happiness and well-being of others is a key part of having an intention of goodwill. Solomon noted this in two proverbs:

> Will they not go astray who devise evil? But kindness and truth will be to those who *devise good.*[63]

> Fools mock at making amends for sin, but *goodwill* is found among the upright.[64]

With great insight, Buddha noted that those who are habitually critical of others are quite prone to the pursuit of sensual pleasures:

> If a man looks after the faults of others, and is always inclined to be offended, his own passions will grow, and he is far from the destruction of passions.[65]

Having high expectations of others, in other words, is a kind of desire that can habitually cause a person to be discontent. It is better to focus on critiquing one's own behavior than that of others.

The Right Intention of Harmlessness

Those who are treacherous seek to harm others to their own benefit, or at least to satisfy their desire for revenge or spite. People of integrity are just that because they value adherence to right behavior over any kind of temporary advantage they might gain by compromising themselves. Solomon noted this:

> The *integrity* of the upright shall guide them, but the *willful contrariness and crookedness of the treacherous* shall destroy them.[66]

Buddha touched on this same issue in two of his proverbs:

> He who, by causing pain to others, wishes to obtain pleasure for himself, he, entangled in the bonds of hatred, will never be free from hatred.[67]

> Let us live happily then, not hating those who hate us!
> Among men who hate us let us dwell free from hatred![68]

The Right Intention of Compassion

Solomon observed that people who are trying to be truly righteous will exhibit compassion for those who are less fortunate than they are. There is something about being truly righteous that makes us sensitive to the suffering of others:

> The righteous is *concerned* for the rights of the poor, the wicked does not understand such concern.[69]

Buddha's primary objective in exhibiting compassion for others was in using self-denial as a path to self-purification. So we see in the next proverb that the emphasis is on the importance of having a detached attitude in the act of helping the less fortunate:

> The world gives according to their faith or according to their pleasure: if a man frets about the food and the drink given to others, he will find no rest either by day or by night.[70]

Though there are distinctions in terms of flavor and emphasis, each element of Buddha's step of Right Intention, like each element of Right View, has evident precursors in Solomon's writings. With both teachers, views and intentions lead to speech and action, subjects to which we now turn.

---

[1] Thomas Knierim, editor and webmaster, "The Noble Eightfold Path," Raison d'Etre, www.thebigview.com/buddhism/eightfoldpath.html, retrieved April 17, 2010.

[2] Ibid. (emphasis added).

[3] Proverbs 4:5a (NIV).

[4] Dhammapada 243.

[5] Ibid., 171.

[6] Ibid., 248.

[7] Ibid., 251.

[8] Proverbs 7:4–23 (NIV).

[9] Dhammapada 317.

[10] Ibid., 318.

[11] Ibid., 319.

[12] Ecclesiastes 1:2 (NIV).

[13] Dhammapada 170a.

[14] Ibid., 174.

[15] Ibid., 254.

[16] Ecclesiastes 1:8 (NIV).

[17] "Siddhartha Gautama: The Historical Siddhartha," Washington State University, "World Civilizations: An Internet Classroom and Anthology," Richard Hooker, author and principal editor, www.wsu.edu/~dee/BUDDHISM/SIDD.HTM.

[18] Dhammapada 277.

[19] Ibid., 278.

[20] Ibid., 279.

[21] Proverbs 11:28 (NASB).

[22] Proverbs 16:8 (NKJV).

[23] Proverbs 11:4 (NIV).

[24] Dhammapada 251.

[25] Ecclesiastes 1:9 (NASB).

[26] Ecclesiastes 3:15 (NIV).

[27] Dhammapada 153-154.

[28] Ibid., 60.

[29] Ecclesiastes 3:18–21 (NIV).

[30] Will Durant, *The Story of Civilization, Part I: Our Oriental Heritage* (New York: Simon and Schuster, 1963), 509.

31 "Buddhist Ethics: Compassion for All," www.all-creatures.org/articles/an-tpr-buddhist.html, retrieved January 27, 2011.

[32] Durant, *The Story of Civilization*, 427.

[33] Proverbs 11:3–8 (NKJV).

[34] Ecclesiastes 11:1–2 (NIV).

[35] John H. Walton, Victor H. Matthews, and Mark W. Chavalas, *The IVP Bible Background Commentary: Old Testament* (Downers Grove, IL: InterVarsity Press, 2000), 575.

[36] Dhammapada 109.

[37] Ibid., 137–140.

[38] Ecclesiastes 7:2 (NASB).

[39] Ecclesiastes 2:14 (NKJV).

[40] Dhammapada 6.

[41] Ibid., 127.

[42] Ibid., 135.

[43] Ecclesiastes 5:15 (NIV).

[44] Dhammapada 41.

[45] Ibid., 148.

[46] Ibid., 174.

[47] Ecclesiastes 6:3–6 (NASB).

[48] Dhammapada 287.

[49] Ibid., 288.

[50] Ibid., 289.

[51] Proverbs 10:25 (NIV).

[52] Dhammapada 21.

[53] Knierim, "The Noble Eightfold Path."

[54] Proverbs 4:3–8 (NKJV) (emphasis added).

[55] Proverbs 6:20–24 (NIV) (emphasis added).

[56] Proverbs 8:10–11 (NIV) (emphasis added).

[57] Dhammapada 282.

[58] Proverbs 6:23–24 (NIV) (emphasis added).

[59] Dhammapada 221.

[60] Ibid., 348.

[61] Ibid., 199.

[62] Ibid., 249.

[63] Proverbs 14:22 (NASB) (emphasis added).

[64] Proverbs 14:9 (NIV) (emphasis added).

[65] Dhammapada 253.

[66] Proverbs 11:3 (AMP) (emphasis added).

[67] Dhammapada 291.

[68] Ibid., 197.

[69] Proverbs 29:7 (NASB) (emphasis added).

[70] Dhammapada 249.

Chapter Five
Precursors to Buddha's Right Speech and Action

Both Buddha and Solomon emphasized a twofold ethical system involving (1) speech, and (2) actions. Every ethical system recognizes the concept of right and wrong actions, but Solomon and Buddha both underscored the enormous power of the tongue. Each pointed out that one's speech could affect one's life, one's relationships, and one's future, as well as the larger world, for good or ill. This chapter covers several components of the ethics of speech and action that are similar in Solomon's writings and Buddha's proverbs.

The discussion of Right Speech is organized into two parts. The first focuses on the power of speech and its consequences. The second details the various types of good and bad speech. Since some proverbs fit into both categories, they may appear in both sections. The second part of the chapter covers the main components of right and wrong in human conduct through the eyes of these two thinkers.

Right Speech: Effects

"Mental purification can only be achieved through the cultivation of ethical conduct. The importance of speech in the context of Buddhist ethics is obvious: **words can break or save lives, make enemies or friends, start war or create peace.**"[1]

Right Speech: Types

"Buddha explained right speech as follows: 1. to abstain from false speech, especially not to tell deliberate lies and not to speak deceitfully, 2. to abstain from slanderous speech and not to use words maliciously against others, 3. to abstain from harsh words that offend or hurt others, and 4. to abstain from idle chatter that lacks purpose or depth. Positively phrased, this means to **tell the truth, to speak friendly, warm, and gently and to talk only when necessary.**"[2]

Both Solomon and Buddha begin with the premise that speech is powerful. With that as a starting point, they detail the effects of speech and describe good and bad forms of speech. By gaining control of the tongue, a person is, in effect, limiting the harm that can come from bad speech and promoting all sorts of positive things in his or her own life and the surrounding world.

Speech Is Powerful, for Good or Ill

To both great wise men, speech could be life changing or death inducing. Solomon stated this quite emphatically:

> Death and life are in the power of the tongue, and they who indulge in it shall eat the fruit of it [for death or life].[3]

Buddha stressed the potential power of just one well-chosen word:

> Even though a speech be a thousand (of words), but made up of senseless words, one word of sense is better, which if a man hears, he becomes quiet.[4]

> Even though a Gatha (poem) be a thousand (of words), but made up of senseless words, one word of a Gatha is better, which if a man hears, he becomes quiet.[5]

Though a man recite a hundred Gathas made up of senseless words, one word of the law is better, which if a man hears, he becomes quiet.[6]

Buddha's repeated reference to peace underscored how important it was to him. To him, the presence or absence of peace at any moment was a summary of one's spiritual condition. Life and peace, or death and, presumably, confusion: For both Solomon and Buddha, this is the choice each person has when deciding how to speak each moment, even before taking any action.

Effects on One's Character

Solomon noted that a person whose speech is perverse will have a devastated spirit:

A soothing tongue is a tree of life, but perversion in it crushes the spirit.[7]

In a similar way, Buddha claimed there would be no limit to the transgressions a person might commit if they were willing to speak falsely:

If a man has transgressed one law, and speaks lies, and scoffs at another world, there is no evil he will not do.[8]

Buddha believed that a person who lied (and/or committed any of four other bad deeds) destroyed the very core of their being:

He who destroys life, *who speaks untruth*, who in this world takes what is not given him, who goes to another man's wife; and the man who gives himself to drinking intoxicating liquors, he, even in this world, digs up his own root.[9]

Buddha went further, plainly stating that the ultimate destiny of hell awaited the liar:

He who says what is not, goes to hell; he also who, having done a thing, says I have not done it. After death both are equal, they are men with evil deeds in the next world.[10]

Solomon painted an illustration of the way that seemingly harmless false speech can affect the very center of one's being, where a person's integrity and worth are either sustained or forfeited:

The words of a talebearer are like tasty trifles, and they go down into the inmost body.[11]

Solomon further noted that when the heart is committed to refusing to be righteous (i.e., the person is wicked), the individual's worth is drastically reduced or badly disfigured:

The tongue of the righteous is choice silver, but the heart of the wicked is of little value.[12]

Buddha went even further, claiming that anyone who lies has already become so corrupted that his or her heart is of little value—so much so that the individual is fully capable of committing every possible type of sin:

If a man has transgressed one law, and speaks lies, and scoffs at another world, there is no evil he will not do.[13]

Other Effects Noted by Solomon

Solomon noted a broader range of specific positive and negative consequences for speech than did Buddha. Those consequences are italicized for emphasis below in proverbs that present vivid contrasts.

1. Effects on Relationships

He who covers over an offense *promotes love*, but whoever repeats the matter *separates close friends*.[14]

There is one who speaks rashly *like the thrusts of a sword,* but the tongue of the wise *brings healing.*[15]

The lips of the righteous *nourish many,* but fools die for lack of judgment.[16]

Through the *blessing* of the upright *a city is exalted,* but by the mouth of the wicked *it is destroyed.*[17]

2. Effects on Health

Pleasant words are like a honeycomb, *sweetness to the soul* and *health to the bones.*[18]

A soothing tongue is *a tree of life,* but perversion in it *crushes the spirit.*[19]

3. Favorable vs. Troublesome Effects

Blessings are on the head of the righteous, but the mouth of the wicked *conceals violence.*[20]

The words of the wicked *lie in wait for blood,* but the speech of the upright *rescues them.*[21]

An evil man is *ensnared by the transgression of his lips,* but the righteous will escape from trouble.[22]

In all labor there is profit, but idle chatter leads only to *poverty.*[23]

Whoever guards his mouth and tongue *keeps his soul from troubles.*[24]

The Downside of Too Many Words

The first three proverbs of Buddha cited at the beginning of this chapter provide dramatic contrasts between the great value of a few powerful, life-changing words and the worthlessness of hundreds, even thousands, of empty words. The following proverbs of Buddha also emphasize the lack of value in a sheer volume of words:

> A man is not learned because he talks much; he who is patient, free from hatred and fear, he is called learned.[25]

> A man is not a supporter of the law because he talks much; even if a man has learnt little, but sees the law bodily, he is a supporter of the law, a man who never neglects the law.[26]

Solomon also highlighted the hazards of prolific, unbridled speech:

> In a multitude of words transgression is not lacking, but he who restrains his lips is prudent.[27]

> A fool vents all his feelings, but a wise man holds them back.[28]

> Idle chatter leads only to poverty.[29]

So, while Buddha saw large quantities of words as worthless, but not necessarily harmful, Solomon detailed their potential negative effect.

Restraint

The importance of restraint exercised over what one says is evident in some of Solomon's proverbs:

> In a multitude of words transgression is not lacking, but he who restrains his lips is prudent.[30]

A fool shows his annoyance at once, but a prudent man overlooks an insult.[31]

He who covers over an offense promotes love, but whoever repeats the matter separates close friends.[32]

Starting a quarrel is like breaching a dam; so drop the matter before a dispute breaks out.[33]

A man of knowledge uses words with restraint, and a man of understanding is even-tempered.[34]

Whoever guards his mouth and tongue keeps his soul from troubles.[35]

A fool vents all his feelings, but a wise man holds them back.[36]

Buddha attached a similar level of importance to restraint in speech:

Silently shall I endure abuse as the elephant in battle endures the arrow sent from the bow: for the world is ill-natured.[37]

The Bhikshu who controls his mouth, who speaks wisely and calmly, who teaches the meaning and the law, his word is sweet.[38]

Types of Good and Bad Speech

If the two paragraphs appearing in boxes at the beginning of this chapter—which describe the effects and types of Right Speech in Buddhism—were used instead as a summary of the content of Solomon's proverbs on right speech, they would be perfectly accurate. Not only that, but most of the key words in those paragraphs (or virtual synonyms of them) are specifically used in Solomon's proverbs on speech. For example, "idle chatter" is cited, and it also appears in a proverb of Solomon:

Idle chatter leads only to poverty.[39]

In the following we will explore specific types of good and bad speech and their parallels in Buddha and Solomon.

1. Tell the Truth—No False or Deceitful Speech or Lies

Solomon gave pointed prohibitions against speaking falsely:

> Put away from you a *deceitful* mouth and put devious speech far from you.[40]

A proverb of Buddha has a very similar flavor, covering a broader range of types of speech:

> Beware of the anger of the tongue, and control thy tongue! Leave the sins of the tongue, and practise virtue with thy tongue![41]

Buddha went further than this in a later proverb of the Dhammapada, plainly stating that the ultimate destiny of hell awaited the liar:

> He who says what is not, goes to hell; he also who, having done a thing, says I have not done it. After death both are equal, they are men with evil deeds in the next world.[42]

2. Only Speak in a Friendly, Warm Manner—No Slander or Malicious Talk

Solomon put great value on keeping interpersonal communications positive:

> He who covers over an offense *promotes love*, but whoever repeats the matter *separates close friends*.[43]

> Pleasant words are like a honeycomb, sweetness to the soul and health to the bones.[44]

The great value of noble, wholesome words cannot be underestimated, in Solomon's view:

> The tongue of the righteous is choice silver, but the heart of the wicked is of little value.[45]

That some speech can be sweet is emphasized in the following proverb of Buddha:

> The Bhikshu who controls his mouth, who speaks wisely and calmly, who teaches the meaning and the law, his word is sweet.[46]

3. Only Speak Gently—No Harsh Words

Solomon encouraged limiting speech to gentle words since harsh words can evoke strong reactions and feelings:

> A *gentle* answer turns away wrath, but a harsh word stirs up anger.[47]

> There is one who speaks rashly *like the thrusts of a sword*, but the tongue of the wise *brings healing*.[48]

> A fool vents all his feelings, but a wise man holds them back.[49]

Buddha elaborated on the consequences harsh words will have on those who utter them:

> Do not speak harshly to anybody; those who are spoken to will answer thee in the same way. Angry speech is painful, blows for blows will touch thee.[50]

4. Talk Only When Necessary—No Idle Chatter

As noted before, one proverb of Solomon's actually refers to "idle chatter":

Idle chatter leads only to poverty.[51]

Though no proverb of Buddha uses these specific words, the importance of not talking too much is clearly emphasized:

A man is not learned because he talks much; he who is patient, free from hatred and fear, he is called learned.[52]

Clearly, practicing wholesome speech and avoiding negative talk was very important to both great wise men. They each devoted many proverbs to this issue. Speech had wide-ranging consequences for the individual, for his or her immediate circle, and for those in the wider community, and good speech was an essential part of the path of wisdom.

Right Action

"1. to abstain from harming sentient beings, especially to abstain from taking life (including suicide) and doing harm intentionally or delinquently, 2. to abstain from taking what is not given, which includes stealing, robbery, fraud, deceitfulness, and dishonesty, and 3. to abstain from sexual misconduct. Positively formulated, right action means **to act kindly and compassionately, to be honest, to respect the belongings of others, and to keep sexual relationships harmless to others.**"[53]

The summary in the box above describes Buddha's notion of Right Action. And yet, it could equally be applied to Solomon. The first two points above are covered in a single proverb of Solomon:

There are six things the LORD hates, seven that are detestable to him: haughty eyes, a lying tongue, hands that shed innocent blood, a heart that devises wicked schemes, feet that are quick to rush into evil, a false witness who pours out lies and a man who stirs up dissension among brothers.[54]

Let's look at this in the form of a chart that puts the different parts of the Buddhist description of Right Action side by side with specific proverbs of Solomon that refer to the same concepts, drawing primarily from Proverbs 6:16–19 quoted above. The second column guides you to the sections of the rest of this chapter that discuss these points. The numbers of the sections correspond to the numbers in the box above.

Buddhist Description	Chapter Subheading	As Described in Proverbs
To abstain from harming sentient beings . . . and doing harm intentionally or delinquently.	(1) Don't Harm, Be Kind; (2) Do Good	A man who stirs up dissension among brothers.[55]
To abstain from taking life (including suicide).	(1) Don't Kill	Hands that shed innocent blood.[56]
To abstain from taking what is not given, which includes stealing, robbery, fraud, deceitfulness and dishonesty.	(2a) Be Generous; (2b) Don't Steal, Defraud, or Lie; (2c) Avoid Hypocrisy	A lying tongue. A heart that devises wicked schemes. Feet that are quick to rush into evil. A false witness who pours out lies.[57]
To abstain from sexual misconduct.	(3) Don't Commit Sexual Misconduct	Why be captivated, my son, by an adulteress?[58]

It is curious that the one part of Proverbs 6:16–19 that is missing from the Buddhist description of Right Action (and from other Right Steps) is the reference to "haughty eyes," or excessive pride. Perhaps this is because the term "haughty eyes" represents an attitude and way of seeing things more than it describes an action. And yet, its absence may not be coincidental. It seems that striving to attain enlightenment carries with it an element of great pride, as discussed in the last section of Chapter Seven on "Right Mindfulness." The following proverb(s) of Buddha seem to epitomize one type of "haughty eyes":

I have conquered all, I know all, in all conditions of life I am free from taint; I have left all, and through the destruction of thirst I am free; having learnt myself, whom shall I teach?[59]

This next proverb of Buddha covers all parts of Right Action, except that harm in a general sense is not mentioned:

He who destroys life, who speaks untruth, who in this world takes what is not given him, who goes to another man's wife; and the man who gives himself to drinking intoxicating liquors, he, even in this world, digs up his own root.[60]

In the rest of this chapter we will look at each of the types of Right Action separately. Each heading includes the number of the type of action cited in the Buddhist definition in the boxed paragraph above.

The word "karma" means action. So, it should not be surprising that many of the proverbs of both Solomon and Buddha have a distinct, often dramatic, karmic essence.

1. Don't Kill

One of the Ten Commandments of Judaism is "You shall not murder."[61] So Solomon felt no need to include this obvious moral prohibition in his proverbs. He did, however, warn against following those who would say:

"Come along with us; let's lie in wait for innocent blood, let's ambush some harmless soul; let's swallow them alive, like the grave, and whole, like those who go down to the pit."[62]

Of these people, he said the following, implying that those who set out to take someone else's life are only destroying their own:

These men lie in wait for their own blood; they ambush only themselves![63]

Buddha emphasized the importance of not taking life by two consecutive proverbs that closely parallel one another:

All men tremble at punishment, all men fear death; remember that you are like unto them, and do not kill, nor cause slaughter.[64]

All men tremble at punishment, all men love life; remember that thou art like unto them, and do not kill, nor cause slaughter.[65]

1. Don't Harm, Be Kind

Unjustified Harm

Solomon stressed the importance of not causing harm, especially if there is no justification for inflicting it:

Do not plot harm against your neighbor, who lives trustfully near you. Do not accuse a man for no reason—when he has done you no harm.[66]

Buddha issued even stronger words against causing harm, citing a list of ten possible dreadful consequences and concluding with a final result—going to hell:

He who inflicts pain on innocent and harmless persons, will soon come to one of these ten states: He will have cruel suffering, loss, injury of the body, heavy affliction, or loss of mind, or a misfortune coming from the king, or a fearful accusation, or loss of relations, or destruction of treasures, or lightning-fire will burn his houses; and when his body is destroyed, the fool will go to hell.[67]

Violence

People automatically associate Buddha with nonviolence and seeking peace. What is less known is that these were also values Solomon espoused. For example:

> Do not envy a violent man or choose any of his ways, for the Lord detests a perverse man but takes the upright into his confidence.[68]

Solomon emphasized that those who are violent will certainly be destroyed—because they have willfully opposed justice:

> The violence of the wicked will destroy them, because they refuse to do justice.[69]

This proverb has a strong karmic flavor. Buddha stressed this same theme in four different proverbs. Here are two of them:

> He who seeking his own happiness punishes or kills beings who also long for happiness, will not find happiness after death.[70]

> He who seeking his own happiness does not punish or kill beings who also long for happiness, will find happiness after death.[71]

The scope of this last proverb must be limited, for certainly unhappiness in the hereafter will be experienced as the result of any of a wide range of wrongdoings, even if someone refrains from tormenting others.

The other two are as follows. The great emphasis Buddha had on always being nonviolent is evident in these two proverbs:

> A man is not an elect (Ariya) because he injures living creatures; because he has pity on all living creatures, therefore is a man called Ariya.[72]

A man is not just if he carries a matter by violence; no, he who distinguishes both right and wrong, who is learned and leads others, not by violence, but by law and equity, and who is guarded by the law and intelligent, he is called just.[73]

Being a Peacemaker

Solomon devoted many more proverbs to the virtues of seeking peace than Buddha did. The Jewish king placed great value on seeking peace and avoiding conflict, and he was known as a man of peace:

It is a man's honor to avoid strife, but every fool is quick to quarrel.[74]

He who covers over an offense promotes love, but whoever repeats a matter separates close friends.[75]

He who is slow to anger is better than the mighty. And he who rules his spirit than he who takes a city.[76]

When a man's ways are pleasing to the Lord, he makes even his enemies live at peace with him.[77]

Buddha praised forbearance, a patient endurance and self-control that refrains from reacting adversely, even when there is ample justification for striking back:

The Awakened call patience the highest penance, long-suffering the highest Nirvana; for he is not an anchorite (pravragita) who strikes others, he is not an ascetic (sramana) who insults others.[78]

Solomon painted sharp contrasts of the karmic consequences of two radically different kinds of people:

The merciful, kind, and generous man benefits himself [for his deeds return to bless him], but he who is cruel and callous [to the wants of others] brings on himself retribution.[79]

Solomon went much further than Buddha did in the positive, lauding the character qualities of mercy, kindness, and generosity. The concepts of mercy, grace, and forgiveness are generally absent in Buddhism. Buddhists regard these as emotion based—a sign of weakness. Instead, Buddha stressed forbearance and refraining from violence and made these one of the cornerstones of his new religion. That he is so closely associated with these values is due in no small way to the Indian emperor Ashoka, whose domain covered nearly all of the Indian subcontinent from 269 to 232 B.C. Ashoka converted to Buddhism after observing the enormous bloodshed of the war of Kalinga, and he devoted himself to the spread of Buddhism throughout India and much of Asia.[80]

Additional proverbs of Buddha on nonviolence are:

He who, by causing pain to others, wishes to obtain pleasure for himself, he, entangled in the bonds of hatred, will never be free from hatred.[81]

Let a man guard himself against irritability in bodily action; let him be controlled in deed. Abandoning bodily misconduct, let him practice good conduct in deed.[82]

Some further sample proverbs of Solomon on nonviolence and peacekeeping follow:

A fool shows his annoyance at once, but a prudent man overlooks an insult.[83]

There is deceit in the hearts of those who plot evil, but joy for those who promote peace.[84]

An offended brother is more unyielding than a fortified city, and disputes are like the barred gates of a citadel.[85]

A gentle answer turns away wrath, but a harsh word stirs up anger.[86]

A hot-tempered man stirs up dissension, but a patient man calms a quarrel.[87]

Starting a quarrel is like breaching a dam, so drop a matter before a dispute breaks out.[88]

Judging Unfairly

Solomon placed great value on upholding justice and rejecting bribes:

The king establishes the land by justice, but he who receives bribes overthrows it.[89]

A wicked man accepts a bribe behind the back to pervert the ways of justice.[90]

Solomon also stressed the need for fairness in administering justice:

A false balance is an abomination to the Lord, but a just weight is His delight.[91]

Buddha asserted that "might does not make right" and that justice requires wise, insightful arbitrators:

A man is not just if he carries a matter by violence; no, he who distinguishes both right and wrong, who is learned and leads others, not by violence, but by law and equity, and who is guarded by the law and intelligent, he is called just.[92]

Be a Good Friend

Some of Solomon's proverbs speak of the sweetness and value of friendships:

> A friend loves at all times, and a brother is born for adversity.[93]

> Ointment and perfume delight the heart, and the sweetness of a man's friend does so by hearty counsel.[94]

> A man who has friends must himself be friendly, But there is a friend who sticks closer than a brother.[95]

Some of Buddha's proverbs likewise make reference to this concept, though in a more subtle way:

> Let him live in charity, let him be perfect in his duties; then in the fulness of delight he will make an end of suffering.[96]

> Kinsmen, friends, and lovers salute a man who has been long away, and returns safe from afar.[97]

> In like manner his good works receive him who has done good, and has gone from this world to the other;—as kinsmen receive a friend on his return.[98]

2. Do Good

Solomon chided people to overcome their reluctance to do good deeds:

> Do not withhold good from those who deserve it, when it is in your power to act. Do not say to your neighbor, "Come back later; I'll give it tomorrow"—when you now have it with you.[99]

Likewise, Buddha urged people to forge ahead in doing good deeds, seeing it as a way to thwart the tendency to do evil:

If a man would hasten towards the good, he should keep his thought away from evil; if a man does what is good slothfully, his mind delights in evil.[100]

As many kinds of wreaths can be made from a heap of flowers, so many good things may be achieved by a mortal when once he is born.[101]

Buddha also noted the relative ease of doing evil deeds versus good ones:

Bad deeds, and deeds hurtful to ourselves, are easy to do; what is beneficial and good, that is very difficult to do.[102]
As the impurity which springs from the iron, when it springs from it, destroys it; thus do a transgressor's own works lead him to the evil path.[103]

2a. Be Generous

Solomon placed great value on generosity:

The sluggard's craving will be the death of him, because his hands refuse to work. All day long he craves for more, but *the righteous give without sparing*.[104]

Cast your bread upon the waters, for you will find it after many days. Give a serving to seven, and also to eight, for you do not know what evil will be on the earth.[105]

One man gives freely, yet gains even more. Another man withholds unduly, but comes to poverty.[106]

This last proverb of Solomon is a precursor to the following saying of Buddha:

The uncharitable do not go to the world of the gods; fools only do not praise liberality; a wise man rejoices in liberality, and through it becomes blessed in the other world.[107]

Additional proverbs of Solomon on generosity include the following:

A generous man will prosper; he who refreshes others will himself be refreshed.[108]

If a man shuts his ears to the cry of the poor, he too will cry out and not be answered.[109]

A good man leaves an inheritance to his children's children.[110]

The righteous man walks in his integrity; blessed (happy, fortunate, enviable) are his children after him.[111]

2b. Don't Steal, Defraud, or Lie

A sense of the inevitable working of bad karma characterizes the next two proverbs of Solomon:

Wealth gained by dishonesty will be diminished, but he who gathers by labor will increase.[112]

Food gained by fraud tastes sweet to a man, but he ends up with a mouth full of gravel.[113]

This next proverb of Buddha, quoted early in this chapter, cites all three forms of bad behavior covered in this section:

He who destroys life, who speaks untruth, who in this world takes what is not given him, who goes to another man's wife; and the man who gives himself to drinking intoxicating liquors, he, even in this world, digs up his own root.[114]

Buddha makes an even more dramatic illustration of karmic consequences:

> Better it would be to swallow a heated iron ball, like flaring fire, than that a bad unrestrained fellow should live on the charity of the land.[115]

2c. Avoid Hypocrisy

Buddha's pronouncements against hypocrisy are much more clear and direct than Solomon's. First, Buddha's:

> Like a beautiful flower, full of colour, but without scent, are the fine but fruitless words of him who does not act accordingly.[116]

> But, like a beautiful flower, full of colour and full of scent, are the fine and fruitful words of him who acts accordingly.[117]

> The thoughtless man, even if he can recite a large portion (of the law), but is not a doer of it, has no share in the priesthood, but is like a cowherd counting the cows of others.[118]

> Let each man direct himself first to what is proper, then let him teach others; thus a wise man will not suffer.[119]

The importance of direct action over oblique religious ceremonies is emphasized by Solomon:

> To do righteousness and justice is more acceptable to the Lord than sacrifice.[120]

> The fruit of the righteous is a tree of life, and he who is wise wins souls.[121]

Winning souls requires both words and action, intention and effort.

3. Don't Commit Sexual Misconduct

Solomon graciously exhorts men to be faithful to their wives:

> Drink water from your own cistern, running water from your
> own well. Should your springs overflow in the streets, your
> streams of water in the public squares? Let them be yours
> alone, never to be shared with strangers. May your fountain be
> blessed, and may you rejoice in the wife of your youth. A
> loving doe, a graceful deer—may her breasts satisfy you always,
> may you ever be captivated by her love. Why be captivated, my
> son, by an adulteress? Why embrace the bosom of another
> man's wife?[122]

As so often in this chapter, Buddha's descriptions of dire karmic
consequences are quite draconian:

> Four things does a wreckless man gain who covets his
> neighbour's wife,—a bad reputation, an uncomfortable bed,
> thirdly, punishment, and lastly, hell.[123]

> There is bad reputation, and the evil way (to hell), there is the
> short pleasure of the frightened in the arms of the frightened,
> and the king imposes heavy punishment; therefore let no man
> think of his neighbour's wife.[124]

We have reviewed about a dozen pairings of similar proverbs on
Right Speech in this chapter and over two dozen on Right Action.
Surprisingly, there are some categories of Right Action where
Solomon had much to say, but Buddha did not. These include
women, family, government, and borrowing and lending, and are
not covered here. However, the subject of Right Action has not by
any means been covered fully: People also carry out actions in
specific kinds of contexts, and one of these is the very important
realm of earning a living. In addition, Right Action is not likely to
happen without conscious attention to Right Effort. Buddha and
Solomon both had much to say on these subjects.

[1] Thomas Knierim, editor and webmaster, "The Noble Eightfold Path," Raison d'Etre, www.thebigview.com/buddhism/eightfoldpath.html, retrieved May 12, 2010.

[2] Ibid. (emphasis added).

[3] Proverbs 18:21 (AMP).

[4] Dhammapada 100.

[5] Ibid., 101.

[6] Ibid., 102.

[7] Proverbs 15:4 (NASB).

[8] Dhammapada 176.

[9] Ibid., 246-247 (emphasis added).

[10] Ibid., 306.

[11] Proverbs 18:8 and 26:22 (NKJV).

[12] Proverbs 10:20 (NIV).

[13] Dhammapada 176.

[14] Proverbs 17:9 (NIV) (emphasis added).

[15] Proverbs 12:18 (NASB) (emphasis added).

[16] Proverbs 10:21 (NIV) (emphasis added).

[17] Proverbs 11:11 (NIV) (emphasis added).

[18] Proverbs 16:24 (NKJV) (emphasis added).

[19] Proverbs 15:4 (NASB) (emphasis added).

[20] Proverbs 10:6 (NASB) (emphasis added).

[21] Proverbs 12:6 (NIV) (emphasis added).

[22] Proverbs 12:13 (NASB) (emphasis added).

[23] Proverbs 14:23b (NKJV) (emphasis added).

[24] Proverbs 21:23 (NKJV) (emphasis added).

[25] Dhammapada 258.

[26] Ibid., 259.

[27] Proverbs 10:19 (AMP).

[28] Proverbs 29:11 (NKJV).

[29] Proverbs 14:23b (NKJV).

[30] Proverbs 10:19 (AMP).

[31] Proverbs 12:16 (NIV).

[32] Proverbs 17:9 (NIV).

[33] Proverbs 17:14 (NIV).

[34] Proverbs 17:27 (NIV).

[35] Proverbs 21:23 (NKJV).

[36] Proverbs 29:11 (NKJV).

[37] Dhammapada 320.

[38] Ibid., 363.

[39] Proverbs 14:23b (NKJV).

[40] Proverbs 4:24 (NASB) (emphasis added).

[41] Dhammapada 232.

[42] Ibid., 306.

[43] Proverbs 17:9 (NIV) (emphasis added).

[44] Proverbs 16:24 (NKJV).

[45] Proverbs 10:20 (NIV).

[46] Dhammapada 363.

[47] Proverbs 15:1 (NIV) (emphasis added).

[48] Proverbs 12:18 (NASB) (emphasis added).

[49] Proverbs 29:11 (NKJV).

[50] Dhammapada 133.

[51] Proverbs 14:23b (NKJV).

[52] Dhammapada 258.

[53] Knierim, "The Noble Eightfold Path."

[54] Proverbs 6:16–19 (NIV).

[55] Proverbs 6:19b (NIV).

[56] Proverbs 6:17b (NIV).

[57] Proverbs 6:17b-19a (NIV).

[58] Proverbs 5:20a (NIV).

[59] Dhammapada 353.

[60] Ibid., 246–247.

[61] Exodus 20:13 (NIV).

[62] Proverbs 1:11–12 (NIV).

[63] Proverbs 1:18 (NIV).

[64] Dhammapada 129.

[65] Ibid., 130.

[66] Proverbs 3:29–30 (NIV).

[67] Dhammapada 137–140.

[68] Proverbs 3:31–32 (NIV).

[69] Proverbs 21:7 (NKJV).

[70] Dhammapada 131.

[71] Ibid., 132.

[72] Ibid., 270.

[73] Ibid., 256-257.

[74] Proverbs 20:3 (NIV).

[75] Proverbs 17:9 (NIV).

[76] Proverbs 16:32 (NKJV).

[77] Proverbs 16:7 (NIV).

[78] Dhammapada 184.

[79] Proverbs 11:17 (AMP).

[80] "Ashoka," New World Encyclopedia, www.newworldencyclopedia.org/entry/Ashoka, retrieved October 8, 2010.

[81] Dhammapada 291.

[82] Ibid., 231; "Kodhavagga: Anger," translated by Acharya Buddharakkhita, Access to Insight, www.accesstoinsight.org/tipitaka/kn/dhp/dhp.17.budd.html, retrieved January 5, 2011.

[83] Proverbs 12:16 (NIV).

[84] Proverbs 12:20 (NIV).

[85] Proverbs 18:19 (NIV).

[86] Proverbs 15:1 (NIV).

[87] Proverbs 15:18 (NIV).

[88] Proverbs 17:14 (NIV).

[89] Proverbs 29:4 (NKJV).

[90] Proverbs 17:23 (NKJV).

[91] Proverbs 11:1 (NKJV).

[92] Dhammapada 256-257.

[93] Proverbs 17:17 (NKJV).

[94] Proverbs 27:9 (NKJV).

[95] Proverbs 18:24 (NKJV).

[96] Dhammapada 376.

[97] Ibid., 219.

[98] Ibid., 220.

[99] Proverbs 3:27–28 (NIV).

[100] Dhammapada 116.

[101] Ibid., 53.

[102] Ibid., 163.

[103] Ibid., 240.

[104] Proverbs 21:25–26 (NIV) (emphasis added).

[105] Ecclesiastes 11:1–2 (NKJV).

[106] Proverbs 11:24 (NIV).

[107] Dhammapada 177.

[108] Proverbs 11:25 (NIV).

[109] Proverbs 21:13 (NIV).

[110] Proverbs 13:22a (NKJV).

[111] Proverbs 20:7 (AMP).

[112] Proverbs 13:11 (NKJV).

[113] Proverbs 20:17 (NIV).

[114] Dhammapada 246–247.

[115] Ibid., 308.

[116] Ibid., 51.

[117] Ibid., 52.

[118] Ibid., 19.

[119] Ibid., 158.

[120] Proverbs 21:3 (NKJV).

[121] Proverbs 11:30 (NASB).

[122] Proverbs 5:15–20 (NIV).

[123] Dhammapada 309.

[124] Ibid., 310.

Chapter Six
Precursors to Buddha's Right Livelihood and Effort

In this chapter, we will focus on proverbs regarding the fifth and sixth steps of Buddha's Noble Eightfold Path: Right Livelihood and Right Effort. In the fifth step we will encounter some ways in which Buddha clearly differed from Solomon. As in all such instances, Buddha's stance coincides with that of Jain ascetics.

Right Livelihood

"One should **earn one's living in a righteous way and that wealth should be gained legally and peacefully**. The Buddha mentions four specific activities that harm other beings and that one should avoid for this reason: **1. dealing in weapons, 2. dealing in living beings (including raising animals for slaughter as well as slave trade and prostitution), 3. working in meat production and butchery, and 4. selling intoxicants and poisons, such as alcohol and drugs**."[1]

These points are discussed below in the order in which they appear in the box.

Earning a Living Righteously

Solomon emphasized the nobility of performing a job with excellence, claiming that those who did so would earn solid recognition from rulers and other famous people:

> Do you see a man who excels in his work? He will stand before kings; He will not stand before unknown men.[2]

This same concept (i.e., mastery producing laudable results) is subtly present in one of Buddha's proverbs:

Well-makers lead the water (wherever they like); fletchers bend the arrow; carpenters bend a log of wood; wise people fashion themselves.[3]

This proverb of Buddha would seem to run counter to the first admonition about inappropriate occupations, in that fletchers make arrows, the purpose of which is either to kill animals or people. Is not a fletcher dealing in weapons? On the other hand, it could well be that Buddha was citing fletchers and their skill in making arrows as an example of skilled craftsmanship taken from Indian society, even though such activity was not acceptable to him.

Gaining Wealth Legally and Peacefully

In the next two proverbs, Solomon spoke against "ill-gotten gains" but did not provide specifics about what kinds of gains would be so regarded:

Such is the end of all who go after ill-gotten gain; it takes away the lives of those who get it.[4]

Ill-gotten gains do not profit, but righteousness delivers from death.[5]

He surely would have thought ill-gotten gains would include those received by means of deceitful trade practices, such as the use of false balances:

A false balance is an abomination to the LORD: but a just weight is his delight.[6]

In the following proverb Solomon stressed the need to acquire wealth honestly through hard work:

Wealth gained by dishonesty will be diminished. But he who gathers by labor will increase.[7]

To Buddha, labor was, at best, a necessary evil to common people. The effort expended in work would generate some kind of karma, whether good or bad, that would need to be dispelled before one could hope to approach enlightenment. We get this sense from the following proverb:

> Let us live happily then, though we call nothing our own! We shall be like the bright gods, feeding on happiness![8]

In another translation, the first sentence links living without possessions to being happy.[9] This is an instance where Buddha differs sharply from Solomon, and, as with nearly all such differences, it probably harkens back to Buddha's involvement with Jain asceticism just prior to his enlightenment. Both Buddha and Solomon warned against gaining livelihood or wealth by illicit means or through any activity that would treat others unjustly. For Solomon, this meant following honest business practices. Buddha took it further and extolled staying away from business, if possible, and making do with less. It is another instance where Buddha takes an issue to a greater extreme than Solomon.

Not Engaging in Activities That Harm Other Beings

In an agrarian society, animal husbandry and care is a leading occupation. Solomon highlighted the importance of considerate diligence in this activity:

> Be diligent to know the state of your flocks, and attend to your herds; for riches are not forever, nor does a crown endure to all generations. When the hay is removed, and the tender grass shows itself, and the herbs of the mountains are gathered in, the lambs will provide your clothing, and the goats the price of a field; you shall have enough goats' milk for your food, for the food of your household, and the nourishment of your maidservants.[10]

Another proverb of Solomon paints a picture of the keeper of livestock taking care of his flock:

> A righteous man cares for the needs of his animal, but the kindest acts of the wicked are cruel.[11]

A different translation adds another twist to the same proverb:

> A righteous man regards the life of his animal, but the tender mercies of the wicked are cruel.[12]

In biblical times, animal sacrifices were a key part of sacred ceremonies in Judaism, as was commanded for the atonement of many sins and for the worship of and reconciliation with God in the writings of Moses. These practices, of course, directly conflicted with the prohibition against the taking of the life of any sentient (conscious) being that was very widespread in Hinduism and integral to Buddhism. The following proverb of Buddha emphasizes this:

> A man is not an elect (Ariya) because he injures living creatures; because he has pity on all living creatures, therefore is a man called Ariya.[13]

Again, Buddha takes an idea to a greater extreme than Solomon, though the root idea (in this case, treating animals well) is the same. Solomon said to take good care of one's animals, but he never forbade animal sacrifices or meat-eating. Buddha took the idea further, promoting complete nonviolence toward animals, as was common among both Hindus and Jains.

Intoxicants

While the Dhammapada is silent about the perils of excess drinking, Solomon devoted some proverbs to the subject:

> Who has woe? Who has sorrow? Who has contentions? Who has complaints? Who has wounds without cause? Who has

redness of eyes? Those who linger long at the wine, those who go in search of mixed wine.[14]

Wine is a mocker, strong drink a brawler, and whoever is intoxicated by it is not wise.[15]

Hear, my son, and be wise; And guide your heart in the way. Do not mix with winebibbers, or with gluttonous eaters of meat.[16]

Right Effort

"The same type of energy that fuels desire, envy, aggression, and violence can on the other side fuel self-discipline, honesty, benevolence, and kindness. Right effort is detailed in four types of endeavors that rank in ascending order of perfection: 1. to *prevent* the arising of unarisen unwholesome states, 2. to *abandon* unwholesome states that have already arisen, 3. to *arouse* wholesome states that have not yet arisen, and 4. to *maintain* and perfect wholesome states already arisen."[17]

Buddhism emphasizes four aspects of Right Effort, as mentioned in the definition above. One of the clearest examples of each of these four types appears in five consecutive verses in Solomon's Proverbs, as detailed in the following table:

Words of Solomon Proverbs 4:23–27, NKJV	Types of Buddhist Moral Endeavor
23. Above all else, keep your heart with all diligence, for out of it spring the issues of life.	Prevent & Maintain
24. Put away from you a deceitful mouth, and put perverse lips far from you.	Abandon
25. Let your eyes look straight ahead, and your eyelids look right before you.	Prevent, Arouse & Maintain

26a. Ponder the path of your feet,	Mindfulness
26b. And let all your ways be established.	Arouse & Maintain
27a. Do not turn to the right or the left;	Prevent
27b. Remove your foot from evil.	Abandon

If Buddha had sought to rewrite the above verses in his own words, the result could well have been the following proverb:

> He who controls his hand, he who controls his feet, he who controls his speech, he who is well controlled, he who delights inwardly, who is collected, who is solitary and content, him they call Bhikshu.[18]

There are clear parallels between all parts of these two sets of proverbs, as is evident in the following chart. Imagery involving feet and speech are common to both as well.

Words of Solomon Proverbs 4:23–27, NKJV	Words of Buddha Dhammapada 362
23. Above all else, keep your heart with all diligence, for out of it spring the issues of life.	He . . . who is well controlled, he who delights inwardly, who is collected, who is . . . content . . .
24. Put away from you a deceitful mouth, and put perverse lips far from you.	. . . he who controls his speech . . .
25. Let your eyes look straight ahead, and your eyelids look right before you.	He . . . who is well controlled, . . . who is collected . . .
26a. Ponder the path of your feet,	He . . . who controls his feet . . .
26b. And let all your ways be established.	. . . him they call Bhikshu.
27a. Do not turn to the right or the left;	He who controls his hand, he who controls his feet . . .
27b. Remove your foot from evil.	He . . . who controls his feet . . .

One of Buddha's proverbs provides a fairly compact presentation of each type of moral effort. To put it in chart form:

Words of Buddha *Dhammapada 293*	Types of Buddhist *Moral Endeavor*
But they whose whole watchfulness is always directed to their body,	Prevent
who do not follow what ought not to be done,	Abandon
who steadfastly do what ought to be done,	Arouse
watchful and wise people,	Maintain (via Mindfulness)
the desires of such watchful and wise people will come to an end.	Maintain

Another series of Solomon's proverbs provides examples of three of the four types of moral effort, with repeated mention of mental activities intended to maintain a high moral state:

Words of Solomon *Proverbs 4:5–9, NKJV*	Types of Buddhist *Moral Endeavor*
5a. Get wisdom! Get understanding!	Arouse
5b. Do not forget, nor turn away from the words of my mouth.	Maintain
6a. Do not forsake her,	Prevent
6b. And she will preserve you.	Maintain
6c. Love her	Arouse & Maintain
6d. And she will keep you.	Maintain
7. Wisdom is the principal thing. Therefore get wisdom. And in all your getting, get understanding.	Arouse & Maintain
8a. Exalt her,	
8b. And she will promote you; she will bring	Maintain

you honor, when you embrace her.

9. She will place on your head an ornament of grace; a crown of glory she will deliver to you.

The following excerpt from Solomon's writings seems to presume the simultaneous application of all four types of moral effort:

> I, the Teacher, was king over Israel in Jerusalem. *I devoted myself to study and to explore by wisdom all that is done under heaven.* . . . I have seen all the things that are done under the sun; all of them are meaningless, a chasing after the wind. . . . I thought to myself, "Look, I have grown and increased in wisdom more than anyone who has ruled over Jerusalem before me; I have experienced much of wisdom and knowledge." Then *I applied myself to the understanding of wisdom,* and also of madness and folly, but I learned that this, too, is a chasing after the wind. For with much wisdom comes much sorrow; the more knowledge, the more grief.[19]

How would it be possible for any person to pursue wisdom and knowledge while reviewing "all the things that are done under the sun"? Surely many of these "things" would involve moral temptations to the investigator. So there would be a great need, before beginning such a sweeping review, to *abandon* any moral weaknesses one had, being objective and ruthless about it. As the investigator encountered various temptations, there would be an ongoing need to *prevent* the arousal of unwholesome feelings and activities. To be able to do that, one would need to deliberately attempt to *arouse* wholesome states of mind and heart to fortify oneself against being drawn into morally hazardous activities. And one would need to *maintain* such wholesome states throughout the whole process.

Solomon called such speculation "vanity," which he says causes much sorrow and grief. Solomon's conclusion, in Ecclesiastes, was that one should just live in the moment, enjoying the simple pleasures of life. The conclusions of his far-reaching investigations are notable:

> Then I realized that it is good and proper for a man to eat and drink, and to find satisfaction in his toilsome labor under the sun during the few days of life God has given him—for this is his lot. Moreover, when God gives any man wealth and possessions, and enables him to enjoy them, to accept his lot and be happy in his work—this is a gift of God. He *seldom reflects* on the days of his life, because God keeps him occupied with gladness of heart.[20]

In other words, partaking in speculation about philosophical issues and questions of religious doctrine is not helpful in trying to become a more ethical person. Huston Smith described Buddha's opinion on this matter: "'Greed for views' on questions of this sort 'tend not to edification.' His practical program was exacting, and he was not going to let his flock be diverted from the hard road of arduous action by the agreeable fields of profitless speculation."[21]

Solomon taught his sons—and he must have had many, for he had three hundred wives—to deeply value (i.e., treasure) his teachings:

> My son, keep [*maintain*] my words and treasure [*arouse*] my commandments within you. Keep [*maintain*] my command-ments and live, and my teaching as the apple of your eye. Bind them on your fingers; write them on the tablet of your heart [*maintain*].[22]

So strong was this emotional valuing to be that his sons were to want to keep his teachings as instinctively as they would protect and value their eyes. And their loyalty to these teachings was to be unshakable—as much as a ring is bound around one of their fingers. Further, Solomon's teachings were to be burnished into the deepest part of their inner being. We also find this kind of intensity of devotion expressed in the following proverb of Buddha:

He in whom a desire for the Ineffable (Nirvana) has sprung up, who is satisfied in his mind, and whose thoughts are not bewildered by love, he is called urdhvamsrotas (carried upwards by the stream) [*arouse*].[23]

Solomon warned his followers to guard their hearts from anything that would weaken their devotion to following the path of pursuing righteousness that he had espoused:

Above all else, guard your heart, for it is the wellspring of life [*all*].[24]

Buddha likewise put great stress on guarding against various things that could easily derail one's spirituality. In the next proverb of Buddha, the word "guard" is also present to describe this mental discipline:

Beware of the anger of the mind, and control thy mind [*prevent*]! Leave the sins of the mind [*abandon*], and practise virtue with thy mind [*arouse*]![25]

An Indian picture of guarding appears in the next proverb of Buddha:

As rain does not break through a well-thatched house, passion will not break through a well-reflecting mind [*prevent*].[26]

Yet other proverbs of Buddha also convey the importance of guarding what one's mind and heart are focused on:

He who holds back rising anger like a rolling chariot, him I call a real driver; other people are but holding the reins [*prevent*].[27]

Those who are ever watchful, who study day and night, and who strive after Nirvana [*arouse*], their passions will come to an end [*prevent*].[28]

This mind of mine went formerly wandering about as it liked, as it listed, as it pleased; but I shall now hold it in thoroughly [*prevent*], as the rider who holds the hook holds in the furious elephant.[29]

If a man would hasten towards the good, he should keep his thought away from evil; if a man does what is good slothfully, his mind delights in evil [*arouse, prevent*].[30]

He who always quiets the evil, whether small or large, he is called a Samana (a quiet man), because he has quieted all evil [*abandon, prevent*].[31]

Solomon underscored the great benefits of going hard after right living and caring deeply about others. These benefits included a fulfilling, satisfying life that others would admire:

He who pursues righteousness and love [*arouse, maintain*] finds life, prosperity and honor.[32]

To Buddha, pursuing one's own righteousness was of paramount importance:

Let no one forget his own duty for the sake of another's, however great [*maintain*]; let a man, after he has discerned his own duty, be always attentive to his duty [*arouse*].[33]

If anything is to be done, let a man do it, let him attack it vigorously [*arouse*]! A careless pilgrim only scatters the dust of his passions more widely.[34]

The importance of intensely seeking wisdom and understanding is emphasized in the following words of Solomon:

My son, if you receive my words, and treasure my commands within you, so that you incline your ear to wisdom, and apply your heart to understanding; yes, if you cry out for discernment, and lift up your voice for understanding, if you seek her as silver, and search for her as for hidden treasures; then you will understand the fear of the Lord and find the knowledge of God. For the Lord gives wisdom, from His mouth come knowledge and understanding.[35]

While Solomon believed, at least during the earlier parts of his reign, that a quest for wisdom and understanding would ultimately lead the seeker to a knowledge of God and God's blessings, Buddha sought to formulate a religion that avoided acknowledgment or reliance upon God or any gods. In Buddha's words:

There is no satisfying lusts, even by a shower of gold pieces; he who knows that lusts have a short taste and cause pain, he is wise; Even in *heavenly pleasures* he finds no satisfaction, *the disciple who is fully awakened delights only in the destruction of all desires.*[36]

The great importance of abandonment among the four types of effort is stressed in the last sentence of Proverb 187 above. Many of Buddha's other proverbs also stress this, a clear departure from Solomon's views and his personal practices later in his life:

Let a wise man blow off the impurities of his self, as a smith blows off the impurities of silver one by one, little by little, and from time to time [*abandon*].[37]

Not only by discipline and vows, not only by much learning, not by entering into a trance, not by sleeping alone, do I earn the happiness of release which no worldling can know. Bhikshu, be not confident as long as thou hast not attained the extinction of desires [*abandon*].[38]

Cut down the whole forest (of lust), not a tree only! Danger comes out of the forest (of lust). When you have cut down both the forest (of lust) and its undergrowth, then, Bhikshus, you will be rid of the forest and free [*abandon*]![39]

So long as the love of man towards women, even the smallest, is not destroyed, so long is his mind in bondage, as the calf that drinks milk is to its mother [abandon].[40]

Is it not conceivable that Buddha had Solomon in mind when he wrote the last proverb? He may have been familiar with the story of how Solomon's hundreds of wives turned the heart of this incredibly wise man away from the values that he had so vigorously advocated and pursued when he was younger. Buddha further stated:

Give up what is before, give up what is behind, give up what is in the middle, when thou goest to the other shore of existence; if thy mind is altogether free, thou wilt not again enter into birth and decay.[41]

Buddha's teaching was that self-purification was utterly central to approaching enlightenment:

You yourself must make an effort. The Tathagatas (Buddhas) are only preachers. The thoughtful who enter the way are freed from the bondage of Mara.[42]

A Bhikshu (mendicant) who delights in earnestness, who looks with fear on thoughtlessness, moves about like fire, burning all his fetters, small or large.[43]

A Bhikshu (mendicant) who delights in reflection, who looks with fear on thoughtlessness, cannot fall away (from his perfect state)—he is close upon Nirvana.[44]

And yet Buddha recognized how difficult and unlikely it is for human beings to purify themselves:

The fault of others is easily perceived, but that of oneself is difficult to perceive; a man winnows his neighbour's faults like chaff, but his own fault he hides, as a cheat hides the bad die from the gambler.[45]

Solomon also portrayed accurately the extreme difficulty and improbability of someone fully exercising effective self-evaluation and self-control:

> There is a way that seems right to a man, but in the end it leads to death.[46]

> He who is slow to anger is better than the mighty. And he who *rules his spirit* than he who takes a city.[47]

This is such a critical issue that we will delve into it more extensively in the next chapter.

---

[1] Thomas Knierim, editor and webmaster, "The Noble Eightfold Path," Raison d'Etre, www.thebigview.com/buddhism/eightfoldpath.html, retrieved May 12, 2010 (emphasis added).

[2] Proverbs 22:29 (NKJV).

[3] Dhammapada 80.

[4] Proverbs 1:19 (NIV).

[5] Proverbs 10:2 (NASB).

[6] Proverbs 11:1 (KJV).

[7] Proverbs 13:11 (NKJV).

[8] Dhammapada 200.

[9] Harischandra Kaviratna, trans., *Dhammapada, Wisdom of the Buddha*, 1980, Theosophical University Press Online, http://www.theosociety.org/pasadena/dhamma/dham15.htm, 200., retrieved May 19, 2011.

[10] Proverbs 27:23–27 (NKJV).

[11] Proverbs 12:10 (NIV).

[12] Proverbs 12:10 (NKJV).

[13] Dhammapada 270.

[14] Proverbs 23:29–30 (NKJV).

[15] Proverbs 20:1 (NASB).

[16] Proverbs 23:19–20 (NKJV).

[17] Knierim, "The Noble Eightfold Path" (emphasis added).

[18] Dhammapada 362.

[19] Ecclesiastes 1:12–13a, 14, 16–18 (NIV) (emphasis added).

[20] Ecclesiastes 5:18–20 (NIV) (emphasis added).

[21] Huston Smith, *The Religions of Man* (New York: Harper and Row, 1965), 105.

[22] Proverbs 7:1–3 (NASB).

[23] Dhammapada 218.

[24] Proverbs 4:23 (NIV).

[25] Dhammapada 233 (emphasis added).

[26] Ibid., 14.

[27] Ibid., 222.

[28] Ibid., 226.

[29] Ibid., 326.

[30] Ibid., 116.

[31] Ibid., 265.

[32] Proverbs 21:21 (NIV).

[33] Dhammapada 166.

[34] Ibid., 313.

[35] Proverbs 2:1–6 (NKJV).

[36] Dhammapada 186–187 (emphasis added).

[37] Ibid., 239.

[38] Ibid., 271–272.

[39] Ibid., 283.

[40] Ibid., 284.

[41] Ibid., 348.

[42] Ibid., 276.

[43] Ibid., 31.

[44] Ibid., 32.

[45] Ibid., 252.

[46] Proverbs 14:12 and 16:25 (NIV).

[47] Proverbs 16:32 (NKJV) (emphasis added).

Chapter Seven
Precursors to Buddha's Right Mindfulness

Ideally, mindful people are able to assess the quality and nature of their own thoughts and feelings with a high level of objectivity. They can stand outside themselves, freed of their own personal biases, and observe and evaluate what is going on inside themselves with a ruthless regard for truth and accuracy. They are also disciplined enough to intercept and tame inappropriate thoughts and feelings, as judged by a preselected set of moral and spiritual values that they believe should apply to all people. Part of this involves quick recognition of the natural tendency to rationalize their own thoughts and actions according to relatively lax standards. In theory, a few rare people are capable of all this.

Right Mindfulness

"**Right mindfulness is anchored in clear perception and it penetrates impressions without getting carried away.** Right mindfulness enables us to be aware of the process of conceptualization in a way that we actively observe and control the way our thoughts go."[1]

Ecclesiastes includes a vivid example of attempted right mindfulness by Solomon:

> *I thought in my heart,* "Come now, I will *test you* with pleasure to find out what is good." But that also proved to be meaningless. "Laughter," I said, "is foolish. And what does pleasure accomplish?" I tried cheering myself with wine, and embracing folly—*my mind still guiding me with wisdom.* I wanted to see what was worthwhile for men to do under heaven during the few days of their lives.
>
> I undertook great projects: I built houses for myself and planted vineyards. I made gardens and parks and planted all kinds of

fruit trees in them. I made reservoirs to water groves of flourishing trees. I bought male and female slaves and had other slaves who were born in my house. I also owned more herds and flocks than anyone in Jerusalem before me. I amassed silver and gold for myself, and the treasure of kings and provinces. I acquired men and women singers, and a harem as well—the delights of the heart of man. I became greater by far than anyone in Jerusalem before me. *In all this my wisdom stayed with me.*[2]

This excerpt illustrates how Solomon attempted to observe and control the way his thoughts were going. He was trying to be vigilant in being ruthlessly objective about his own thoughts and feelings. He sought to have wisdom guide him in his mind as he was tempted in various ways. And he believed that his wisdom stayed with him.

Solomon sought to *objectively* evaluate his own heart and mind as they were being pushed and pulled by feelings, temptations, and rationalizations. He sought to stand outside of himself and yet to be very nearby, carefully observing his own actions, feelings, and thoughts and impartially judging them on the basis of "wisdom." Perhaps Solomon was the first "Buddhist." He once wrote:

The simple believes every word, but the prudent considers well his steps.[3]

Being king, Solomon had no human authority to report to, so he reported directly to himself, just as Buddha advocated doing. And he exhorted his sons to do likewise:

Hear, my son, and be wise. And guide your heart in the way . . .[4]

His early life was an ancient example of a number of Buddha's proverbs. Compare what Buddha later had to say with the quotations of Solomon above:

If a man make himself as he teaches others to be, then, being himself well subdued, he may subdue (others); one's own self is indeed difficult to subdue.[5]

If a man hold himself dear, let him watch himself carefully; during one at least out of the three watches a wise man should be watchful.[6]

Self is the lord of self, who else could be the lord? With self well subdued, a man finds a lord such as few can find.[7]

By oneself the evil is done, by oneself one suffers; by oneself evil is left undone, by oneself one is purified. Purity and impurity belong to oneself, no one can purify another.[8]

Late in life Solomon's exercise of mindfulness became quite cavalier. As king, he seemed to think that he was above succumbing to the sordid effects of various worldly temptations—as long as he was mindfully guided by "wisdom." Solomon had so much confidence in his ability to do this that he exposed himself to a broad range of the delights of mankind and this world. As he did so, he seemed to view the overall process in a way that foreshadowed the Seventh Step of Buddha's Noble Path:

He who is slow to anger is better than the mighty. And he who *rules his spirit* than he who takes a city.[9]

Buddha said the same thing, in so many words, in these proverbs, using very similar imagery:

If one man conquer in battle a thousand times thousand men, and if another conquer himself, he is the greatest of conquerors.[10]

One's own self conquered is better than all other people.[11]

Not even a god, a Gandharva, not Mara with Brahman could change into defeat the victory of a man who has vanquished himself, and always lives under restraint.[12]

If a man for a hundred years sacrifice month after month with a thousand, and if he but for one moment pay homage to a man whose soul is grounded (in true knowledge), better is that homage than sacrifice for a hundred years.[13]

If a man for a hundred years worship Agni (fire) in the forest, and if he but for one moment pay homage to a man whose soul is grounded (in true knowledge), better is that homage than sacrifice for a hundred years.[14]

Is it really possible to rule your own spirit? Apparently Solomon thought so, as the proverb quoted earlier states. However, this proverb also implies that only an exceptional person could do it. To rule one's spirit is naturally very difficult and challenging, but still attainable. Buddha believed it was not only possible, but an important part of the path to enlightenment, as expressed in the following proverbs:

Well-makers lead the water (wherever they like); fletchers bend the arrow; carpenters bend a log of wood; wise people fashion themselves.[15]

Let a wise man blow off the impurities of his self, as a smith blows off the impurities of silver one by one, little by little, and from time to time.[16]

Rouse thyself by thyself, examine thyself by thyself, thus self-protected and attentive wilt thou live happily, O Bhikshu![17]

One major difficulty of relying on the self to observe and evaluate and discipline the self is the wayward, unreliable nature of the self, as Buddha admitted in these proverbs:

As a fletcher makes straight his arrow, a wise man makes straight his trembling and unsteady thought, which is difficult to guard, difficult to hold back.[18]

It is good to tame the mind, which is difficult to hold in and flighty, rushing wherever it listeth; a tamed mind brings happiness.[19]

Let the wise man guard his thoughts, for they are difficult to perceive, very artful, and they rush wherever they list: thoughts well guarded bring happiness.[20]

If a man make himself as he teaches others to be, then, being himself well subdued, he may subdue (others); *one's own self is indeed difficult to subdue.*[21]

The fault of others is easily perceived, but that of oneself is difficult to perceive; a man winnows his neighbour's faults like chaff, but *his own fault he hides*, as a cheat hides the bad die from the gambler.[22]

Did Solomon ever make such admissions? Consider this verse, which appears twice, with identical wording, in his Proverbs:

There is a way that seems right to a man, but in the end it leads to death.[23]

So, how, according to Solomon, can one avoid following such a destructive path? His answer is that when one is truly righteous, then one will see all things objectively and clearly:

The righteousness of the blameless makes a straight way for them, but the wicked are brought down by their own wickedness.[24]

A wicked man puts up a bold front, but an upright man gives thought to his ways.[25]

The problem with all this is that one must be totally righteous for it to work, and human beings have always had a notoriously difficult time being totally righteous throughout their entire lifetimes. As soon as a bit of wickedness creeps in, it muddies one's mindfulness. Since that bit of wickedness is typically pleasurable, or of immediate benefit to one's self, at least temporarily, it is natural to want to continue doing just a bit of it. And as one continues doing just a bit of it, one's mindfulness becomes less acute. Then it seems all right to do it again, but more extensively. A downward spiral has begun, and what is to stop it? It is questionable that either Solomon or Buddha adequately addressed this perilous difficulty. Each offered the same sources of help to deal with the problem, but these sources may not be sufficient. The later years of Solomon's life are a prime illustration of temptations and failings ruining a life that had begun quite nobly.

The sources of help each espoused were:

1. The support and honest critique of like-minded seekers;

2. Companionship with righteous people;

3. Avoidance of relations with women;

4. The power of proverbs memorized and much meditated upon (as discussed in the next chapter); and

5. The "trinity" of Buddhism (or Judaism). (p. 54)

First Aid: The Support and Honest Critique of Like-Minded Seekers

The great worth of having righteous friends who care enough about you to encourage you and to exhort you when you are heading off in the wrong direction was emphasized by Solomon:

> Ointment and perfume delight the heart, and the sweetness of a man's friend does so by hearty counsel.[26]

> Iron sharpens iron, so one man sharpens another.[27]

> Faithful are the wounds of a friend, but the kisses of an enemy are deceitful.[28]

Buddha stressed the same idea clearly in these proverbs:

> If you see an intelligent man who tells you where true treasures are to be found, who shows what is to be avoided, and administers reproofs, follow that wise man; it will be better, not worse, for those who follow him.[29]

> Let him admonish, let him teach, let him forbid what is improper!—he will be beloved of the good, by the bad he will be hated.[30]

> And this is the beginning here for a wise Bhikshu: watchfulness over the senses, contentedness, restraint under the law; keep noble friends whose life is pure, and who are not slothful.[31]

Second Aid: Companionship with Righteous People

The second aid in maintaining righteousness is closely related to the first, but there is a slight shift in emphasis. The first aid, having the support and honest critique of like-minded seekers, emphasizes friends consciously keeping each other on track through intentional dialogue and vigilance on each other's behalf. It involves keeping each other accountable.The second aid emphasizes the more subtle good and bad influences that friends can have on each other. The point here is that if you "hang out" with people who are wicked, they will have an influence on you, possibly entangling you in evil deeds. Likewise, if you associate with righteous people, they will influence you to do good things and pursue wisdom.

Solomon stressed the importance of having the right kind of friends in this proverb:

> The righteous should choose his friends carefully, for the way of the wicked leads them astray.[32]

Buddha offered essentially the same counsel:

> Do not have evil-doers for friends, do not have low people for friends: have virtuous people for friends, have for friends the best of men.[33]

> He who walks in the company of fools suffers a long way; company with fools, as with an enemy, is always painful; company with the wise is pleasure, like meeting with kinsfolk.[34]

> If a man find a prudent companion who walks with him, is wise, and lives soberly, he may walk with him, overcoming all dangers, happy, but considerate.[35]

As much as possible, Buddha said, one should seek friends who are more righteous than oneself. If such cannot be found, solitude is better. He observed:

> If a traveller does not meet with one who is his better, or his equal, let him firmly keep to his solitary journey; there is no companionship with a fool.[36]

One possible concern about Buddha's proverb is that it does not include an exhortation for genuine seekers to mentor friends who are not quite as far along the path as they are, and there is a great need for that. Perhaps this omission is intentional and is based on the realization that just being a "genuine seeker" is not enough to qualify someone to mentor others. Such a seeker is presumably very well-intentioned and highly motivated, but is only beginning to truly understand Buddha's teachings.

Solitude is always better than associating with fools and wicked people. Buddha made this clear in the next proverb:

> If a man find no prudent companion who walks with him, is wise, and lives soberly, let him walk alone, like a king who has left his conquered country behind, —like an elephant in the forest. It is better to live alone, there is no companionship with a fool; let a man walk alone, let him commit no sin, with few wishes, like an elephant in the forest.[37]

One should avoid spending time with wicked or evil people, for their influence most likely will be corrosive, or worse. Solomon made this emphatically clear in the following proverbs:

> Do not be envious of evil men, nor desire to be with them; for their heart devises violence, and their lips talk of troublemaking.[38]

> Make no friendship with an angry man, and with a furious man do not go, lest you learn his ways and set a snare for your soul.[39]

> Do not set foot on the path of the wicked or walk in the way of evil men. Avoid it, do not travel on it; turn from it and go on your way. For they cannot sleep till they do evil; they are robbed of slumber till they make someone fall. They eat the bread of wickedness and drink the wine of violence. . . . But, the way of the wicked is like deep darkness; they do not know what makes them stumble.[40]

Buddha lived out his later years much more true to his teachings than Solomon did, probably because he so completely renounced worldly riches and attachments and surrounded himself with like-spirited monks. Solomon not only did not renounce his great wealth, but augmented it beyond all reason, also adding to it hundreds of foreign wives, most of whom did not share his religious beliefs.

Third Aid: Avoidance of Relations with Women

To Buddha, the critical worth of radical renunciation extended to relationships with women:

> So long as the love of man towards women, even the smallest, is not destroyed, so long is his mind in bondage, as the calf that drinks milk is to its mother.[41]

> But they whose whole watchfulness is always directed to their body, who do not follow what ought not to be done, and who steadfastly do what ought to be done, the desires of such watchful and wise people will come to an end.[42]

Solomon offered similar words with respect to immoral women:

> For these commands are a lamp, this teaching is a light, and the corrections of discipline are the way to life, keeping you from the immoral woman, from the smooth tongue of the wayward wife. Do not lust in your heart after her beauty or let her captivate you with her eyes, for the prostitute reduces you to a loaf of bread, and the adulteress preys upon your very life. Can a man scoop fire into his lap without his clothes being burned? Can a man walk on hot coals without his feet being scorched? So is he who sleeps with another man's wife; no one who touches her will go unpunished.[43]

To Solomon, an immoral woman symbolized all of the perilous attractions of this world. However, he did not by any means advocate renunciation of all relations with women. In fact, one of his proverbs is unabashedly pro-marriage:

> An excellent wife is the crown of her husband.[44]

Fourth Aid: The Power of Proverbs Memorized and Much Meditated Upon

As noted above, this aid is discussed quite extensively in the next chapter.

Fifth Aid: The "Trinity" of Buddhism (or Judaism)

Both Buddha and Solomon looked to three sources of teaching. For Solomon, as noted near the end of Chapter Three, they were Moses, the Torah, and the Levites. In Buddhism, they were the "Three Jewels." Consecutive proverbs recite the three central helps for the Buddhist:

> The disciples of Gotama (Buddha) are always well awake, and their thoughts day and night are always set on Buddha . . . the law [the teachings]. . . the church [the Order of Monks].[45]

Each of the elements is parallel: Moses/Buddha (a person); Torah/Dhamma (sacred writings); and Levites/Monks (a priestly order).

An Unrealistic Confidence in the Self?

Buddha offered a way of salvation—that is, attaining enlightenment and nirvana—based on being utterly fixated on a radical pursuit of morality and renunciation involving intense, prolonged sessions of meditation. He openly admitted that this was something most people would not do (and perhaps were not capable of):

> Few are there among men who arrive at the other shore (become Arhats); the other people here run up and down the shore.[46]

> This world is dark, few only can see here; a few only go to heaven, like birds escaped from the net.[47]

Bad deeds, and deeds hurtful to ourselves, are easy to do; what is beneficial and good, that is very difficult to do.[48]

So perilous is the journey of the soul to enlightenment that Buddha believed that there was "no other path" than the one he prescribed:

The best of ways is the eightfold; the best of truths the four words; the best of virtues passionlessness; the best of men he who has eyes to see.[49]

This is the way, *there is no other* that leads to the purifying of intelligence. Go on this way! Everything else is the deceit of Mara (the tempter).[50]

Buddhism is characterized by an intense drive to fashion a self-made path of spirituality. Reaching nirvana is something only an elite few can hope to realize. It is reserved for the handful of people who are exceptionally gifted in being able to maintain a lifelong, intense effort to rid oneself of all self:

You yourself must make an effort. The Tathagatas (Buddhas) are only preachers. The thoughtful who enter the way are freed from the bondage of Mara.[51]

Again and again, Buddha asserted that his followers would have to have the strength and tenacity of self-will to pursue the path he had charted, with no substantive help or assistance from others:

If a man delights in quieting doubts, and, always reflecting, dwells on what is not delightful (the impurity of the body, &c. [etc.]), he certainly will remove, nay, he will cut the fetter of Mara.[52]

They depart with their thoughts well-collected, they are not happy in their abode; like swans who have left their lake, they leave their house and home.[53]

A wise man should leave the dark state (of ordinary life), and follow the bright state (of the Bhikshu). After going from his home to a homeless state, he should in his retirement look for enjoyment where there seemed to be no enjoyment. Leaving all pleasures behind, and calling nothing his own, the wise man should purge himself from all the troubles of the mind.[54]

Those whose mind is well grounded in the (seven) elements of knowledge, who without clinging to anything, rejoice in freedom from attachment, whose appetites have been conquered, and who are full of light, are free (even) in this world.[55]

He alone who, without ceasing, practises the duty of sitting alone and sleeping alone, he, subduing himself, will rejoice in the destruction of all desires alone, as if living in a forest.[56]

Rouse thyself by thyself, examine thyself by thyself, thus self-protected and attentive wilt thou live happily, O Bhikshu![57]

Not the perversities of others, not their sins of commission or omission, but his own misdeeds and negligences should a sage take notice of.[58]

Is there anything similar in Solomon's writings to the level of intense self-discipline and critical self-evaluation that Buddha espoused? Two proverbs come to mind. First:

Above all else, guard your heart, for it is the wellspring of life.[59]

When Solomon wrote, "Above all else," isn't that like saying there is no higher priority than that? In the second proverb he wrote:

He who is slow to anger is better than the mighty. And he who *rules his spirit* than he who takes a city.[60]

How can someone rule his own spirit? In some sense, that person must be motivated by an abhorrence of what will befall him if he does not succeed in doing this. Solomon himself failed to rule his spirit, having become unwilling to renounce his power, wealth, and hundreds of wives and concubines. He had a royal, legal prerogative to have as many wives and concubines as he desired, and he took full advantage of this while ignoring a very explicit biblical prohibition against it:

> The king, moreover, must not acquire great numbers of horses for himself or make the people return to Egypt to get more of them, for the LORD has told you, "You are not to go back that way again." He must not take many wives, *or his heart will be led astray*. He must not accumulate large amounts of silver and gold. When he takes the throne of his kingdom, he is to write for himself on a scroll a copy of this law, taken from that of the priests, who are Levites.[61]

As history records, Solomon's heart was "led astray." The wellsprings of his spiritual life became very polluted.

To Buddha's great credit, he remained true to his commitment to renounce the treasures of this world until he died. Could it be that his awareness of how great a failure Solomon was helped motivate him to continue his intense practice of renunciation? Or was it simply that he was so taken by his own new religion, and of his need to stay true to it for it to spread, that he was able to perform this difficult feat?

Spiritual Pride

Both Solomon and Buddha fell prey to particular kinds of spiritual pride. Though the two forms of pride to which they succumbed were quite different, they undoubtedly were both very real. The evidence for this is substantial.

An extraordinary sense of spiritual pride is a natural byproduct of the intense mental and moral discipline required to truly practice Buddhism, despite its rejection of "ego-consciousness," or "the feeling of a separate 'I'."[62] This is exhibited in several of Buddha's proverbs:

When the learned man drives away vanity by earnestness, he, the wise, climbing the terraced heights of wisdom, looks down upon the fools, serene he looks upon the toiling crowd, as one that stands on a mountain looks down upon them that stand upon the plain.[63]

As on a heap of rubbish cast upon the highway the lily will grow full of sweet perfume and delight, thus the disciple of the truly enlightened Buddha shines forth by his knowledge among those who are like rubbish, among the people that walk in darkness.[64]

He whose conquest is not conquered again, into whose conquest no one in this world enters, by what track can you lead him, the Awakened, the Omniscient, the trackless?[65]

He whom no desire with its snares and poisons can lead astray, by what track can you lead him, the Awakened, the Omniscient, the trackless?[66]

Difficult (to obtain) is the conception of men, difficult is the life of mortals, difficult is the hearing of the True Law, difficult is the birth of the Awakened (the attainment of Buddhahood).[67]

I have conquered all, I know all, in all conditions of life I am free from taint; I have left all, and through the destruction of thirst I am free; having learnt myself, whom shall I teach?[68]

Solomon, too, must have been overtaken by spiritual pride when he concluded that he was exempt from the clear biblical prohibitions against hoarding horses, wives, and gold. For him, this was the way that seemed right to him, although it led to his spiritual death. He also allowed worship of foreign gods, in part, as mentioned earlier, to satisfy his numerous wives who came from other traditions. In this way he violated the teachings of Moses, the Torah, and the Levites, the very authorities he had earlier revered. These actions would have been perceived by fellow Jews who knew the Torah as offenses to God himself, and thus extremely prideful.

[1] Thomas Knierim, editor and webmaster, "The Noble Eightfold Path," Raison d'Etre, www.thebigview.com/buddhism/eightfoldpath.html, retrieved May 12, 2010 (emphasis added).

[2] Ecclesiastes 2:1–9 (NIV) (emphasis added).

[3] Proverbs 14:15 (NKJV).

[4] Proverbs 23:19 (NIV).

[5] Dhammapada 159.

[6] Ibid., 157.

[7] Ibid., 160.

[8] Ibid., 165.

[9] Proverbs 16:32 (NKJV) (emphasis added).

[10] Dhammapada 103.

[11] Ibid., 104.

[12] Ibid., 105.

[13] Ibid., 106.

[14] Ibid., 107.

[15] Ibid., 80.

[16] Ibid., 239.

[17] Ibid., 379.

[18] Ibid., 33.

[19] Ibid., 35 (emphasis added).

[20] Ibid., 36 (emphasis added).

[21] Ibid., 159 (emphasis added).

[22] Ibid., 252 (emphasis added).

[23] Proverbs 14:12 and 16:25 (NIV).

[24] Proverbs 11:5 (NIV).

[25] Proverbs 21:29 (NIV).

[26] Proverbs 27:9 (NKJV).

[27] Proverbs 27:17 (NASB).

[28] Proverbs 27:6 (NKJV).

[29] Dhammapada 76.

[30] Ibid., 77.

[31] Ibid., 375.

[32] Proverbs 12:26 (NKJV).

[33] Dhammapada 78.

[34] Ibid., 207.

[35] Ibid., 328.

[36] Ibid., 61.

[37] Ibid., 329–330.

[38] Proverbs 24:1–2 (NKJV).

[39] Proverbs 22:24–25 (NKJV).

[40] Proverbs 4:14–17, 19 (NIV).

[41] Dhammapada 284.

[42] Ibid., 293.

[43] Proverbs 6:23–29 (NIV).

[44] Proverbs 12:4a (NKJV).

[45] Dhammapada 296–298.

[46] Ibid., 85.

[47] Ibid., 174.

[48] Ibid., 163.

[49] Ibid., 273.

[50] Ibid., 274 (emphasis added).

[51] Ibid., 276.

[52] Ibid., 350.

[53] Ibid., 91.

[54] Ibid., 87-88.

[55] Ibid., 89.

[56] Ibid., 305.

[57] Ibid., 379.

[58] Ibid., 50.

[59] Proverbs 4:23 (NIV) (emphasis added).

[60] Proverbs 16:32 (NKJV) (emphasis added).

[61] Deuteronomy 17:16–18 (NIV) (emphasis added).

[62] "Ego and Desire," Gal Viharaya (Rock Temple) Polonnaruwa, Sri Lanka, Maithri Publications, www.maithri.com/articles_new/ego_desire.htm.

[63] Dhammapada 28.

[64] Ibid., 58–59.

[65] Ibid., 179.

[66] Ibid., 180.

[67] Ibid., 182.

[68] Ibid., 353.

Today it seems that meditation and Buddhism are synonymous. Statues of the meditating Buddha number well into the billions. One would think that Buddha either invented, or perfected, the art and practice of meditation. Buddhists commonly believe that a person who does not meditate cannot progress spiritually. It's that critical. In conversations between Buddhists and non-Buddhists, if the discussion gets spiritual at all, the Buddhist invariably asks the non-Buddhist if he or she meditates. It's very important to them.

We know for certain that Buddha did not invent meditation. Meditation was a long-standing Hindu and Jain practice for centuries before Buddha. In addition, Jews practiced meditation centuries before either Solomon or Buddha lived.

In Buddhism, meditation is part of the last step of the Noble Eightfold Path, called "Right Concentration."

Right Concentration

"Concentration . . . is . . . one-pointedness of mind, meaning a state where all mental faculties are unified and directed onto one particular object. Right concentration for the purpose of the eightfold path means *wholesome concentration,* i.e., concentration on wholesome thoughts and actions. The Buddhist method of choice to develop right concentration is through the practice of meditation. The meditating mind focuses on a selected object. It first directs itself onto it, then sustains concentration, and finally intensifies concentration step by step. Through this practice it becomes natural to apply elevated levels of concentration also in everyday situations."[1]

The practice of meditation goes to the very roots of the Jewish culture. Genesis 24 mentions that Isaac (circa 1900 B.C., the son of Abraham, the father of the Jewish people) meditated:

Isaac went out to *meditate* in the field toward evening; and he lifted up his eyes and looked, and behold, camels were coming.[2]

The context text offers no clue as to what kind of meditation Isaac was practicing, or of what he was focusing on. This incident occurred over 1,360 years before Buddha became a monk.

In a well-known passage, Joshua (circa 1250–1450 B.C., Moses' successor as leader of the Jews as they reached the Promised Land) exhorted the children of Israel to meditate:

This Book of the Law shall not depart from your mouth, but you shall *meditate* on it day and night, that you may observe to do according to all that is written in it. For then you will make your way prosperous, and then you will have good success.[3]

Psalm 39, written by Solomon's father, David, also refers to meditation:

I said, "I will watch my ways and keep my tongue from sin; I will put a muzzle on my mouth as long as the wicked are in my presence." But when I was silent and still, not even saying anything good, my anguish increased. My heart grew hot within me, and as I *meditated*, the fire burned; then I spoke with my tongue: "Show me, O LORD, my life's end and the number of my days; let me know how fleeting is my life. You have made my days a mere handbreadth; the span of my years is as nothing before you. Each man's life is but a breath. Man is a mere phantom as he goes to and fro: He bustles about, but only in vain."[4]

David reigned from 1007 to 967 B.C. The above psalm clearly expresses some opinions that coincide with the Right View of a Buddhist: (1) Life is fleeting; (2) A person's days are a mere handbreadth; (3) A man's life is an illusion and we hustle around in vain. Furthermore, David exhorts himself to practice Right Mindfulness ("I will watch my ways."[5]).

Psalm 1 (apparently written by an author other than David) underscores meditation as the key practice in inducing spiritual and physical blessings:

> Blessed is the man who does not walk in the counsel of the wicked or stand in the way of sinners or sit in the seat of mockers. But his delight is in the law of the LORD, and on his law he *meditates* day and night. He is like a tree planted by streams of water, which yields its fruit in season and whose leaf does not wither. Whatever he does prospers.[6]

Notice that the opening verse of Psalm 1 is also a strong exhortation to renounce keeping company with unworthy people, of three different types. But more importantly, for the purposes of our current discussion, is that this psalm is a precursor to one of Buddha's proverbs about meditation:

> Even the gods envy those who are awakened and not forgetful, who are given to *meditation*, who are wise, and who delight in the repose of retirement (from the world).[7]

So great are the blessings of those who seriously meditate on the laws of the Jews, as those blessings are symbolized in Psalm 1, that crooked, pleasure-seeking people would likely be envious of them. This same theme was expressed by Buddha:

> He who gives himself to vanity, and does not give himself to meditation, forgetting the real aim (of life) and grasping at pleasure, will in time envy him who has exerted himself in *meditation*.[8]

It is believed that most of the psalms written by authors other than David were composed before or during Solomon's reign [967–938 B.C.]. At a minimum, Solomon was quite aware of meditation as it was practiced in his day. As further evidence, we can cite Asaph, an important tabernacle musician during King David's reign.[9] He referred to meditation in Psalm 77:

I will also *meditate* on all Your work, and talk of Your deeds.[10]

In addition, the sons of Korah were known as temple singers. David put them in charge of the service of song in the tabernacle (the "tent of meeting" used for worship before the temple was built) after the Ark of the Covenant, the sacred box covered with gold containing the tablets of Moses and other sacred items, was brought to Jerusalem.[11] In Psalm 48, the Korahites refer to meditation:

> Within your temple, O God, we *meditate* on your unfailing love.[12]

The belief that those who meditate deeply, habitually, and for prolonged periods of time attain some rarefied spiritual state has definite precursors in Psalm 119:

> Oh, how I love your law! I meditate on it all day long. Your commands *make me wiser than my enemies*, for they are ever with me. I have *more insight than all my teachers*, for I meditate on your statutes. I have *more understanding than the elders*, for I obey your precepts. I have kept my feet from every evil path so that I might obey your word. I have not departed from your laws, for you yourself have taught me. How sweet are your words to my taste, sweeter than honey to my mouth! I gain understanding from your precepts; therefore I hate every wrong path. Your word is a *lamp* to my feet and a *light* for my path.[13]

This Jewish outpouring of pride ends with a claim to have attained a modest form of enlightenment.[14]

One of Buddha's proverbs extols being "radiant in meditation," a state approaching that of the Awakened One, who showers his entire surroundings with light:

> The sun is bright by day, the moon shines by night, the warrior is bright in his armour, the Brahmana is bright in his *meditation*; but Buddha, the Awakened, is bright with splendour day and night.[15]

Many precursors to Buddha's practice of meditation are evident in pre-Solomon Judaism. What is less clear is whether there are also close similarities in the nature of meditative practice.

Solomon and Meditation

Solomon never directly referred to meditation. However, the following proverb of Solomon presumes some kind of meditation as a central, critical element in living a moral life:

> My son, keep my words and store up my commands within you. Keep my commands and you will live; guard my teachings as the apple of your eye. Bind them on your fingers; write them on the tablet of your heart.[16]

How would one go about writing Solomon's words and commands "on the tablet of your heart"? Surely the most obvious way would be through dedicated repetition and memorization, as is done in guided meditation on a text.

Solomon's exhortation is immediately followed by strong warnings against the seductress, who symbolizes the temptations of the senses:

> Say to wisdom, "You are my sister," and call understanding your kinsman; they will keep you from the adulteress, from the wayward wife with her seductive words. . . . Do not let your heart turn to her ways or stray into her paths. Many are the victims she has brought down; her slain are a mighty throng. Her house is a highway to the grave, leading down to the chambers of death.[17]

Solomon concludes his exhortation with strong warnings of ugly eternal consequences. Buddha makes similar warnings. The above verses from Proverbs 7 are precursors to this proverb of Buddha:

> *Meditate*, O Bhikshu, and be not heedless! Do not direct thy thought to what gives pleasure that thou mayest not for thy

heedlessness have to swallow *the iron ball (in hell)*, and that thou mayest not cry out when *burning*, "This is pain."[18]

Buddha's imagery is akin to Solomon's in the verses immediately preceding Chapter 7:

> For these commands are a lamp, this teaching is a light, and the corrections of discipline are the way to life, keeping you from the immoral woman, from the smooth tongue of the wayward wife. Do not lust in your heart after her beauty or let her captivate you with her eyes, for the prostitute reduces you to a loaf of bread, and the adulteress preys upon your very life. Can a man *scoop fire into his lap* without his clothes being *burned*? Can a man walk on *hot coals* without his feet being *scorched*?[19]

The similarities between these two sets of proverbs are apparent. There are remarkable correspondences not only in the ideas but in the very images used to express the importance of maintaining the right state of mind.

Psalm 119 Patterns

The longest chapter in the Bible by far is Psalm 119. Its authorship is unstated. Throughout its 176 verses is one common theme: the critical importance and benefits of meditating, cherishing, and obeying the Law. Its core substance could be summarized succinctly in Proverb 364 of Buddha:

> He who dwells in the law, delights in the law, meditates on the law, follows the law, that Bhikshu will never fall away from the true law.[20]

Psalm 119, a key centerpiece of Judaism, and Buddha's proverb both highlight the importance of upholding a whole system of laws (codes of conduct) as critical to self-purification. For the author of Psalm 119, "the Law" would mean the Law of Moses as presented in the Torah (discussed in more detail below). For Buddhists, the Law consists of Buddha's teachings. But although the source of the law referred to is different, the approach to it and commitment to it is the same. Curiously, meditation is mentioned in seven sections of Psalm 119. In every instance, the verse about meditation, and its adjacent verses, tightly parallel the content of Buddha's 364th proverb. In the third, fifth, and seventh sections, the order of the content is identical to the order in Buddha's 364th proverb, highlighted below in gray.

Psalm 119: 3rd Section	Psalm 119: 5th Section	Psalm 119: 7th Section	Buddha's Dhammapada 364
I am laid low in the dust; preserve my *life* according to your word. I *recounted my ways and you answered me*; *teach me* your decrees.[21]	Let your compassion come to me that I may *live*.[22]	I call out to you; save me and I will *keep your statutes*.[23]	He who *dwells* in the law . . .[24]
Let me *understand* the teaching of your precepts.[25]	For your law is my *delight*.[26]	I rise before dawn and cry for help; I have *put my hope* in your word.[27]	. . . *delights* in the law . . .[28]
Then I will *meditate* on your wonders.[29]	But I will *meditate* on your precepts.[30]	My eyes stay open through the watches of the night, that I may *meditate* on your promises.[31]	. . . *meditates* on the law . . .[32]
I have chosen the way of truth; I have *set my heart* on your laws.[33]	May my heart *be blameless toward your decrees*.[34]	*Preserve* my life, O Lord, according to your laws.[35]	. . . *follows* the law . . .[36]

I run in the *path* of your commands, for you have set my heart free.[37]	That I may *not be put to shame*.[38]	Long ago I learned from your statutes that you established them *to last forever*.[39]	. . . will *never fall away* from the true law.[40]

In the following table are displayed the verses from each of the remaining four sections of Psalm 119 that focus on meditation. Each part of Buddha's 364th proverb, quoted in the headers highlighted in gray, has evident precursors within the indicated sections of Psalm 119.

Psalm 119: 1st Section	Psalm 119: 2nd Section	Psalm 119: 4th Section	Psalm 119: 6th Section
He who *dwells* in the law . . .			
How can a young man keep his way pure? By *living* according to your word.[41]	Do good to your servant, and I will live; I will *obey* your word.[42]	I will *walk about* in freedom, for I have sought out your precepts.[43]	Your commands make me wiser than my enemies, for *they are ever with me*.[44]

. . . *delights* in the law . . .			
I *seek* you with all my heart. I *delight* in your decrees.[45]	Open my eyes that I may *see wonderful things* in your law. My soul is *consumed with longing* for your laws at all times. Your statutes are my *delight*.[46]	For I *delight* in your commands because I *love* them. I *lift up my hands* to your commands, which I *love*.[47]	Oh, how I *love* your law! How *sweet* are your words *to my taste*, sweeter than honey to my mouth![48]
. . . *meditates* on the law . . .			
I have *hidden your word in my heart.* I *meditate* on your precepts and consider your ways.[49]	Your servant will *meditate* on your decrees.[50]	And I *meditate* on your decrees.[51]	I *meditate* on it all day long. For I *meditate* on your statutes.[52]
. . . *follows* the law . . .			
I rejoice in *following* your statutes as one rejoices in great riches.[53]	For I *keep* your statutes. Your statutes . . . are my counselors.[54]	I will *always obey* your law, for *ever* and *ever*.[55]	I *have not departed* from your laws.[56]
. . . will *never fall away* from the true law.			
That I might *not sin* against you.[57]	*Though rulers sit together and slander me*, your servant will meditate on your decrees. Your statutes are *my delight*.[58]	I will speak of your statutes before kings and will *not be put to shame*.[59]	I *hate every wrong path*.[60]

The Jewish author(s) of Psalm 119 elaborated extensively on the key elements of spiritual practice that relate to meditation. In a psalm written around the time of Solomon's reign, we have seven expansions for each component of Buddha's 364th proverb. It would appear that the state of meditative practice of the Jews who wrote this psalm was quite elaborate and advanced.

Seven is the most important number in the Bible. In hundreds of examples, it is a symbol of completion or spiritual perfection. That the above pattern appears in seven sections of the longest chapter in the Bible may not be a coincidence. It may have been an intentional device used by the author(s) of Psalm 119 to emphasize the central importance of meditation on the Law as a critical part of seeking spiritual perfection.

We can also gain an appreciation for this by focusing on the content of all the verses in these sections of Psalm 119 that cover just one component. For example, we see from Psalm 119 that the component of "glorying in the Law" involves the following (noted by verse number):

10. Seeking God with all your heart.

10, 16, 77. Delighting in God's decrees.

18. Praying that God would open your eyes to see wonderful things in his Law.

18. Being consumed with longing for God's laws at all times.

26. Praying that you would understand the teachings of the Law.

47. Delighting in God's commands because you love them.

48. Lifting up your hands to God's commands out of love for them.

97. Loving God's Law.

103. Regarding the words of the Law as sweeter than honey in your mouth.

147. Rising before dawn and crying for help because you have put your hope in God's words.

Doing similar reviews of all the verses in Psalm 119 from the sections that explicitly mention meditation is also worthwhile. For example, doing this for "dwelling in the Law" is also fascinating.

What Kind of Meditation Was Being Practiced?

With few exceptions, meditation as practiced by Jews prior to and during Solomon's reign (as described in the Old Testament) was focused on the Law, or Torah, the first five books of the Hebrew Bible. There are two exceptions. Asaph meditated on God's work and God's deeds (Psalm 77) and the sons of Korah meditated on God's unfailing love (Psalm 48). These are instances of focused meditation on external phenomena, as contrasted with many of the inner phenomena that are often the objects of meditation in Buddhism (e.g., one's breathing, specific parts of the body, or sheer emptiness of mind).

Only six of Buddha's proverbs mention meditation. The 364th proverb is the only one that mentions an object of meditation, and that object is the law, just as in the Hebrew scriptures. The other proverbs do not disclose the object of meditation but only mention elements involved in its practice. Those proverbs tell us that one's mind should not wander during meditation, but should be absorbed in the meditation, "taking delight in the inner calm of renunciation." For example:

> Meditate, O Bhikshu, and be not heedless! Do not direct thy thought to what gives pleasure that thou mayest not for thy heedlessness have to swallow the iron ball (in hell), and that thou mayest not cry out when burning, "This is pain."[61]

> Even the gods envy those who are awakened and not forgetful, who are given to meditation, who are wise, and who delight in the repose of retirement (from the world).[62]

Also, they tell us that meditation involves exertion:

> He who gives himself to vanity, and does not give himself to meditation, forgetting the real aim (of life) and grasping at pleasure, will in time envy him who has exerted himself in meditation.[63]

The remaining proverb about meditation that has not yet been cited in this chapter is the following:

> You yourself must make an effort. The Tathagatas (Buddhas) are only preachers. The thoughtful who enter the way are freed from the bondage of Mara.[64]

This proverb makes it clear that meditation involves solitary self-effort and entering "the path."

There is only one clear difference between the kinds of meditation practiced by the Jews around Solomon's time and that described in Buddha's earliest published work, the Dhammapada: Jewish meditation directly or indirectly involved God.

Psalm 119 is broken up into twenty-two sections, each labeled by one of the twenty-two letters of the Hebrew alphabet. In most of these sections, there is mention of some kind of spiritual activity that directly or indirectly involves meditation. All seven of the sections that directly mention meditation focus on self-effort. Many of the remaining sections are direct prayers from the seeker to receive help from God, rather than about using self-effort alone. It is these sections that clearly distinguish Judaic from Buddhist practice. *Buddhism is "I will do this." Judaism is "Help me, God, to love and obey your laws."* We see that in this excerpt from Psalm 119, where the author's petitions for help from God are emphasized:

> *Teach me*, O LORD, to follow your decrees; then I will keep them to the end. *Give me* understanding, and I will keep your law and obey it with all my heart. *Direct me* in the path of your commands, for there I find delight. *Turn my heart* toward your statutes and not toward selfish gain. *Turn my eyes away from* worthless things; *preserve my life* according to your word. *Fulfill*

your promise to your servant, so that you may be feared. *Take away the disgrace* I dread, for your laws are good. How I long for your precepts! *Preserve my life* in your righteousness.[65]

God and God's laws were a critical part of Jewish meditation in Solomon's time. Divine involvement in Jewish meditation adds numerous enriching elements to this spiritual practice. The importance of meditation is illustrated by the following verses from Psalm 119:

45. I will walk about in *freedom,* for I have sought out your precepts.

46. I will *speak* of your statutes *before kings* and will *not be put to shame.*

54. Your decrees are the *theme of my song* wherever I lodge.

58a. I have *sought your face* with all my heart.

64. The earth is filled with your love, O LORD; teach me your decrees.

71. It was *good for me to be afflicted* so that I might learn your decrees.

120. My flesh trembles in fear of you; I stand in awe of your laws.

135. Make your face shine upon your servant and teach me your decrees.

161b. But my heart trembles at your word.

162. I rejoice in your promise like one who finds great spoil.

164a. Seven times a day I praise you.

171. May *my lips overflow with praise,* for you teach me your decrees.

172. May *my tongue sing* of your word, for all your commands are righteous.

Judaic meditation in Solomon's time was a practice rich in vitality and diversity of experience. Buddha's proverbs achieve this richness in only one proverb, where it is a virtual copy of a framework of spiritual practice accompanying meditation that appears seven times in Psalm 119:

> He who dwells in the law, delights in the law, meditates on the law, follows the law, that Bhikshu will never fall away from the true law.[66]

We have seen that several key facets of meditation fundamental to Buddhism have precursors in Judaic texts written centuries before Buddha lived. Chief among those facets are:

- The consistent practice of deep meditation as a central, critical element in living a moral life.
- The importance of renunciation and extended absorption in meditation.
- The idea that those who fail to seriously practice meditation will be particularly susceptible to the temptations offered by immoral women and other worldly pleasures.
- The claim that persistent, prolonged meditation can enable a practitioner to achieve a state of enlightenment far above the spiritual condition even of generally devout people. This notion, detailed in Psalm 119:99, is very central to Buddhism.

In Chapters Three through Eight, we have seen that every one of the Four Noble Truths and steps in the Noble Eightfold Path (including meditation) are major parts of the teachings of Solomon and Judaism.

---

[1] Thomas Knierim, editor and webmaster, "The Noble Eightfold Path," Raison d'Etre, www.thebigview.com/buddhism/eightfoldpath.html, retrieved May 12, 2010 (emphasis added).

[2] Genesis 24:63 (NASB) (emphasis added).

[3] Joshua 1:8 (NKJV) (emphasis added).

[4] Psalm 39:1–6a (NIV) (emphasis added).

[5] Psalm 39:1a (NIV).

[6] Psalm 1:1–3 (NIV) (emphasis added).

[7] Dhammapada 181 (emphasis added).

[8] Ibid., 209 (emphasis added).

[9] 1 Chronicles 6:31–32, 39.

[10] Psalm 77:12 (NKJV) (emphasis added).

[11] 1 Chronicles 6:31–33.

[12] Psalm 48:9 (NIV) (emphasis added).

[13] Psalm 119:97–105 (NIV) (emphasis added).

[14] Psalm 119:105.

[15] Dhammapada 387 (emphasis added).

[16] Proverbs 7:1–3 (NIV).

[17] Proverbs 7:4–5, 25–27 (NIV).

[18] Dhammapada 371 (emphasis added).

[19] Proverbs 6:23–28 (NIV) (emphasis added).

[20] Dhammapada 364.

[21] Psalm 119:25–26 (NIV) (emphasis added).

[22] Psalm 119:77a (NIV) (emphasis added).

[23] Psalm 119:146 (NIV) (emphasis added).

[24] Dhammapada 364a.

[25] Psalm 119:27a (NIV) (emphasis added).

[26] Psalm 119:77b (NIV) (emphasis added).

[27] Psalm 119:147 (NIV) (emphasis added).

[28] Dhammapada 364b.

[29] Psalm 119:27b (NIV) (emphasis added).

[30] Psalm 119:78b (NIV) (emphasis added).

[31] Psalm 119:148 (NIV) (emphasis added).

[32] Dhammapada 364c.

[33] Psalm 119:30 (NIV) (emphasis added).

[34] Psalm 119:80a (NIV) (emphasis added).

[35] Psalm 119:149b (NIV) (emphasis added).

[36] Dhammapada 364d.

[37] Psalm 119:32 (NIV) (emphasis added).

[38] Psalm 119:80b (NIV) (emphasis added).

[39] Psalm 119:152 (NIV) (emphasis added).

[40] Dhammapada 364e.

[41] Psalm 119:9 (NIV) (emphasis added).

[42] Psalm 119:17 (NIV) (emphasis added).

[43] Psalm 119:45 (NIV) (emphasis added).

[44] Psalm 119:98 (NIV) (emphasis added).

[45] Psalm 119:10a, 16a (NIV) (emphasis added).

[46] Psalm 119:18, 20, 24a (NIV) (emphasis added).

[47] Psalm 119:47–48a (NIV) (emphasis added).

[48] Psalm 119:97a, 103 (NIV) (emphasis added).

[49] Psalm 119:11a, 15 (NIV) (emphasis added).

[50] Psalm 119:23b (NIV) (emphasis added).

[51] Psalm 119:48b (NIV) (emphasis added).

[52] Psalm 119:97b, 99b (NIV) (emphasis added).

[53] Psalm 119:14 (NIV) (emphasis added).

[54] Psalm 119:22b, 24 (NIV) (emphasis added).

[55] Psalm 119:44 (NIV) (emphasis added).

[56] Psalm 119:102a (NIV) (emphasis added).

[57] Psalm 119:11b (NIV) (emphasis added).

[58] Psalm 119:23–24a (NIV) (emphasis added).

[59] Psalm 119:46 (NIV) (emphasis added).

[60] Psalm 119:104b (NIV) (emphasis added).

[61] Dhammapada 371.

[62] Ibid., 181.

[63] Ibid., 209.

[64] Ibid., 276.

[65] Psalm 119:33–40 (NIV) (emphasis added).

[66] Dhammapada 364.

Chapter Nine
Origins of the Law of Karma

The concept of karma was a key component of classical Hinduism, which flourished from around 200 B.C. through A.D. 1100, but evidence suggests that it did not appear in India before about 800 B.C.[1] Since Solomon reigned as King of Israel from 967 to 938 B.C., it is quite possible that the concept of karma, which is clearly present in many of his proverbs, could have come to India through the spread of his writings. As noted in Chapter Two, the literal text of the Old Testament makes a bold claim about this kind of possibility:

> King Solomon was greater in riches and wisdom than all the other kings of the earth. *The whole world* sought audience with Solomon to hear the wisdom God had put in his heart.[2]

Did Solomon come up with, or at least champion prior beliefs in, the Law of Karma, an integral part of both Hinduism and Buddhism? To convey a sense of this possibility, key proverbs will be reviewed in this chapter that clearly express the essence of this law. Although "karma" is not a Jewish word, the implicit presence of the concept is quite common in Solomon's writings. We will also see that there is a very strong correspondence between the content of the karma proverbs of Solomon and Buddha.

Historian Will Durant defined karma as "that universal law by which every act of good or of evil will be rewarded or punished in this life, or in some later incarnation of the soul."[3] Belief in this law may have had its roots in the Jewish culture of Solomon's time, or it may have been imported into Solomon's culture from earlier or neighboring cultures.

The Law of Karma is not exactly the same in Judaism as it is in Hinduism and Buddhism. The different versions of the concept relate to differing beliefs about life after death. The Jewish style of application may have naturally shifted when transplanted to a Hindu culture as Hindus adapted it to their way of thinking and integrated it with their other beliefs. Jews believed in a single life after death, if they believed in an afterlife at all, whereas Hindus believed in reincarnation. It would have been an easy matter to extend the concept of good and bad consequences to the long view of many lives as opposed to one lifetime.

Hindus were captivated by the far-reaching implications of a belief in repeated reincarnation. If you believe you are the reincarnation of a prior being, which could have been some kind of animal, and you are an heir to the good or bad karma of that prior being, you look at the tragedies and good fortunes of your life quite differently than if you did not believe you could have existed previously. To a Hindu, the misfortunes of this life are most likely the result of bad deeds from one of your prior lives. Because of this belief, it is not uncommon in India for people to choose not to help someone who is struggling—to do so would be to interfere in the natural consequences of their bad karma. Buddha disagreed with this perspective, calling his followers to help those in need—not to subvert the workings of karma, but to practice compassion for all sentient beings. However, Buddha assumed reincarnation as a fact, as we will see in many of his proverbs quoted in this chapter.

The Law of Karma is evident in dozens of vivid proverbs of Solomon. For example:

> The house of the wicked will be destroyed, but the tent of the upright will flourish.[4]

In proverbs like this, it is very evident that being righteous produces the consequences of good karma, while being wicked produces bad karma. This concept also appears in the book of Ecclesiastes:

> Be generous: Invest in acts of charity. Charity yields high returns."[5]

Karma is so key to Buddhism that Buddha's *first two* proverbs in the Dhammapada highlight it:

> All that we are is the result of what we have thought: it is founded on our thoughts, it is made up of our thoughts. If a

man speaks or acts with an evil thought, pain follows him, as the wheel follows the foot of the ox that draws the carriage.[6]

All that we are is the result of what we have thought: it is founded on our thoughts, it is made up of our thoughts. If a man speaks or acts with a pure thought, happiness follows him, like a shadow that never leaves him.[7]

The Law of Karma is strongly implied by other proverbs of Buddha:

The evil-doer mourns in this world, and he mourns in the next; he mourns in both. He mourns and suffers when he sees the evil of his own work. The virtuous man delights in this world, and he delights in the next; he delights in both. He delights and rejoices, when he sees the purity of his own work.[8]

An evil deed is better left undone, for a man repents of it afterwards; a good deed is better done, for having done it, one does not repent.[9]

If a man offend a harmless, pure, and innocent person, the evil falls back upon that fool, like light dust thrown up against the wind.[10]

He who inflicts pain on innocent and harmless persons, will soon come to one of these ten states: He will have cruel suffering, loss, injury of the body, heavy affliction, or loss of mind, Or a misfortune coming from the king, or a fearful accusation, or loss of relations, or destruction of treasures, Or lightning-fire will burn his houses; and when his body is destroyed, the fool will go to hell.[11]

Karmic Proverbs

Almost all of the karmic proverbs of Solomon and Buddha fall into one of three categories:

- Those in which the karmic result is *security* or lack of it.
- Those in which the karmic result is *happiness* or its opposite.
- Those in which the karmic result is impact, or *influence*, on other people.

What is curious is that, within each of these groupings, the individual verses can easily be paired off, much as if each separate proverb of Solomon had inspired a specific proverb of Buddha. Naturally, some of Buddha's karmic proverbs have their own Indian twist. Yet there tended to be a nearly direct relationship, one-to-one, with a corresponding proverb of Solomon.

Security Karmic Proverbs

In each source there are numerous proverbs that focus on good karma resulting in security and bad karma in a lack of security. Let's review examples of these side by side.

Solomon	Buddha
The righteous shall never be removed: but the wicked shall not inhabit the earth.[12]	By rousing himself, by earnestness, by restraint and control, the wise man may make for himself an island which no flood can overwhelm.[14]
The wicked are overthrown, and are not: but the house of the righteous shall stand.[13]	

To Solomon, a person's righteousness results in deep and lasting security. Such a person will never be uprooted, and his house, both physically and spiritually, will stand firm. Buddha's proverb is similar, but more limited in two respects. First, security is provided against only one type of misfortune (a flood), though, arguably, a flood could symbolize any kind of catastrophe or attack. Second, security is assured by the inevitable, impersonal operation of the Law of Karma.

What is vigilance? It is commonly defined as including watchfulness, alertness, attention, heedfulness, concern, and care. By being vigilant, as well as diligent, self-restrained, and disciplined in subjugating one's senses, Buddhists aspire to insulate themselves from disaster.

Solomon	*Buddha*
For though a righteous man *falls* seven times, he rises again. The wicked are brought down by calamity.[15]	A Bhikshu (mendicant) who delights in reflection, who looks with fear on thoughtlessness, cannot *fall* away (from his perfect state)--he is close upon Nirvana.[16]

Both proverbs refer to falling, presumably in a spiritual sense. For Solomon, if someone is fundamentally righteous, he or she will be restored seven times. In other words, though the righteous person may experience troubles or setbacks, he or she will recover. Seven, as the number of perfection in the Bible, likely represents an unlimited number of restorations rather than seven per se. Buddha's proverb conveys the sense that there is some chance the bhikshu could fall back, but it is not likely; there is no mention of the bhikshu, once fallen, being able to recover. However, the closer the bhikshu is to nirvana, the less likely he is to regress spiritually.

"Wandering" is mentioned by each wise man as a key weakness of fools. For Solomon, "integrity" is its opposite, and the man of integrity is guarded by righteousness. According to Buddha, one must control the wandering mind in the "inner cavern"; those who do so liberate themselves from evil.

Solomon	Buddha
Righteousness guards the man of integrity, but wickedness overthrows the sinner.[17] A discerning man keeps wisdom in view, but a fool's eyes *wander* to the ends of the earth.[18]	Those who bridle their mind which *travels* far, *moves* about alone, is without a body, and hides in the chamber (of the heart), will be free from the bonds of Mara (the tempter).[19]

Note that no protection or liberation is provided for the wicked person. In Solomon, the wicked are overthrown. For Buddha, the shackles of the evil one remain.

For both Solomon and Buddha, keeping "wisdom in view" is an essential activity of the vigilant. For Buddha, it is the "supreme treasure," as noted below. Why? Because it ensures the protection described above for the righteous, for Solomon, and freedom from evil, for Buddha.

Solomon	Buddha
A discerning man keeps *wisdom* in view, but a fool's eyes wander to the ends of the earth.[20]	Fools follow after vanity, men of evil wisdom. The *wise* man keeps earnestness as his best jewel.[21]

Below, we repeat one of Solomon's proverbs to show another parallel proverb from Buddha.

Solomon	Buddha
Righteousness guards the man of integrity, but wickedness overthrows the sinner.[22]	Of the people who possess these virtues, who live without thoughtlessness, and who are emancipated through true knowledge, Mara, the tempter, never finds the way.[23]

What precisely is the man of integrity guarding against? The word "guard" implies deliberate attacks. Solomon's proverb may assume that this protection will be provided by God. Solomon may also be referring to the kind of protection the righteous one has because there are no weak areas that would be chinks in his or her armor. Buddha's proverb claims very strong protection, wherein the Evil One cannot even come close to the virtuous, vigilant person. Mara's schemes will be seen for what they are by those who are wise.

An important difference between Solomon and Buddha is that, for Solomon, the source of protection is assumed to be God, whereas in Buddha the source is clearly the self.

Solomon	Buddha
The [uncompromisingly] righteous is delivered out of trouble, and the wicked gets into it instead.[24]	Self is the lord of self, who else could be the lord? With self well subdued, a man finds a lord such as few can find.[25]

The question in the second sentence of Buddha's proverb implies that God is not a candidate for being the master of one's self. Solomon's proverb presumes God's role as the rescuer, as well as the one who diverts disaster away from the righteous and onto the wicked. The righteous person "is delivered"; in other words, rescued by someone other than the self. Although Solomon does not specifically say so, what we know about Jewish culture and beliefs strongly suggests that he meant that God was the one who would do the delivering. Buddha's proverb implies that each person is his or her own worst enemy as well as his or her own deliverer. The phrase "the fully subdued self" implies that there is a self that must be subdued to begin with; somehow, self must overcome self by a sheer act of will. It's no wonder that, for Buddha, this kind of mastery is "very difficult to achieve."

And yet, because of the consequences described by these verses, the righteous have no reason to fear or envy the wicked. Ultimately, in both Buddha and Solomon, righteousness brings a reward, while evil brings a downfall. So fear and envy can be put to rest.

Solomon	Buddha
Do not *fret* because of evildoers, nor be envious of the wicked; for there will be no prospect for the evil man; the lamp of the wicked will be put out.[26]	If a man's thoughts are not dissipated, if his mind is not perplexed, if he has ceased to think of good or evil, then there is no *fear* for him while he is watchful.[27]

Solomon exhorted us to not be concerned with or jealous of evil people because in the end they will encounter their undoing. Buddha's focus was on each person thoroughly insulating himself or herself from the debilitating effects of any kind of fear.

Furthermore, the righteous need not fear because the positive consequences of wisdom are permanent.

Solomon	Buddha
The wicked are overthrown and are no more, but the house of the righteous will stand.[28]	As a solid rock is not shaken by the wind, wise people falter not amidst blame and praise.[29]

Buddha's goal was to attain impenetrable insulation from the manipulative efforts of others, whether by praise or criticism. His imagery of a solid rock that the wind cannot shake is quite analogous to Solomon's symbol of a house that stands firm against severe weather. In both cases, the righteous are seen as invincible.

Solomon	Buddha
The wicked are overthrown and are no more, but the house of the righteous will stand.[30]	One's own self conquered is better than all other people.[31] Not even a god, a Gandharva, not Mara with Brahman could change into defeat the victory of a man who has vanquished himself, and always lives under restraint.[32]

Buddha's goal was to become spiritually impervious to the attacks and impacts of spiritual powers through a long-lasting act of spiritual anesthesia. Solomon had confidence that the righteous would prevail against the attacks of both hostile people and spiritual powers.

So long-lasting are the effects of righteousness and wickedness that they have clear implications for immortality. Solomon's proverbs about immortality are based on being "righteous," and Buddha's, on "vigilance."

Solomon	Buddha
When the whirlwind passes, the wicked is no more, but the righteous has an everlasting foundation.[33] A kind man benefits himself, but a cruel man brings trouble on himself. The wicked man earns deceptive wages, but he who sows righteousness reaps a sure reward. The truly righteous man attains life, but he who pursues evil goes to his death.[34]	Earnestness is the path of immortality (Nirvana), thoughtlessness the path of death. Those who are in earnest do not die, those who are thoughtless are as if dead already.[35]

The next comparison lays Buddha's succession of four consecutive proverbs next to parallel proverbs of Solomon.

Solomon	Buddha
He who *leads the upright along an evil path* will fall into his own trap, but the blameless will receive a good inheritance.[36] The *violence* of the wicked will drag them away, for they refuse to do what is right.[37] He who *sows iniquity* will reap *calamity* and futility, and the rod of his wrath [with which he smites others] will fail.[38]	He who *inflicts pain* on innocent and harmless persons, will soon come to one of these ten states: He will have cruel suffering, loss, injury of the body, heavy affliction, or loss of mind, or a misfortune coming from the king, or a fearful accusation, or loss of relations, or destruction of treasures, or lightning-fire will burn his houses; and when his body is destroyed, the fool will go to hell.[39]

The last of Solomon's proverbs above talks about reaping calamity. Buddha heaped up a daunting list of eleven vivid calamities that could await anyone who punished or harmed blameless people. That is the essence of karma in action.

Solomon also included the following, for which no parallel can be found in the Dhammapada. Nevertheless, it, too, shows a karmic-style effect:

> Whoever shuts his ears to the cry of the poor will also cry himself and not be heard.[40]

Happiness Karmic Proverbs

The results of good karma are quite different for the follower of Solomon's teachings than for the Buddhist. For the former, wholesome, fulfilling connectedness with others is the result, whereas for the Buddhist, the desired result is solitary bliss. Though the source of happiness was different, the operation of karma in bringing about the happiness was similar.

Solomon	Buddha
He who pursues righteousness and love finds life, prosperity and honor.[41]	If a man does what is good, let him do it again; let him delight in it: happiness is the outcome of good.[42]
	If a man speaks or acts with a pure thought, happiness follows him, like a shadow that never leaves him.[43]

Solomon urged people to "pursue righteousness and love." How would one do that? Probably by doing good deeds and truly caring for other people, without significant ulterior motives. Buddha pointed out, in the first of the two proverbs quoted above, that one could accumulate happiness by finding a good deed and performing it repeatedly. Those who did, he implied, would find it so satisfying that they might develop a longing to keep doing it.

Solomon told us that the righteous would *find* life, prosperity, and honor. Buddha stated that happiness would never leave him.

Solomon	Buddha
He who pursues righteousness and love finds life, prosperity and honor.[44] The wicked man earns deceptive wages, but he who sows righteousness reaps a sure reward.[45]	The virtuous man delights in this world, and he delights in the next; he delights in both. He delights and rejoices, when he sees the purity of his own work.[46] The virtuous man is happy in this world, and he is happy in the next; he is happy in both. He is happy when he thinks of the good he has done; he is still more happy when going on the good path.[47]

How can a person sow righteousness? Some ways that come to mind are teaching, training, and mentoring. One's motivation can be love or a sense of caring or obedience to religious commands, which is a definition of pursuing righteousness.

For Solomon, the rewards seem to come from external as well as internal sources. For Buddha, a good life consists, to a fair degree, in the doing of good, wholesome deeds, so that, afterward, you will feel good about what you have done. Recollection of recent good deeds will bring good memories that will make you feel happier. Isn't that what pursuing righteousness and love is all about? Nevertheless, it takes effort to pursue this kind of happiness, as keeping focused on doing good deeds often goes against man's natural inclinations.

Solomon	Buddha
The righteousness of the blameless will smooth his way, but the wicked will fall by his own wickedness.[48] A discerning man keeps wisdom in view, but a fool's eyes wander to the ends of the earth.[49]	Let the wise man guard his thoughts, for they are difficult to perceive, very artful, and they rush wherever they list: thoughts well guarded bring happiness.[50]

Taken together, the quotations of Solomon and the quotation from Buddha above suggest that for the righteous, purity of mind can create clarity of vision, which in turn enables one to advance along a smooth path. Conversely, the impurities in one's mind can cause one's path to become crooked and treacherous. To the Jew, God orchestrates these karmic consequences:

> With the pure You will show Yourself pure; and with the devious You will show Yourself shrewd.[51]

The straight way is the path taken by those who do not wander—wherever their desires might motivate them to go.

Solomon	Buddha
The integrity of the upright guides them. The unfaithful are destroyed by their duplicity.[52]	It is good to tame the mind, which is difficult to hold in and flighty, rushing wherever it listeth; a tamed mind brings happiness.[53]

Buddha's notion of a "flighty" mind is similar, though potentially more innocent, than Solomon's notion of the "duplicity" of the "unfaithful." After all, duplicity, or double-mindedness, could be described in terms of a mind that is "difficult to hold in and flighty," prone to wander wherever it desires. Integrity, in contrast, requires being single-minded. It means being mentally and spiritually disciplined by a set of ethical standards and a desire to rein in rogue desires and thoughts. Integrity stabilizes a flighty, meandering mind.

Solomon	Buddha
Though they join forces, the wicked will not go unpunished; but the posterity of the righteous will be delivered.[54]	If a man's thoughts are not dissipated, if his mind is not perplexed, if he has ceased to think of good or evil, then there is no fear for him while he is watchful.[55]

For Solomon, freedom involves an escape from punishment or judgment. Buddha, too, describes what it is (to him) to go free: "There is no fear for him," he says of the vigilant man. It is fear that imprisons people spiritually, and both Solomon and Buddha recognize this, describing the positive consequences of doing good deeds in terms of deliverance, freedom, and rejoicing and the negative consequences of being wicked in terms of being fearful or being entrapped or punished.

Both Buddha and Solomon point out that we are members of a community and our greatest deeds involve our relationships with or impact on others.

Solomon	Buddha
The fruit of the righteous is a tree of life, and he who wins souls is wise.[56]	Happy is the arising of the awakened, happy is the teaching of the True Law, happy is peace in the church, happy is the devotion of those who are at peace.[57]
	The disciples of Gotama are always well awake, and their thoughts day and night are always set on the church.[58]

For Solomon, one of the wisest things a person can do is to "win souls." Doing that doesn't involve preaching on street corners, but rather living a life that others find attractive, and then being there to help when people are struggling with specific needs or questions. To a Buddhist, encouraging people to join a monastic order (sangha) is an act of "winning a soul."

Although for Buddha, the consequences of our actions can extend over many lifetimes, they can also be quite immediate, as they are for Solomon.

Solomon	Buddha
The house of the wicked will be destroyed, but the tent of the upright will flourish.[59]	Those whose mind is well grounded in the (seven) elements of knowledge, who without clinging to anything, rejoice in freedom from attachment, whose appetites have been conquered, and who are full of light, are free (even) in this world.[60]

The tent (i.e., mind and life) will flourish in amazing ways, Solomon claimed, for the upright, and dozens of his proverbs give us clues about what is involved in being upright. In a single proverb, Buddha describes five states of being that would hasten the attainment of nirvana during a person's lifetime on earth (listed below in the second column). Each of these elements have a precursor in one or more of the proverbs of Solomon.

Solomon (Various Proverbs)	Buddha (Dhammapada, 89)
But the path of the righteous is like the light of dawn, that shines brighter and brighter until the full day.[61]	Those whose mind is well grounded in the (seven) elements of knowledge . . .[62]
A sound heart is life to the body, but envy is rottenness to the bones.[63]	. . . who without clinging to anything . . .[64]
Better one handful with tranquility than two handfuls with toil and chasing after the wind.[65]	. . . rejoice in freedom from attachment . . .[66]

. . . cast off the troubles of your body, for youth and vigor are meaningless.[67]	. . . whose appetites have been conquered . . . [68]
But the path of the righteous is like the light of dawn, that shines brighter and brighter until the full day.[69]	. . . who are full of light, are free (even) in this world.[70]

Buddha's single proverb, broken into the parts shown above, is a wonderful, compact version of the essence of the ideal life of a Buddhist. And every element of it is also present in Solomon's writings.

The richness of a life of joy and honor is expressed in other proverbs of Solomon and Buddha as well.

Solomon	*Buddha*
Great wealth is in the house of the righteous, but trouble is in the income of the wicked.[71] Better one handful with tranquility than two handfuls with toil and chasing after the wind.[72]	He who drinks in the law lives happily with a serene mind: the sage rejoices always in the law, as preached by the elect (Ariyas).[73]

The wealth Solomon refers to above may be much broader than just a collection of expensive things in one's house. Having a good marriage, children, neighbors, and friends and living contentedly in a peaceful neighborhood may also be involved. The implication is that even if "the income of the wicked" is high, it is not equivalent to the "great wealth" of the righteous. The proverb quoted below provides additional evidence that for Solomon, "riches" involve more than material things. For Buddha, happiness and peace are all that really matter, and little materially is needed.

Solomon	Buddha
He who trusts in his riches will fall, but the righteous will flourish like foliage.[74]	Wise people, after they have listened to the laws, become serene, like a deep, smooth, and still lake.[75]

Both use appropriate symbols for their respective culture: For Solomon, the righteous are like "a thriving plant," whereas Buddha advocates attaining a state of mind like a very quiet lake.

Both have specific things in mind when they consider the goals or rewards worth striving for. They each feel that these specific forms of goodness will come to the person who actively seeks to do good.

Solomon	Buddha
The desire of the righteous ends only in good, but the hope of the wicked ends only in wrath.[76] Do they not err who devise evil and wander from the way of life? But loving-kindness and mercy, loyalty and faithfulness, shall be to those who devise good.[77]	A wise man should leave the dark state (of ordinary life), and follow the bright state (of the Bhikshu). After going from his home to a homeless state, he should in his retirement look for enjoyment where there seemed to be no enjoyment.[78]

The specific types of goodness that Solomon believes await the righteous are expressed in the second proverb of his above: loving-kindness, mercy, loyalty, and faithfulness, from both God and other righteous people. His focus was on relationships. To Buddha, the goal of the enlightened person is to shed all desire for worldly things and pleasures and position and become content with very little. His focus was on solitude rather than relationship.

Both also emphasize an additional benefit of righteousness and wisdom: longevity.

Solomon	Buddha
Honor your father and your mother, that *your days may be long* upon the land which the LORD your God is giving you.[79]	He who always greets and constantly reveres the aged, four things *will increase* to him, viz. *life*, beauty, happiness, power.[80]

For both, long life is a clear consequence of honoring one's parents or the aged.

Both Buddha and Solomon link laziness to negative consequences. It is one of the most direct forms of good versus bad karma.

Solomon	Buddha
The way of the sluggard is blocked with thorns, but the path of the upright is a highway.[81]	He who lives looking for pleasures only, his senses uncontrolled, immoderate in his food, idle, and weak, Mara (the tempter) will certainly overthrow him, as the wind throws down a weak tree.[82]

A sluggard is "a person who is habitually inactive or lazy." Each of the above proverbs focuses on this type of person and the difficulties they bring on themselves.

However, not all bad karma is so direct or immediate. As the following proverbs make clear, some bad deeds at first seem to be accompanied by sweetness.

Solomon	Buddha
Food gained by deceit is *sweet* to a man, but afterward his mouth will be filled with gravel.[83]	As long as the evil deed done does not bear fruit, the fool thinks it is *like honey*; but when it ripens, then the fool suffers grief.[84]
	An evil deed, like newly-drawn milk, does not turn (suddenly); smouldering, like fire covered by ashes, it follows the fool.[85]

The above proverbs are quite parallel in their usage of sweet food as an analogy, as well as in the implied delay between doing a bad deed and seeing its undesirable consequences.

Influence Karmic Proverbs

Right living and right views may seem like personal matters, but both Solomon and Buddha point out that they can have a big impact on other people, sometimes affecting an entire city.

Solomon	Buddha
When it goes well with the righteous, the city rejoices; and when the wicked perish, there is jubilation. By the blessing of the upright the city is exalted, but it is overthrown by the mouth of the wicked.[86]	The scent of flowers does not travel against the wind, nor (that of) sandal-wood, or of Tagara and Mallika flowers; but the odour of good people travels even against the wind; a good man pervades every place.[88]
A wicked messenger falls into trouble, but a faithful ambassador brings health.[87]	

Solomon envisioned the ways that upright people can "exalt" an entire city. This same concept is expressed by Buddha, though perhaps in a more localized manner, in the above proverb. The scope of the influence of the virtuous is described much more expansively in two proverbs of Buddha immediately following the one quoted above:

> Sandal-wood or Tagara, a lotus-flower, or a Vassiki, among these sorts of perfumes, the perfume of virtue is unsurpassed.[89]

> Mean is the scent that comes from Tagara and sandal-wood;— the perfume of those who possess virtue rises up to the gods as the highest.[90]

Buddha spent forty-five years of his life attempting to help others reach the awakened state he believed he had attained. In Buddhism, those who reach enlightenment are liberated from the cycle of birth and death and can go to nirvana; choosing to come back to earth in another incarnation in order to help others reach it is regarded as the ultimate act of selfless compassion.

The curious thing about Solomon's proverbs is that, although he believed in God, only a few of his proverbs directly refer to God as the one who causes the Law of Karma to operate. The sense that the vast majority of Solomon's proverbs leave is that they are statements of universal laws that operate automatically, without the direct involvement of God. They are natural or logical consequences that follow from prior acts and intentions. This facet of Solomon's proverbs would have made Buddha comfortable with much of their content. He did not have to accept Solomon's god in order to value his teachings.

---

[1] "Karma," http://en.wikipedia.org/wiki/Karma, retrieved December 6, 2010.

[2] 1 Kings 10:23–24 (NIV) (emphasis added).

[3] Will Durant, *The Story of Civilization, Part I: Our Oriental Heritage* (New York: Simon and Schuster, 1963), 427.

[4] Proverbs 14:11 (NASB).

[5] Ecclesiastes 11:1 (The Message).

[6] Dhammapada 1.

[7] Ibid., 2.

[8] Ibid., 15–16.

[9] Ibid., 314.

[10] Ibid., 125.

[11] Ibid., 137–140.

[12] Proverbs 10:30 (KJV).

[13] Proverbs 12:7 (KJV).

[14] Dhammapada 25.

[15] Proverbs 24:16 (NIV) (emphasis added).

[16] Dhammapada 32 (emphasis added).

[17] Proverbs 13:6 (NIV) (emphasis added).

[18] Proverbs 17:24 (NIV) (emphasis added).

[19] Dhammapada 37 (emphasis added).

[20] Proverbs 17:24 (NIV) (emphasis added).

[21] Dhammapada 26 (emphasis added).

[22] Proverbs 13:6 (NIV).

[23] Dhammapada 57.

[24] Proverbs 11:8 (AMP).

[25] Dhammapada 160.

[26] Proverbs 24:19–20 (NKJV) (emphasis added).

[27] Dhammapada 39 (emphasis added).

[28] Proverbs 12:7 (NKJV).

[29] Dhammapada 81.

[30] Proverbs 12:7 (NKJV).

[31] Dhammapada 104.

[32] Ibid., 105.

[33] Proverbs 10:25 (NASB).

[34] Proverbs 11:17–19 (NIV).

[35] Dhammapada 21.

[36] Proverbs 28:10 (NIV) (emphasis added).

[37] Proverbs 21:7 (NIV) (emphasis added).

[38] Proverbs 22:8 (AMP) (emphasis added).

[39] Dhammapada 137–140.

[40] Proverbs 21:13 (NKJV).

[41] Proverbs 21:21 (NIV).

[42] Dhammapada 118.

[43] Ibid., 2b.

[44] Proverbs 21:21 (NIV).

[45] Proverbs 11:18 (NIV).

[46] Dhammapada 16.

[47] Ibid., 18.

[48] Proverbs 11:5 (NASB).

[49] Proverbs 17:24 (NIV).

[50] Dhammapada 36.

[51] Psalm 18:26 and 2 Samuel 22:27 (NKJV).

[52] Proverbs 11:3 (NIV).

[53] Dhammapada 35.

[54] Proverbs 11:21 (NKJV).

[55] Dhammapada 39.

[56] Proverbs 11:30 (NKJV).

[57] Dhammapada 194.

[58] Ibid., 298.

[59] Proverbs 14:11 (NASB).

[60] Dhammapada 89.

[61] Proverbs 4:18 (NASB).

[62] Dhammapada 89a.

[63] Proverbs 14:30 (NKJV).

[64] Dhammapada 89b.

[65] Ecclesiastes 4:6 (NIV).

[66] Dhammapada 89c.

[67] Ecclesiastes 11:10b (NIV).

[68] Dhammapada 89d.

[69] Proverbs 4:18 (NASB).

[70] Dhammapada 89e.

[71] Proverbs 15:6 (NASB).

[72] Ecclesiastes 4:6 (NIV).

[73] Dhammapada 79.

[74] Proverbs 11:28 (NKJV).

[75] Dhammapada 82.

[76] Proverbs 11:23 (NIV).

[77] Proverbs 14:22 (AMP).

[78] Dhammapada 87.

[79] Exodus 20:12 (NKJV).

[80] Dhammapada 109 (emphasis added).

[81] Proverbs 15:19 (NIV).

[82] Dhammapada 7.

[83] Proverbs 20:17 (AMP) (emphasis added).

[84] Dhammapada 69 (emphasis added).

[85] Ibid., 71.

[86] Proverbs 11:10–11 (NKJV).

[87] Proverbs 13:17 (NKJV).

[88] Dhammapada 54.

[89] Ibid., 55.

[90] Ibid., 56.

Chapter Ten
Transitioning from Solomon to Buddha

Wise men from diverse cultures of necessity have similar views on many of the fundamental issues and questions of life. And so, it should be expected that there would be many areas of agreement between the sayings of Solomon and Buddha. Nevertheless, it is surprising that Solomon's writings thoroughly cover every key tenet in the Four Noble Truths and the Noble Eightfold Path of Buddhism. Because of this it is natural to wonder if Solomon's teachings somehow influenced Buddha.

The fact is that if you start with the wisdom of Solomon's proverbs and the cynicism of his Ecclesiastes, remove all references to God—occasionally replacing God with "mind"—make a few departures based on traditional Hindu beliefs in reincarnation, and advocate a general renunciation of the world, you end up with Buddhism.

Despite the remarkable similarities, there are some key topics covered in Solomon that receive little or no mention in the Dhammapada. Renunciation involves withdrawal from life in some very important areas. While Solomon's proverbs offer advice on the important subjects of women, marriage, family, children, government, and God quite extensively, Buddha's proverbs say little or nothing on these topics. All of them would be areas of life in which it would be important to apply an ethical consciousness. What are we to make of the relative absence of these topics in the earliest known collection of Buddha's writings?

The story of Buddha's life offers some possible explanations. Buddha was forced to marry at a very early age and was sequestered by his controlling, possessive father even into his late twenties. Buddha chose to eject himself from all of this by abandoning his wife, child, palace, and future kingship and withdrawing from life to meditate and seek enlightenment. It is no wonder that Buddha's proverbs have scarcely anything to say on the topics named above. Buddha's life experiences predisposed him to have an obsessive resistance to authority and avoidance of close relationships.

Is it possible for a philosopher to avoid expounding on these key areas of life and to still be regarded as a real philosopher? Buddha demonstrated that it was. However, he should be viewed as a philosopher whose perspective and realm of expertise was noticeably constrained. But both Buddha and Solomon had limitations. On one hand, Buddha essentially became a "dropout" from Indian society, while Solomon tenaciously held on to his position as king. As a result, Solomon's proverbs are rich in insights regarding topics about which Buddha had little or nothing to say. On the other hand, it was Solomon's obsessive zeal to remain king, while also attempting to be a philosopher without equal, that led to his moral downfall. His willingness to honor the wide array of religions brought to Israel by his many foreign wives caused him to betray his loyalty to the one true God of the Jews. By so doing, he violated the very system of beliefs he had so ably delineated.

What we have in Buddha is a philosopher traumatized by many disturbing phenomena, including suffering, oppression, disease, and death. And what we have in Solomon is a corrupted, double-minded philosopher. When we compare and contrast the two sets of proverbs, many intriguing observations emerge. Buddha's ways are comparatively existentialist and stridently antiestablishment. Relationally, to westerners they feel somewhat akin to Asperger's syndrome. For example, Buddha's love of homelessness is quite extreme:

> A wise man should leave the dark state (of ordinary life), and follow the bright state (of the Bhikshu). After going from his home to a homeless state, he should in his retirement look for enjoyment where there seemed to be no enjoyment.[1]

In great contrast, Solomon took a very dim view of people who would make solitude a great priority:

> A man who isolates himself seeks his own desire; he rages against all wise judgment.[2]

The ways that Solomon advocated (but often did not practice later in his life) were temperate and balanced:

> Do not be overrighteous, neither be overwise—why destroy yourself? Do not be overwicked, and do not be a fool—why die before your time? It is good to grasp the one and not let go of the other. The man who fears God will avoid all extremes.[3]

Yet Solomon's desire to try to please everyone meant that, at the end of his life, no one was happy with him. It is possible that the tragic story of Solomon's end-of-life failures to uphold his own beliefs, known throughout the world, were part of what motivated Buddha to be an intense fanatic about remaining utterly righteous in everything he did and taught. Perhaps this was one of the obsessions (fears) that Buddha struggled with, leading him to develop an entire religion of compulsions and rituals to calm his anxiety. We know that Buddha was obsessed with fears of moral failure, disease, endless suffering, and death, as these are well chronicled in his proverbs:

> Is there in this world any man so restrained by humility that he does not mind reproof, as a well-trained horse the whip?[4]

> This body is wasted, full of sickness, and frail; this heap of corruption breaks to pieces, life indeed ends in death.[5]

Some of the writings of Solomon stand in sharp contrast to virtually all of the rest of the Old Testament. Most of this distinctive writing is in the book of Ecclesiastes. We see these areas of dramatic difference:

Bulk of Old Testament	Solomon's Ecclesiastes	Buddha's Dhammapada
Life is linear.	Life is cyclical.	Life is cyclical.
God is personal.	God is impersonal.	If God exists, God is impersonal.
Life is very meaningful because of our relationship with a personal God.	Life is meaningless, so enjoy life's simple pleasures when you can, and don't expect more.	Life is meaningless, so it is best to withdraw from this world to escape its pervasive suffering.
Salvation is attainable through love of and obedience to the laws and direction of a personal God.	Salvation is by works (righteousness), as defined by specific proverbs authored by the wise and discerning.	Enlightenment is attainable by works— via the Four Noble Truths and the Noble Eightfold Path.
Authored by prophets instead of royalty, with the exceptions of King David and King Solomon.	Authored by the richest and most powerful king of his time.	Authored by a man who had rejected the life of royalty his father had given him.
Written with a true fear of a powerful God.	Written with an attitude of spiritual certitude.	Written with an attitude of spiritual certitude.

What is intriguing is that in each of the above areas, Buddha's views are much closer to Solomon's than to those of the vast majority of the Old Testament. Perhaps Buddha had access to Solomon's writings but not to most of the rest of the Old Testament. Or perhaps he had seen much of the Old Testament, but found that his views resonated with Solomon's writings much more readily than with the rest of Judaism's holy book. Or it could be just a coincidence that his ideas matched Solomon's at all.

Ecclesiastes is clearly labeled as Solomon's opinions, not as a "Thus says the Lord" type of document. It contradicts other books in the Bible. For example, Solomon's assessment that "All is meaningless" conflicts with Psalm 139, which depicts man as a creation that is deeply precious to his Creator, who plays an overwhelmingly integral part in fashioning each person.

The great majority of the Old Testament was written by prophets, not kings. Solomon became a king not by conquest but by succession to the throne as his father, David, was dying. He accumulated an enormous amount of power and wealth and a large number of wives and concubines during his reign. He hungered for wisdom and, in his search for meaning and truth, ultimately despaired of the emptiness of a life where he was able to have everything he wanted. In the process, he lost the personal relationship with God that he had enjoyed early in his reign. The shift from relying on God to spiritual self-reliance occurred sometime before he wrote the book of Ecclesiastes.

Buddha was raised to be a prince and rebelled against his father's determined efforts to make him a captive of the life of the rich at the complete expense of his identity and independence. If Buddha read Solomon's writings during his years of discontent, those writings may have inspired him to shun the established order and find his own way in a search for truth and meaning in life. Buddha would not have had to exercise much imagination to progress from Solomon's teachings to his own. He would have only had to make three departures from Solomon's path:

1. God was not necessary. After all, the Hindu universe, teaming with millions of deities, both great and weak, was fraught with suffering and struggles.

2. As one who grew up in Hindu India, Buddha assumed that reincarnation was real, which was not a Jewish belief.

3. Intense spiritual self-reliance (something like a spiritual form of Asperger's syndrome) was elevated as being superior to the "wisdom of the ages," or the accumulated learning of mankind, so that one need only look deep within for real truth, as long as one was mentally

disciplined enough to exclude all outside thoughts and influences.

Other than these departures, every one of the Four Noble Truths and the individual steps of the Noble Eightfold Path have numerous precursors in the writings of Solomon. We observed this in extensive detail in Chapters Three through Eight. Some of the emphases shift, to be sure. While there is no literal mention of meditation in Solomon's writings, his descriptions of how one should focus on his proverbs sound like guided meditation.

Right View, Intention, Speech, Action, Livelihood, Effort, Mindfulness, and Concentration—we have seen that each step in this progression is illustrated by precursor proverbs from Solomon. According to one summary of Buddhist thinking, Buddhism has this view of the steps: "The eight aspects of the path are not to be understood as a sequence of single steps[;] instead they are highly interdependent principles that have to be seen in relationship with each other."[6]

The opening verses of Solomon's Proverbs enumerate the same purposes that Buddhists seek, saying the proverbs are:

1. For attaining wisdom and discipline;

2. For understanding words of insight;

3. For acquiring a disciplined and prudent life; and

4. For doing what is *right* and just and fair.[7]

Where Buddha Parted Company from Solomon

In the remainder of this chapter, we will focus on areas where Buddha's beliefs are clear departures from Solomon's. We will look at the following areas in turn:

1. An absence of references to God

2. Replacing God with mind

3. Acknowledging the existence of evil (e.g., Mara, the Devil)

4. Self instead of God at the center

5. Truth lies deep within

6. An absence of positive references to the family

7. A lack of positive references to government

8. A form of spirituality somewhat analogous to Asperger's syndrome

An Absence of References to God

There are only two references to a god or to gods in the Dhammapada:

> Through vigilance, did Maghavan (Indra) attain to the sovereignty of the gods.

> By earnestness did Maghavan (Indra) rise to the lordship of the gods. People praise earnestness; thoughtlessness is always blamed.[8]

> Who shall overcome this earth, and the world of Yama (the lord of the departed), and the world of the gods? Who shall find out the plainly shown path of virtue, as a clever man finds out the (right) flower?[9]

It is clear from these proverbs that Buddha is making reference to many gods.

In contrast, in Solomon's Book of Proverbs (excluding Chapters 30 and 31, which are attributed to other authors), God is mentioned 5 times and the Lord is mentioned 90 times, and in Solomon's Ecclesiastes, God is mentioned 37 times. We see in the next quote that Solomon sees God as the one who administers the workings of karma:

> Rescue those being led away to death; hold back those staggering toward slaughter. If you say, "But we knew nothing about this," does not he who weighs the heart perceive it? Does not he who guards your life know it? Will he not repay each person according to what he has done?[10]

Replacing God with Mind

The first two proverbs of Buddha at the beginning of the Dhammapada are:

> All that we are is the result of what we have thought: it is founded on our thoughts, it is made up of our thoughts. If a man speaks or acts with an evil thought, pain follows him, as the wheel follows the foot of the ox that draws the carriage.[11]

> All that we are is the result of what we have thought: it is founded on our thoughts, it is made up of our thoughts. If a man speaks or acts with a pure thought, happiness follows him, like a shadow that never leaves him.[12]

These proverbs greatly conflict with biblical views. Buddha's "thought" is not interchangeable with the God of the Jews. The latter was the only true creator, whereas, in Buddha's view, each person's mind creates their own unique reality.

Acknowledging the Existence of Evil (e.g., Mara, the Devil)

While Solomon made very frequent mention of wicked people, he never directly referred to any spiritual being who was distinctly evil. In sharp contrast, Buddha made fifteen references to Mara (the Evil One) in his proverbs. Three of these provide characterizations of indulgent pleasure-seekers that Mara will overcome:

> He who lives looking for pleasures only, his senses uncontrolled, immoderate in his food, idle, and weak, Mara (the tempter) will certainly overthrow him, as the wind throws down a weak tree.[13]

> Death carries off a man who is gathering flowers and whose mind is distracted, as a flood carries off a sleeping village.[14]

> Death subdues a man who is gathering flowers, and whose mind is distracted, before he is satiated in his pleasures.[15]

Next are three proverbs providing descriptions of the types of people against whom Mara will not prevail:

> He who lives without looking for pleasures, his senses well controlled, moderate in his food, faithful and strong, him Mara will certainly not overthrow, any more than the wind throws down a rocky mountain.[16]

> Those who bridle their mind which travels far, moves about alone, is without a body, and hides in the chamber (of the heart), will be free from the bonds of Mara (the tempter).[17]

> Of the people who possess these virtues, who live without thoughtlessness, and who are emancipated through true knowledge, Mara, the tempter, never finds the way.[18]

There are also seven proverbs of Buddha that describe how one is to fight Mara.

Knowing that this body is (fragile) like a jar, and making this thought firm like a fortress, one should attack Mara (the tempter) with the weapon of knowledge, one should watch him when conquered, and should never rest.[19]

One's own self conquered is better than all other people; not even a god, a Gandharva, not Mara with Brahman could change into defeat the victory of a man who has vanquished himself, and always lives under restraint.[20]

This is the way, there is no other that leads to the purifying of intelligence. Go on this way! Everything else is the deceit of Mara (the tempter).[21]

You yourself must make an effort. The Tathagatas (Buddhas) are only preachers. The thoughtful who enter the way are freed from the bondage of Mara.[22]

This salutary word I tell you, `Do ye, as many as are here assembled, dig up the root of thirst, as he who wants the sweet-scented Usira root must dig up the Birana grass, that Mara (the tempter) may not crush you again and again, as the stream crushes the reeds.[23]

If a man delights in quieting doubts, and, always reflecting, dwells on what is not delightful (the impurity of the body, &c. [etc.]), he certainly will remove, nay, he will cut the fetter of Mara.[24]

Two proverbs of Buddha describe the kind of view of reality that is needed in defeating Mara:

He who knows that this body is like froth, and has learnt that it is as unsubstantial as a mirage, will break the flower-pointed arrow of Mara, and never see the king of death.[25]

Look upon the world as a bubble, look upon it as a mirage: the king of death does not see him who thus looks down upon the world.[26]

Finally, one proverb provides an illustration of what the struggle against Mara is like:

As a fish taken from his watery home and thrown on dry ground, our thought trembles all over in order to escape the dominion of Mara (the tempter).[27]

The above proverbs may come as a surprise to many people interested or involved in Buddhism, since it generally teaches today that in reality All is One, and any appearance of evil is only temporary or illusory. Nevertheless, the distinct flavor of the above proverbs of Buddha is that Mara is quite real—so much so that Buddha devoted twelve of his proverbs to espousing ways of defeating him. These proverbs also make it clear that some (if not all) people have the ability, without the help of God, to resist and turn away the Evil One.

Curiously, Buddha depicts Mara as a god (or spirit being) who is dedicated to ensnaring and enslaving *every* person who pursues pleasure or other worldly desires, or who is undisciplined in controlling his or her mind. So Mara is everywhere and quite powerful, and yet any person, by following Buddha's path, can escape Mara's entanglements entirely by themselves, without the help of any "good" deity.

Self Instead of God at the Center

Buddha's approach to purifying himself was to rely on himself:

> Self is the lord of self, who else could be the lord? With self well subdued, a man finds a lord such as few can find.[28]

This is in complete contrast with the following words of Solomon:

> Trust in the Lord with all your heart and lean not on your own understanding; in all your ways acknowledge him, and he will make your paths straight. Do not be wise in your own eyes.[29]

Solomon's verses talk of a personal God who directs those who trust and revere him. They also speak of a need for the self to admit that it doesn't have "the answers." Solomon continues by painting a picture of extensive interaction between a Jew and the personal God that he worships:

> Fear the LORD and shun evil. This will bring health to your body and nourishment to your bones. Honor the LORD with your wealth, with the firstfruits of all your crops; then your barns will be filled to overflowing, and your vats will brim over with new wine. My son, do not despise the LORD's discipline and do not resent his rebuke, because the LORD disciplines those he loves, as a father the son he delights in.[30]

In this passage Solomon portrays God as being quite personal. He loves and delights in his followers. He gives health and nourishment to the bodies of his followers, and lavishly fills their barns and vats.

Another proverb openly states that this personal God loves people who follow his commandments:

> The way of the wicked is an abomination to the Lord, but He loves him who follows righteousness.[31]

This personal God who loves his followers: (1) gives them secret counsel, (2) blesses their homes, (3) gives grace to those who are humble, and (4) gives them an inheritance of glory:

> Do not envy the oppressor, and choose none of his ways; for the perverse person is an abomination to the Lord, but His secret counsel is with the upright. The curse of the Lord is on the house of the wicked, but He blesses the habitation of the just. Surely He scorns the scornful, but gives grace to the humble. The wise shall inherit glory, but shame shall be the legacy of fools.[32]

Surely, if such a loving god exists and really cares personally for people, then a religion focused on following that god would be superior to the lone-ranger approach of Buddha in dealing with the suffering of life. Buddhists, however, do not believe such a god exists.

Truth Lies Deep Within

For Buddha, the search for wisdom began by looking deep within, and nowhere else. Solomon advocated a totally opposite approach, saying one must begin by acknowledging God:

> The fear of the Lord is the beginning of wisdom.[33]

To Solomon, great danger lay in relying on the self to improve the self:

> Every way of a man is right in his own eyes, but the Lord weighs the hearts.[34]

Further, Solomon said, self-reliance can easily lead to much pride, which is also a dangerous place to be spiritually:

> Everyone who is proud in heart is an abomination to the Lord. Though they join forces, none will go unpunished.[35]

Buddha, in contrast to Solomon, became thoroughly self-justified in his own eyes, taking on an intense form of pride:

> I have conquered all, I know all, in all conditions of life I am free from taint; I have left all, and through the destruction of thirst I am free; having learnt myself, whom shall I teach?[36]

From this lofty perspective, Buddha looked down on the bulk of mankind:

> When the learned man drives away vanity by earnestness, he, the wise, climbing the terraced heights of wisdom, looks down upon the fools, serene he looks upon the toiling crowd, as one that stands on a mountain looks down upon them that stand upon the plain.[37]

> Earnest among the thoughtless, awake among the sleepers, the wise man advances like a racer, leaving behind the hack.[38]

Solomon's belief in God led him to advise us to recognize our own very humble position in the order of things. God is the one who is above everyone, who knows all things, and made all things. He is a sovereign judge ruling the affairs of men, and his understanding of events is far beyond ours. In acknowledging him we see our own shortcomings:

> Do not be quick with your mouth, do not be hasty in your heart to utter anything before God. God is in heaven and you are on earth, so let your words be few.[39]

> He has made everything beautiful in its time. He has also set eternity in the hearts of men; yet they cannot fathom what God has done from beginning to end.[40]

> I know that everything God does will endure forever; nothing can be added to it and nothing taken from it. God does it so that men will revere him.[41]

As you do not know the path of the wind, or how the body is formed in a mother's womb, so you cannot understand the work of God, the Maker of all things.[42]

For the ways of man are before the eyes of the Lord, and He ponders all his paths.[43]

I also thought, "As for men, God tests them so that they may see that they are like the animals."[44]

Indeed, there is not a righteous man on earth who continually does good and who never sins.[45]

When times are good, be happy; but when times are bad, consider: God has made the one as well as the other. Therefore, a man cannot discover anything about his future.[46]

This only have I found: God made mankind upright, but men have gone in search of many schemes.[47]

To the man who pleases him, God gives wisdom, knowledge and happiness, but to the sinner he gives the task of gathering and storing up wealth to hand it over to the one who pleases God.[48]

Moreover, when God gives any man wealth and possessions, and enables him to enjoy them, to accept his lot and be happy in his work—this is a gift of God.[49]

Guard your steps when you go to the house of God. Go near to listen rather than to offer the sacrifice of fools, who do not know that they do wrong.[50]

Now all has been heard; here is the conclusion of the matter: Fear God and keep his commandments, for this is the whole duty of man.[51]

For God will bring every deed into judgment, including every hidden thing, whether it is good or evil.[52]

An Absence of Positive References to the Family

In his own life, Buddha left his family to pursue wisdom. According to Buddhist tradition, he set out on the night of his son's birth or soon thereafter. His wife, Yasodhara, who was also his cousin, grieved initially but then began a life of renunciation, following his example. Eventually she became a Buddhist nun, and the son became a monk.[53]

This background goes a long way to explaining why, in his teachings, Buddha preferred the wandering homelessness of a holy man to the institution of the family:

They depart with their thoughts well-collected, they are not happy in their abode; like swans who have left their lake, they leave their house and home.[54]

Buddha's proverbs hardly placed any emphasis on the importance of family. Instead, whatever proverbs he has about family tend to be rather negative in tone:

"These sons belong to me, and this wealth belongs to me," with such thoughts a fool is tormented. He himself does not belong to himself; how much less sons and wealth?[55]

Death comes and carries off that man, praised for his children and flocks, his mind distracted, as a flood carries off a sleeping village.[56]

Sons are no help, nor a father, nor relations; there is no help from kinsfolk for one whom death has seized.[57]

Even the one proverb of Buddha's with a positive slant about family does not elevate parenthood above being a homeless recluse, or "Samana":

> Pleasant in the world is the state of a mother, pleasant the state of a father, pleasant the state of a Samana, pleasant the state of a Brahmana.[58]

This proverb may also be translated as follows:

> To render service unto a mother in this world is bliss; to render service unto a father in this world is bliss; to render service unto a homeless recluse in this world is bliss, and to render service unto a Brahman sage in this world is bliss.[59]

One gets the sense that Buddha had a very unhappy childhood and young adulthood.

In great contrast, Solomon's proverbs include many very positive portrayals of family relationships. Proverbs focusing on family relationships take up twenty-eight pages of a popular topical collection of Solomon's Proverbs.[60] Consider these examples:

> An excellent wife is the crown of her husband.[61]

> A wise son makes a father glad.[62]

> Children's children are the crown of old men, and the glory of children is their father.[63]

> The father of the righteous will greatly rejoice, and he who begets a wise child will delight in him. Let your father and mother be glad, and let her who bore you rejoice.[64]

> A righteous man who walks in his integrity—how blessed are his sons after him.[65]

Judaism so greatly values the family that the Hindu and Buddhist practice of forswearing marriage and family is quite foreign to Jews.

Jewish rabbis, unlike Hindu holy men and Buddhist monks, typically marry and have children. In fact, a website on Jewish marriage practices says that "not only are rabbis allowed to marry, they are obligated to marry. 'Be fruitful and multiply' is a command to all, regardless of career or position in the community."[66]

Even though the Dhammapada lacks clear supportive references to marriage and family, some of Buddha's other writings document his acceptance of marriage as a common institution. However, he tended to view marriage not as a union but as a circumstance defined by the personality and morals of the individual partici-pants. "Householders, there are these four kinds of marriages. What four? A wretch lives together with a wretch; a wretch lives together with a goddess; a god lives together with a wretch; a god lives together with a goddess."[67]

It is evident from Buddha's writings that what is important are the separate practices of individuals involved in a marriage rather than the marriage itself having significance. In Buddhist societies, the lives of monks and nuns are of central importance, while those of common householders are of little consequence, save that of being a source of food to begging monks.

A Lack of Positive References to Government

Solomon's proverbs include ethical admonitions to earthly kings. Solomon's view is that kings are under the sovereign authority of God. As such, they are subject to moral laws and their karmic consequences, just as other people are. Like the common people, they can be righteous or wicked:

> It is an abomination for kings to commit wickedness, for a throne is established by righteousness. Righteous lips are the delight of kings, and they love him who speaks what is right.[68]

> When the righteous are in authority, the people rejoice; but when a wicked man rules, the people groan.[69]

Mercy and truth preserve the king, and by lovingkindness he upholds his throne.[70]

Buddha's proverbs do not depict earthly kings in a positive light:

If, whether for his own sake, or for the sake of others, a man wishes neither for a son, nor for wealth, nor for lordship, and if he does not wish for his own success by unfair means, then he is good, wise, and virtuous.[71]

They lead a tamed elephant to battle, the king mounts a tamed elephant; the tamed is the best among men, he who silently endures abuse.[72]

In the second proverb quoted above, Buddha is almost mocking the easy life that a king enjoys. The implication is that this easy life is insufficient for attaining enlightenment, for it presents no real challenges. According to Solomon, a king can be righteous; for Buddha, this would be nearly impossible. Perhaps that is why "one should not long for . . . a kingdom."

Two of Buddha's proverbs that refer to kings do so in a spiritually symbolic way. In the following proverbs, father symbolizes egotism, mother symbolizes craving, two valiant kings symbolize the two false doctrines of eternalism and annihilation of the soul and the subjects symbolize the bases of sense perception and objects of attachment.[73]

A true Brahmana goes scatheless, though he have killed father and mother, and two valiant kings, though he has destroyed a kingdom with all its subjects.[74]

A true Brahmana goes scatheless, though he have killed father and mother, and two holy kings, and an eminent man besides.[75]

Kings and kingdoms, in other words, are something to be renounced, not revered.

A Form of Spirituality

Asperger's syndrome is defined as "a pervasive developmental disorder, usually of childhood, characterized by impairments in social interactions and repetitive behavior patterns."[76] Arguably, the practice of Buddhism bears resemblance to some types of obsessive-compulsive behavior. It involves excessively repeated acts of meditation aimed at achieving emotional detachment and mental rigidity. One might go further to hypothesize that, by shunning the outpouring of emotions stirred by harms of the past, Buddhist practice hampers healthy communication between people and blunts emotional and spiritual healing resulting from confessions of feelings about past negative events.

Buddhism espouses a suppression and avoidance of all emotions. This naturally leads to impairments in social interactions. Lorin Roche, Ph.D., a longtime advocate of meditation and counselor to those who have encountered life problems while they have been trying to adopt a deep meditative practice, noted several aspects of Buddhism and Hinduism that foster a form of spirituality analogous to Asperger's syndrome:

> Many of the best, most brilliant and articulate teachers working in the West are from Hindu and Buddhist lineages, and even when they are talking to women who have families, they tend to use language and techniques that were designed only for monks, such as: detachment, renunciation, silencing the mind. These attitudes are harmful to people who are not monks, because *they injure one's ability to be intimate with another human being*. . . . Just because recluses and renunciates by definition have a sour grapes attitude toward bodies, the senses, sensual enjoyment, is very damaging to non-monks. It's like studying cooking with someone with an eating disorder, who conveys a conflicted, problem-laden attitude toward food with every look and word . . .

Many spiritual teachers whine continually about "attachments." Decoded, this is an attack on your attachment or bonding to anything or anyone other than the teacher . . .

Another damaging aspect of meditation teachers is that they do not have peer relationships. No one is their equal.[77]

Buddhism champions intense practices that bear resemblance to the compulsions of people suffering from Asperger's syndrome. Dr. Roche made the following observations regarding meditators who suffered from depression:

They have interpreted the Buddhist or Hindu teachings they are studying in such a way as to detach themselves from their desires, their ego, their loves, and their passion. In other words, they have cut themselves off from everything interesting and thrilling in life. Depression is a natural result of loss, and if you internalize teachings that poison you against the world, then you will of course become depressed.[78]

The point of all this is not that intense meditation is harmful, but rather that it should be engaged in with moderation. In a real sense, the intensive meditation Buddhism espouses is like a painkiller. Taken in small, prescribed doses, it can have very beneficial effects. Downing an entire bottle of any painkiller, however, will cause death.

Buddhism's emphasis on solitude and the fact that it does not address the need for confession stand in sharp contrast to Solomon's Judaism. For Solomon, confession plays an important and positive role in our lives:

He who conceals his sins does not prosper, but whoever confesses and renounces them finds mercy.[79]

Where there is confession, there is mercy, grace, and forgiveness. These concepts are virtually absent in Buddhism. Furthermore, Buddhism's avoidance of God and the need to turn to him for guidance and correction are opposites of Solomon's teachings. Recall that Solomon wrote:

> All a man's ways seem innocent to him, but motives are weighed by the Lord.[80]

> Trust in the Lord with all your heart, and lean not on your own understanding. In all your ways acknowledge Him, and He will direct your paths.[81]

As a consequence of taking God out of the equation, Buddhism must give up corollaries such as forgiveness, grace, and mercy, and it must give up humility before an all-knowing being who can offer guidance and correction. It forswears relationships at all levels, including those between man and wife, parent and child, and man and God, causing the seeker to desire a state analogous to Asperger's syndrome.

As we have seen in this chapter, there are several areas of major difference between Buddha's teachings and Solomon's writings. However, this does not mean that Buddha was not influenced by Solomon. For the most part, these differences are quite predictable and fall into a few well-defined categories, as presented above.

---

[1] Dhammapada 87.

[2] Proverbs 18:1 (NKJV).

[3] Ecclesiastes 7:16–18 (NIV).

[4] Dhammapada 143.

[5] Ibid., 148.

[6] Thomas Knierim, editor and webmaster, "The Noble Eightfold Path," Raison d'Etre, www.thebigview.com/buddhism/eightfoldpath.html, retrieved November 19, 2010.

[7] Proverbs 1:2–3, paraphrased from the NLT and Today's New International Version (emphasis added).

[8] Dhammapada 30.

[9] Ibid., 44.

[10] Proverbs 24:11–12 (NIV).

[11] Dhammapada 1.

[12] Ibid., 2.

[13] Ibid., 7.

[14] Ibid., 47.

[15] Ibid., 48.

[16] Ibid., 8.

[17] Ibid., 37.

[18] Ibid., 57.

[19] Ibid., 40.

[20] Ibid., 104–105.

[21] Ibid., 274.

[22] Ibid., 276.

[23] Ibid., 337.

[24] Ibid., 350.

[25] Ibid., 46.

[26] Ibid., 170.

[27] Ibid., 34.

[28] Dhammapada 160.

[29] Proverbs 3:5–7a (NIV).

[30] Proverbs 3:7b–12 (NIV).

[31] Proverbs 15:9 (NKJV).

[32] Proverbs 3:31–35 (NKJV).

[33] Proverbs 9:10 (NKJV).

[34] Proverbs 21:2 (NKJV).

[35] Proverbs 16:5 (NKJV).

[36] Dhammapada 353.

[37] Ibid., 28.

[38] Ibid., 29.

[39] Ecclesiastes 5:2 (NIV).

[40] Ecclesiastes 3:11 (NIV).

[41] Ecclesiastes 3:14 (NIV).

[42] Ecclesiastes 11:5 (NIV).

[43] Proverbs 5:21 (NKJV).

[44] Ecclesiastes 3:18 (NIV).

[45] Ecclesiastes 7:20 (NASB).

[46] Ecclesiastes 7:14 (NIV).

[47] Ecclesiastes 7:29 (NIV).

[48] Ecclesiastes 2:26a (NIV).

[49] Ecclesiastes 5:19 (NIV).

[50] Ecclesiastes 5:1 (NIV).

[51] Ecclesiastes 12:13 (NIV).

[52] Ecclesiastes 12:14 (NIV).

[53] For more on Buddha's wife, see, for example, "Yasodhara," http://en.wikipedia.org/wiki/Yasodhar%C4%81; Patricia M. Herbert, *The Life of the Buddha* (Petaluma, CA: Pomegranate Communications, 2005).

[54] Dhammapada 91.

[55] Ibid., 62.

[56] Ibid., 287.

[57] Ibid., 288.

[58] Ibid., 332.

[59] This alternate translation is from Harischandra Kaviratna, trans., *Dhammapada, Wisdom of the Buddha*, 1980, Theosophical University Press Online, www.theosociety.org/pasadena/dhamma/dham-hp.htm, retrieved April 14, 2011.

[60] *God's Wisdom for Daily Living* (Nashville: Thomas Nelson, 1984), 28–56.

[61] Proverbs 12:4a (NKJV).

[62] Proverbs 15:20a (NKJV).

[63] Proverbs 17:6 (NKJV).

[64] Proverbs 23:24–25 (NKJV)

[65] Proverbs 20:7 (NASB).

[66] Aron Moss, "Can a Rabbi Get Married?" Jewish Marriage: Becoming One, Chabad.org Lifecycles, www.chabad.org/library/article_cdo/aid/248162/jewish/Can-a-Rabbi-Get-Married.htm.

[67] Bhikkhu Bodhi, ed., *In the Buddha's Words* (Boston: Wisdom Publications, 2005), 120.

[68] Proverbs 16:12–13 (NKJV).

[69] Proverbs 29:2 (NKJV).

[70] Proverbs 20:28 (NKJV).

[71] Dhammapada 84.

[72] Ibid., 321.

[73] Harischandra Kaviratna, trans., *Dhammapada, Wisdom of the Buddha*, 1980, Theosophical University Press Online, www.theosociety.org/pasadena/dhamma/dham-hp.htm, retrieved May 23, 2011.

[74] Ibid., 294.

[75] Ibid., 295.

[76] Definition from www.dictionary.com, retrieved November 17, 2010.

[77] Lorin Roche, "The Dangers of Meditation," www.lorinroche.com/page8/page8.html, retrieved September 18, 2010 (emphasis added).

[78] Ibid.

[79] Proverbs 28:13 (NIV).

[80] Proverbs 16:2 (NIV).

[81] Proverbs 3:5–6 (NIV).

Part Two: Buddha and Jesus

Chapter Eleven
Similarities Between Buddha and Jesus

A number of recent books have proposed the idea that Buddha and Jesus are practically brothers. Close to the end of *Living Buddha, Living Christ*, Buddhist monk Thich Nhat Hanh asserted, "When you are a truly happy Christian, you are also a Buddhist. And vice versa."[1]

In the controversial book *Jesus and Buddha: The Parallel Sayings*, New Testament scholar Marcus J. Borg claimed that both religious founders espoused a "world-subverting wisdom that undermined and challenged conventional ways of seeing and being in their time and in every time." Borg claimed that both were teachers of wisdom, not only regarding "moral behavior, but about the 'center,' the place from which moral perception and moral behavior flow." Both, according to Borg, "were teachers of the way less traveled. 'Way' or 'path' imagery is central to both bodies of teaching."[2]

And in a Catholic magazine devoted to apologetics called *This Rock*, authors Carl E. Olson and Anthony E. Clark, citing Thich Nhat Hanh's assertion, noted that "some Catholics agree." They cited as evidence that "Jesuit Father Robert E. Kennedy . . . holds Zen retreats at Morning Star Zendo in Jersey City." Further, "The St. Francis Chapel at Santa Clara University hosts the weekly practice of 'mindfulness and Zen meditation.' Indeed, the number of Buddhist retreats and workshops being held at Catholic monasteries and parishes is growing." Olson and Clark went on to point out serious differences between Buddhism and Christianity. The title of their article in *The Rock* was "Are Jesus and Buddha Brothers? If So, There's a Serious Family Feud."[3]

The article mentions Borg's *Jesus and Buddha*; another book by Thich Nhat Hanh, entitled *Going Home: Jesus and Buddha as Brothers*; and *Zen Spirit, Christian Spirit: The Place of Zen in Christian Life*, by Robert E. Kennedy, all of which espouse the viewpoint that Buddhism and Christianity are compatible.

Is it true that on a spiritual level Buddha and Jesus are quite similar? In this chapter and the ones that follow, we will look at this question broadly, covering the areas of moral behavior, spirituality, and beliefs about the nature of reality, sin and evil, and God as well as the degree to which variations in the teachings of Buddha and Jesus could be acceptable (that is, compatible enough that a Buddhist could continue to maintain Buddhism while at the same time accepting Christianity, or vice versa). Were Buddha and Jesus almost identical in their ideas—spiritual brothers—or were they quite similar in some ways but very different in others? In other words, can someone be both fully Buddhist and fully Christian without sacrificing any of the tenets or beliefs of either religion?

We will first explore this question by comparing conservative Christianity and conservative (Theravada) Buddhism, in large part because these two systems are well known and reasonably well defined. Comparisons of liberal Christianity and other branches of Buddhism are covered in Chapter Thirteen, where answers to frequently asked questions are provided. In this chapter we will look at some obvious similarities between Buddha and Christ and the two religions they inspired.

Remarkable Similarities

It is not surprising to find speculation about Buddha and Jesus somehow being linked. There are, to be sure, many remarkable similarities between them. Both espoused altruism, emphasizing that it is more blessed to give than to receive. Both said that love is the best way to overcome hatred. Both taught the Golden Rule, and both urged their followers not to judge others.

Buddha urged people to lose self to gain nirvana; Jesus exhorted people to lose self to gain eternal life through a personal relationship with him. Buddha emphasized the importance of ceasing existence as an individual to escape suffering; Jesus offered the hope of a heaven where there would be no suffering.

Similarities in Ethics

In the area of ethics, it is quite easy to see many close parallels, because altruism is at the heart of the teachings of both Buddha and Christ.

Buddha	Christ
"Consider others as yourself."[4]	"Treat others the same way you want them to treat you."[5] "You shall love your neighbor as yourself."[6]
"If you do not tend to one another then who is there to tend to you? Whoever would tend me, he should tend the sick."[7]	"Truly I say to you, to the extent that you did not do it to one of the least of these, you did not do it to Me."[8]
"Just as a mother would protect her only child at the risk of her own life, even so, cultivate a boundless heart towards all beings. Let your thoughts of boundless love pervade the whole world."[9]	"This is my commandment, that you love one another as I have loved you. No one has greater love than this, to lay down one's life for one's friends."[10]
"Hard it is to understand: By giving away our food, we get more strength; by bestowing clothing on others, we gain more beauty; by founding abodes of purity and truth, we acquire great treasures. The charitable man has found the path of liberation. He is like the man who plants a sapling securing thereby the shade, the flowers and the fruit in future years. Even so is the result of charity, even so is the joy of him who helps those that are in need of assistance; even so is the great nirvana."[11]	"Remember this: Whoever sows sparingly will also reap sparingly, and whoever sows generously will also reap generously. Each man should give what he has decided in his heart to give, not reluctantly or under compulsion, for God loves a cheerful giver. And God is able to make all grace abound to you, so that in all things at all times, having all that you need, you will abound in every good work. . . . You will be made rich in every way so that you can be generous on every occasion, and through us your generosity will result in thanksgiving to God."[12]

"The charitable man has found the path of liberation."[13]

"In everything I showed you that by working hard in this manner you must help the weak and remember the words of the Lord Jesus, that He Himself said, 'It is more blessed to give than to receive.'"[14]

"The fault of others is easily perceived, but that of oneself is difficult to perceive; a man winnows his neighbour's faults like chaff, but his own fault he hides, as a cheat hides the bad die from the gambler."[15]

"Judge not, that you be not judged. For with what judgment you judge, you will be judged; and with the measure you use, it will be measured back to you. And why do you look at the speck in your brother's eye, but do not consider the plank in your own eye? Or how can you say to your brother, 'Let me remove the speck from your eye'; and look, a plank *is* in your own eye? Hypocrite! First remove the plank from your own eye, and then you will see clearly to remove the speck from your brother's eye."[16]

"Hatred does not ever cease in this world by hating, but by love; this is an eternal truth. . . . Overcome anger by love, overcome evil by good, overcome the miser by giving, overcome the liar by truth."[17]

"Love your enemies, do good to those who hate you, bless those who curse you, pray for those who mistreat you."[18]

"You have heard that it was said, 'Eye for eye, and tooth for tooth.' But I tell you, Do not resist an evil person. If someone strikes you on the right cheek, turn to him the other also. And if someone wants to sue you and take your tunic, let him have your cloak as well. If someone forces you to go one mile, go with him two miles. Give to the one who asks you, and do not turn away from the one who wants to borrow from you."[19]

"The world gives according to their faith or according to their pleasure: if a man frets about the food and the drink given to others, he will find no rest either by day or by night."[20]	"Be careful not to do your 'acts of righteousness' before men, to be seen by them. If you do, you will have no reward from your Father in heaven. So when you give to the needy, do not announce it with trumpets, as the hypocrites do in the synagogues and on the streets, to be honored by men. I tell you the truth, they have received their reward in full. But when you give to the needy, do not let your left hand know what your right hand is doing, so that your giving may be in secret. Then your Father, who sees what is done in secret, will reward you."[21]
Lose self to gain nirvana and escape from suffering.	Lose self to gain Christ and entrance into heaven, where there will be no suffering.

We can summarize the above by listing the following areas of close agreement between Buddha and Christ:

- Altruism
- The Golden Rule
- Don't judge others
- Love your enemies
- Overcome hate with love
- More blessed to give than to receive
- Avoid being religious for show

Other Significant Parallels

As covered in Chapters Three through Nine, Buddhism's Four Noble Truths and Noble Eightfold Path are composed almost entirely of elements that have parallels in Judaism and Christianity. To these we can add the fact that both Buddha and Jesus emphasized the very serious nature of sin and its consequences. For example, Buddha's proverbs include the following:

> He who inflicts pain on innocent and harmless persons, will soon come to one of these ten states: He will have cruel suffering, loss, injury of the body, heavy affliction, or loss of mind, or a misfortune coming from the king, or a fearful accusation, or loss of relations, or destruction of treasures, or lightning-fire will burn his houses; and when his body is destroyed, the fool will go to hell.[22]

Similarly, in the Sermon on the Mount, Jesus said:

> You have heard that the ancients were told, "You shall not commit murder" and "Whoever commits murder shall be liable to the court." But I say to you that everyone who is angry with his brother shall be guilty before the court; and whoever says to his brother, "You good-for-nothing," shall be guilty before the supreme court; and whoever says, "You fool," shall be guilty enough to go into the fiery hell. Therefore if you are presenting your offering at the altar, and there remember that your brother has something against you, leave your offering there before the altar and go; first be reconciled to your brother, and then come and present your offering.[23]

There are also many parallels between Jesus and Christianity, on one hand, and Buddha and Buddhism, on the other, beyond the area of ethics, as summarized in the following chart.

Buddha/Buddhism	Jesus/Christianity
Rejected parts of Hinduism while retaining some of its elements.	Rejected parts of Judaism while retaining some of its elements.
Spread by Indian Emperor Ashoka after his conversion from Hinduism.	Spread by Roman Emperor Constantine after his conversion to Christianity.
Some branches of Buddhism evolved into a highly ceremonial religion, with monks who withdrew from secular life (monasticism).	Catholicism evolved into a highly ceremonial religion, with monks who withdrew from secular life (monasticism).
Primary activities are meditating, chanting, listening to teachings and mentoring.	Primary activities are worship, singing, listening to sermons, and engaging in prayer (both group and individual), fellowship, Bible study, and discipleship.
Buddha said, "As the impurity which springs from the iron, when it springs from it, destroys it; thus do a transgressor's own works lead him to the evil path."[24]	"But those things which proceed out of the mouth come from the heart, and they defile a man. For out of the heart proceed evil thoughts, murders, adulteries, fornications, thefts, false witness, blasphemies. These are the things which defile a man, but to eat with unwashed hands does not defile a man."[25]
Buddha said, "Let the wise man guard his thoughts, for they are difficult to perceive, very artful, and they rush wherever they list: thoughts well guarded bring happiness."[26]	Part of being righteous is to watch over the mind. The apostle Paul urged people to bring "every thought into captivity to the obedience of Christ."[27]

In view of all of the above, it would be easy to conclude that Buddha and Jesus were practically brothers. However, as we will see in the next chapter, there are ten areas of major difference between Buddhism and Christianity. And the opposing elements of each of these differences are basically irreconcilable.

---

[1] Carl E. Olson and Anthony E. Clark, "Are Jesus and Buddha Brothers?" This Rock 16, no. 5 (May-June 2005), www.catholic.com/thisrock/2005/0505fea1.asp, retrieved February 17, 2011.

[2] Marcus Borg, ed., with coeditor Ray Riegert and an Introduction by Jack Kornfield, *Jesus and Buddha: The Parallel Sayings* (Berkeley: Ulysses Press, 1997), 8–9.

[3] Olson, "Are Jesus and Buddha Brothers?"

[4] Heartland Sangha American Buddhism, "Parallel Sayings of Buddha and Christ," www.heartlandsangha.org/parallel-sayings.html, retrieved October 12, 2010.

[5] Luke 6:31 (NASB).

[6] Mark 12:31b (NASB).

[7] Heartland Sangha American Buddhism, "Parallel Sayings."

[8] Matthew 25:45b (NASB).

[9] Heartland Sangha American Buddhism, "Parallel Sayings."

[10] John 15:12–13 (NKJV).

[11] Exotic India, "Buddha and Christ: Two Gods on the Path to Humanity" (November 2003), www.exoticindiaart.com/article/buddhaandchrist, retrieved October 12, 2010.

[12] 2 Corinthians 9:6–8,11 (NIV).

[13] Exotic India, "Buddha and Christ."

[14] Acts 20:35 (NASB).

[15] Dhammapada 252.

[16] Matthew 7:1–5 (NKJV).

[17] Heartland Sangha American Buddhism, "Parallel Sayings."

[18] Luke 6:27–28 (NIV).

[19] Matthew 5:38–42 (NIV).

[20] Dhammapada 249.

[21] Matthew 6:1–4 (NIV).

[22] Dhammapada 137–140.

[23] Matthew 5:21–24 (NASB).

[24] Dhammapada 240.

[25] Matthew 15:18–20 (NKJV).

[26] Dhammapada 36.

[27] 2 Corinthians 10:5b (NKJV).

Chapter Twelve
Differences Between Buddha and Jesus

For all the similarities detailed in the previous chapter, there are ten areas of major difference between Buddhism and Christianity. The next table summarizes these. In this comparison, every effort has been made to present each religion in as positive and objective a light as possible, consistent with the beliefs of conservative practitioners of that religion.[1]

The phrases in the first column of the table correspond to the topics we will look at in more detail throughout this chapter.

Type of Difference	Buddhism	Christianity
1. What It Is All About	A method of right living and self-guided mind control via meditation modeled by Buddha. The goal is to be freed from reincarnation and suffering. God is not relevant to one's ability to do this.	A personal relationship with God's crucified and risen Son, Jesus, that empowers believers with the Spirit of God. The goal is to love God and all people and to gain eternal life in heaven.
2. Journey of the Soul	Repeated reincarnation. Life is largely predetermined by past lives' karma. One has little free will, and it is very hard to work off bad karma.	Resurrection once to eternal life. Free will is pervasive. God can quickly forgive all past and future deeds that create bad karma.
3. Accessibility to Liberation	Only a very select few attain it.	Readily available to everyone.
4. Mercy, Grace, and Forgiveness	These concepts are foreign to Buddhism.	God is eager to extend these and people should, too.

5. Losing One's Self and Dealing with Suffering	The goal is to become detached. The existence of the soul is an illusion.	The goal is to lose the self in a relationship with a personal God. The soul is eternal.
6. Works vs. Faith	One reaches enlightenment through meditation and right living.	Salvation is by faith alone.
7. Being a Follower	Truth lies deep within. Follow Buddha's example and teachings.	Sin lies within; Jesus is the Truth. Follow the Holy Spirit and the Bible.
8. Many Paths vs. One Path	Many paths are possible: Buddha is only one of many enlightened ones. Occult beliefs and practices are okay.	Jesus, who is divine, is the only way to God. All occult beliefs and practices are evil and forbidden.
9. Nature of the Universe	The universe always existed. All is one. All conscious beings (humans and animals) are basically equal.	God created the universe. Reality has two opposite natures. There is a clear hierarchy among beings.
10. Women	Men are almost always superior to women.	Women are frequently regarded as being equal, or nearly equal, to men.

Given the contrasts highlighted above, it would be difficult to see how someone could be both a Buddhist and a Christian at the same time. These are not minor issues that could easily be compromised. Instead, they are major tenets of each religion that are mutually exclusive. The reality is that both religions are very narrow, but in radically different ways. The narrowness of Buddhism, which is its ultimate impracticality, is highlighted in number 3 above. The narrowness of Christianity, which is its doctrinal intolerance, is underscored in number 8.

In the discussion below, we look in detail at each of these areas of contrast.

Major Contrast #1: What It Is All About

Buddhism	Christianity
A method of right living and self-guided mind control via meditation modeled by Buddha. The goal is to be freed from reincarnation and suffering. God is not relevant to one's ability to do this.	A personal relationship with God's crucified and risen Son, Jesus, that empowers believers with the Spirit of God. The goal is to love God and all people and to gain eternal life in heaven.

Buddhism is all about the practitioner eliminating himself or herself in an effort to escape being reborn as another sentient (conscious) being, either animal or human, struggling in a world full of suffering. The Christian, in contrast, believes that God has a unique plan for each individual. God wishes to bless each individual and has given gifts, talents, and opportunities to each person. To the extent the believer seeks God's involvement in his or her life, its scope can go far beyond the basic assurance of salvation to the cultivation of a personal, interactive relationship with Jesus and the Holy Spirit. One may suffer for a time, but God works everything together for good and gives the believer peace and joy in the midst of suffering.[2]

Buddha's entire approach to spirituality intentionally deferred (or avoided) theological issues. He did this to put the focus on what he believed was the highest priority — finding a humanistic way to bring an end to suffering. He explained this in a parable, which Huston Smith summarized as follows:

It is as if a man had been wounded by an arrow thickly smeared with poison, and his friends and kinsmen were to get a surgeon to heal him, and he were to say, I will not have this arrow pulled out until I know by what man I was wounded, whether he is of the warrior caste, or a Brahmin, or of the agricultural, or the lowest caste. . . . Similarly, it is not on the view that the world is eternal, that it is finite, that body and soul are distinct, or that the Buddha exists after death that a religious life depends. . . . I have not spoken to these views because they do not conduce to absence of passion, tranquility, and Nirvana. And what have I explained? Suffering have I explained, the cause of suffering, the destruction of suffering, and the path that leads to the destruction of suffering have I explained. For this is useful.[3]

In other words, the main problem confronting each individual is that life entails suffering, and the main goal is to follow Buddha's teachings (about meditation, renunciation, and so on) in order to eliminate it from one's life. The solution is not a matter of what one believes about doctrine, but what one can do to become detached from the suffering. This perspective contrasts sharply with that of Jesus, who warned his followers not to be surprised if they were persecuted for their faith, but to see it as a good thing that would yield great rewards in their lives in heaven. The main thing was to believe in him, and suffering for one's beliefs was to be expected and even desired:

> Blessed are you when people insult you, persecute you and falsely say all kinds of evil against you because of me. Rejoice and be glad, because great is your reward in heaven, for in the same way they persecuted the prophets who were before you.[4]

Major Contrast #2: Journey of the Soul

Buddhism	Christianity
Buddha assumed repeated reincarnation and many past lives, during some of which one may have been some kind of animal.	Jesus proclaimed resurrection to eternal life (in heaven or hell) after one life on earth. Each individual lives as a unique person either in the presence of God or fully separated from him.
Each person is the product of good and bad karma from their	There is no prior life and no

various past lives. This leaves very little room to exercise free will.

It is very difficult to work off negative karma, which can haunt a person into many future lives. Attaining enlightenment is the only way out of endless cycles of life and death.

burden of bad karma from it. Each person was created by God in his image with the free will to choose his or her own direction.

Anyone can have all the bad karma of past actions completely forgiven by God by admitting past sins, desiring to repent, and receiving Jesus as Lord and Savior. (Though the individual is then spiritually freed, he or she may still have to face the natural consequences of past misdeeds.)

Each of the above differences originates from predecessor religions. The influences of Hinduism on Buddhism are far reaching, as are the influences of Judaism on Christianity.

Buddha's own birth records provide a vivid example of his belief in reincarnation: "According to these records," wrote an authority on Eastern religions, "Buddha has gone through numerous transmigrations; that is, he was 83 times ascetic, 43 times Deva (a divine being), 18 times ape, 6 times elephant, 1 time thief, 1 time frog, 1 time snipe (a bird), 58 times king, 24 times Brahman, 10 times deer, 10 times lion, 1 time gambler and 1 time hare."[5]

Major Contrast #3: Accessibility to Liberation

Buddhism

Liberation (enlightenment) can only be attained through many years (or lifetimes) of focused effort. Only a very small number of people have ever attained it. Making progress spiritually is very slow. Liberation is not available to those who cannot or will not meditate intensively for very long periods of time.

Christianity

Liberation (salvation) can be rapid and radical. It is quickly available to everyone, regardless of their level of intelligence or self-discipline.

While one can adopt basic Buddhist beliefs and practices quickly, this does not result in liberation (enlightenment). Progress toward liberation requires many years, if not many lifetimes, of consistent, intense meditation and moral discipline. Only an elite few are capable of this. Even fewer have lived the kind of morally pure lives (both in this life and in all past lives) necessary to set them free from the persistent drag of negative karma. So, for all practical purposes, Buddhism is a path most people are incapable of following to completion, making it extremely narrow. For example, those with attention deficit disorder (ADD) have absolutely no hope of liberation. The stark reality is that, in the world as Buddhism perceives it, the vast majority of people will spend an endless number of lifetimes reincarnating back into a suffering world.

In contrast, liberation through Christ is universally accessible, and attaining liberation (salvation) as a result of a commitment based on faith often is very quick. The thief on the cross next to Jesus received salvation instantly after his confession of faith.[6] Because it emphasizes faith, rather than works and discipline, Christianity has ready appeal to people of ordinary or even lower levels of intelligence. It may even be hard for highly disciplined self-achievers to accept it because they are susceptible to believing that their superior efforts should be rewarded specifically.

While the Buddhist who attains liberation is only ushered into a state of peace and nothingness after death, the true Christian gains immediate access to a personal, interactive relationship with a loving, compassionate Jesus in this life and an eternity with him and other believers in heaven.

Chapter Fourteen provides an extended discussion of this key area of difference.

Major Contrast #4: Mercy, Grace, and Forgiveness (from God and Other People)

Buddhism	Christianity
Mercy, grace, and forgiveness are concepts that are virtually absent in Buddhism. There is no mercy, grace, or forgiveness to be received from a loving God or	A supreme God who controls the universe loves every person and is eager to show mercy, grace, and forgiveness to those who approach him in faith and

from other people. If "God" exists, it is impersonal and everywhere, like gravity.	humility. The Bible exhorts Christians (and Jews) to practice mercy, grace, and forgiveness toward one another.

The Buddhist sees mercy, grace, and forgiveness as violations of the inevitable working out of karma for each person. Facing the consequences of one's past deeds is part of karmic conditioning, as emphasized in Buddha's First Noble Truth. In Christianity, when God exhibits mercy, grace, and forgiveness toward a believer, it is intended to free the individual from the spiritual burden of past misdeeds so that his or her relationship with God and with other people can be restored.

Major Contrast #5: Losing One's Self and Dealing with Suffering

Buddhism	Christianity
Desire is the cause of suffering. Thus, all desire is bad and must be eliminated.	Rejoicing in God and desiring to help others are very good. Christians should rejoice when they are persecuted. When it causes spiritual growth, some suffering can be good.
Buddhist practices are ways of "checking out" of present reality to find peace and freedom from suffering. The goal is to become detached, impervious, and numbed from the pains of life.	One is called to lose one's self in the care, direction, inspiration, and protection of a loving, gracious, merciful, forgiving, all-powerful God.
The idea that man has a soul is an illusion.	A personal God created each person with an eternal soul and unique personality so that he or she might have a rich and satisfying relationship with others and with God, both now and forever.
Everyone is a closely interconnected part of the universe.	

The natural reaction of a Buddhist seeker to the above claims of Christianity is that they are too good to be true. Alternatively, the natural reaction of a Christian to the above claims of Buddhism is that they are too bleak.

Yet there are more areas of contrast to consider regarding desire and suffering. To the Buddhist, any kind of desire is bad, because desire is the cause of suffering. To the Christian, though many desires are sinful, many others are clearly good. This is implied by a verse in the Psalms: "Delight yourself also in the LORD, and He shall give you the desires of your heart."[7] Such desires are good, because God gave them to believers. It is God's will that one rejoice in him and in his blessings.[8] Yet, Jesus also said, "In the world you will have tribulation."[9]

In addition, to the Buddhist, all suffering is bad. That's just the way it is. Christians have something quite different to say about the cause and purposes of suffering. As for the cause, mankind (via Adam and Eve) chose to rebel against God and to live independently of him. God responds by pulling back and withholding many of his blessings, as well as much of his protection, from us. Typically the result is suffering. Not all suffering is due to sin, however. Some kinds of suffering can be good. For example, people serving God will experience persecution. And God can also allow suffering in a person's life to bring about personal growth and maturity. It is through suffering that we learn patience and become more like Christ.[10]

For the Buddhist, eliminating expectations for selfish gain can create contentment. To the Christian, praising and thanking God, and caring for others, causes contentment.

Buddhists practice compassion out of a belief in the interconnectedness of all living beings. They also see acts of kindness as a means of creating good karma in order to become liberated from the self. Christian compassion is empowered by the filling and enabling of the Holy Spirit. Christians practice compassion as a response to God's love for mankind.

Major Contrast #6: Works vs. Faith

Buddhism	Christianity
Buddhism is a *method* of making progress toward becoming enlightened via persistent meditation and self-directed efforts to live righteously. It can be useful to followers of any religion in trying to overcome and eliminate the self. Buddha said, "Self is the lord of self, who else could be the lord? With self well subdued, a man finds a lord such as few can find."[11]	No human being can save themselves from the mortal consequences of their sins. Christianity is a rescue operation, initiated by God, to reconcile to himself everyone who will truly accept Jesus as Lord and Savior by faith. It is also a *personal relationship* with Christ which is sustained by the indwelling of the Holy Spirit in those who believe. Jesus said, "Apart from me you can do nothing."[12]

Major Contrast #7: Being a Follower

Buddhism	Christianity
Buddha taught that truth lies deep within each person. To find truth, outside sources must be excluded. In each spiritual practice and moment of life, the focus is on looking deep within one's self and strictly controlling one's thoughts, guided by the example of the Buddha, the counsel of his teachings, and the mentorship of a monk/guru.	Christians believe that at the core of every person is a sinful soul. The follower should look instead to Jesus in his or her search for truth. In each spiritual practice and moment of life, the focus is on following the leading of the Holy Spirit and the counsel of the Bible as the key parts of a personal relationship with Jesus.

Christians believe that since Adam and Eve rejected God in the Garden of Eden, every person has a strongly ingrained lower nature that rebels against God and seeks its own way. Truth is objective in nature, existing outside of and independent of the self. Christ said, "I am the truth." The Buddhist's focus is within the self in each spiritual practice followed on the path to enlightenment, whereas the Christian's focus is on God. It is not possible to do both at the same time. We see this clearly as we contrast each type of spiritual practice in the table below.

Buddhism	Christianity
Meditation is an essential element of the process of spiritual growth.	Bible study and prayer are essential elements of the process of spiritual growth. Meditation is not commonly practiced.
Meditation involves focusing one's attention on a single point of reference, such as one's breathing, some part of one's body, a mantra, or visualization of compassion or peace, for extended periods of time.	Christian meditation involves willfully choosing to focus the mind and spirit on specific attributes of God or on specific Bible verses, seeking deeper insight and understanding of their meaning and applicability to life.
A goal of meditation is to empty the mind.	A goal of meditation is to engage the mind and to draw on its own creativity and the leading of the Holy Spirit.
Prayers consist of words expressing intentions for blessings, peace, or protection. One's spoken words have the power to directly change reality.	Prayers consist of words directed to God seeking his blessings, guidance, enabling, and protection. One's spoken words, per se, have only limited power to change reality.
Chanting is the traditional means of preparing the mind for meditation. It can also be used for ritualistic purposes. Buddha warned against reciting the Dhamma with a musical intonation, out of concern that participants would become attached to the music rather than the content.[13]	Songs praising God for his attributes and deeds are usually an integral part of worship services. Experiencing an emotional liking to such music is considered quite wholesome and very beneficial to loving God and growing spiritually. The repertoire of Christian music is vast and very rich, including hundreds of masterpieces.

Major Contrast #8: Many Paths vs. One Path

Buddhism	Christianity
To Buddha many paths to eliminating the self were beneficial.	Jesus claimed the only way to God was through him.
Buddha denied his own divinity, seeing himself as being only one of many enlightened ones.	Jesus proclaimed his own divinity (i.e., saying he was one with God). He asserted his own uniqueness and spiritual supremacy over all people and spiritual beings.
Readily accommodates a very broad range of occult beliefs and practices.	Views all occult beliefs and practices as evil and forbidden.

Many Paths?

To the Buddhist, there are many paths to transcending the self. Each path is individual, with each person guided by a guru. In contrast, Jesus said, "I am the way and the truth and the life. No one comes to the Father except through me."[14]

Buddhists have a wide variety of different gurus and bodhisattvas to choose from for guidance in developing their own path to enlightenment. Christians have a tightly defined core text, the Bible, as a consistent source of guidance in seeking and following God. Parts of the Bible have been construed in diverse ways, and extrabiblical sources are also used as a guide by some (e.g., Catholics who heed dictums of the papacy). However, the central belief in Jesus as the Savior of the world through his death on the cross and resurrection to life on the third day is common to all mainstream Christians.

Since Buddhists recognize many paths to enlightenment, they see tolerance of different beliefs and peace with all people as paramount virtues. If others have different beliefs, there is no pressing need to try to change those beliefs as long as others are seeking tolerance and peace with everyone. Buddhists often will, however, encourage others to adopt some form of meditation as a practice.

Christ taught his followers to love their enemies and to care for and pray for them, leaving the struggle against opponents up to God. He taught that he alone was the judge of people; no one else should assume that role. Some Christians tend to see people who have different beliefs as the enemy, but in the New Testament, people are not the true enemies. Instead, a spiritual battle is going on in "the heavenly realms," and the enemy is Satan, along with the other fallen angels—the demons—who followed him in a rebellion against God and attempt to manipulate people.[15]

Buddhists are comparatively subjective. They believe that they can change their experience of the world by changing how they choose to view it. Christians are comparatively objective. They believe that they can change the world by earnest prayer if it is in accord with the will of God.

Were They Divine?

Theravada Buddhists usually do not believe in the divinity of Buddha. Buddha believed he was the same as every other enlightened being. Some Buddhists believe he was more enlightened than any other buddha in history. However, many Mahayana Buddhists believe in his divinity.

Conservative Christians believe in the divinity of Christ. In the Gospels, Jesus claimed to be one with God on several occasions. Mainstream Christianity from its earliest times has viewed God as a "triune" being consisting of the Father, the Son, and the Holy Spirit. The Gospel of John says of Jesus that "all things were made through him, and without him was not anything made that was made."[16] Thus, as the second person of the Trinity, he shared in the role of creator of the universe. Some liberal Christians do not regard Jesus as divine, viewing him as a great moral teacher instead.

Occult

In many Asian countries, Buddhism intentionally blended in the beliefs and practices of native populations as it expanded. Typically, this included superstitions and occult practices. Vajrayana Buddhists adopted many native Tibetan beliefs (in a wide range of deities) as an integral part of their spiritual practices.

Conservative Christians view all occult beliefs and activities as evils that should be completely avoided. Many liberal Christians are more open to blending in some of these views.

Near the end of Chapter Fifteen, in a section labeled, "Only One Way?" there is an extensive discussion of this entire area of contrast.

Major Contrast #9: Nature of the Universe

Buddhism	Christianity
The universe has always existed. It was never created.	God created the universe suddenly, as the Big Bang theory depicts.
Buddha taught that any appearance of dualism is an illusion and is not part of ultimate reality, which has only one nature (monism).	Jesus taught dualism (i.e., that reality consists of two opposite natures). He believed in the reality of good vs. evil, virtue vs. sin, and heaven vs. hell.
Buddha claimed that all sentient beings (i.e., people and animals) are interconnected and nearly equal. People are capable of attaining enlightenment, whereas animals are not.	Jesus emphasized a clear hierarchy among beings: God the Creator, then angels and demons, then people, then animals and plants, and finally, inanimate matter.
Why would God create a world where suffering is pervasive? It makes more sense to believe that the world, and the universe, were never created. They always existed.	In response to mankind's rejection of God in the Garden of Eden, God withdrew from active control of the world. In God's absence, Satan became "prince of this world."[17] This left mankind exposed to inherent, persistent suffering and misfortune.

To Buddha, any appearance of "good" or "evil" is an illusion that exists only in the realm of seeming reality. To Jesus, good and evil are opposites engaged in a battle for the eternal destiny of every soul.

Buddhism denies the ultimate existence of sin and the necessity of grace. Choosing to cast off the illusions of self and dualism is necessary to become enlightened. In Christianity, sin is not an illusion; it is a state of rebellion against and alienation from God. How one's sin is dealt with will determine a person's eternal destiny. Jesus, who is one with God as the second person of the Trinity and existed with God in heaven before he came to earth, took the initiative to seek and rescue mankind from a fallen world— in which all people are inherently sinful.

Buddhism denies the ultimate existence of evil. However, forms of "evil" appear in the relative reality of this world. Christianity stresses the active presence of evil in the world and the need to confess one's own sinful nature and need of a savior as a basis for escaping the power that evil now has in this world.

Monists look for truth within themselves, since they believe they are a central part of a universal whole. Dualists look for truth outside of themselves—for example, to a sacred book, to a specific church, or by direct appeal to a personal God far superior to themselves.

The life and worship of a dualist is rich and varied because it involves the interaction of a human soul with something other than itself. In the case of Christianity, this interaction is with a personal God who loves every human being and desires to be actively involved in each person's life. To the extent that any individual is willing to invite God into his or her life, that individual will experience an intimate relationship with him. If someone who is not a dualist believes in God, that God is impersonal. Hence the degree of richness of religion *as an exercise of man relating to God* is much greater for the dualist than for the monist, much as life in a world with both men and women is much richer than one in a society consisting only of men or only of women. The apostle Paul referred to the church as the bride of Christ.[18] Buddhism has not inspired great works of music, such as Handel's Messiah or Bach's B Minor Mass, or the large body of hymns and songs of worship present within Christianity. Such works are expressions of individual people with their own personalities who were inspired by their interaction with a personal God. The chants and meditations of a Buddhist, in contrast, are designed to help the seeker to transcend self and to minimize or eliminate personal identity.

Major Contrast # 10: Women

Buddhism	Christianity
Buddha's attitude toward women could best be summarized by saying that any kind of contact should be avoided whenever possible. "So long as the love of man towards women, even the smallest, is not destroyed, so long is his mind in bondage, as the calf that drinks milk is to its mother."[19]	In over a dozen instances during Jesus' ministry, he demonstrated a level of deference toward and concern for women that was astonishing in the ancient world. Jesus' ministry was supported to a large degree by women of means.[20]
Buddhist nuns have 311 vows to take, in contrast to the 227 for monks.[21] "There is no gender equality in Buddhism."[22]	"There is neither Jew nor Greek, there is neither slave nor free, there is neither male nor female; for you are all one in Christ Jesus."[23]
"It is always better to be reincarnated as a man than a woman. That's one reason why Chinese parents have been known to throw away their baby girls, long before the communists' 'one birth policy.'"[24]	Catholic monks and priests have clear authority over nuns. In many conservative Protestant churches, women are not allowed to preach to men.

Jesus lived in a patriarchal society where women were regarded as chattel. The Gospels contain many examples of Jesus respecting and caring for women in a way that was revolutionary for his day.

Apart from his twelve disciples, some of his closest followers were women:

> After this, Jesus traveled about from one town and village to another, proclaiming the good news of the kingdom of God. The Twelve were with him, and also some women who had been cured of evil spirits and diseases: Mary (called Magdalene) from whom seven demons had come out; Joanna the wife of Cuza, the manager of Herod's household; Susanna; and many others. These women were helping to support them out of their own means.[25]

In addition, Mary Magdalene was the first person to whom Jesus appeared after his resurrection.[26]

Jesus willingly risked his reputation by choosing to publicly minister to women of dubious reputation.[27] He healed women who sought healing for themselves[28] or others.[29] He also raised a woman from the dead[30] and raised a man from the dead at the plea of a group of women.[31] He also honored poor women who donated what little they had.[32] It is unfortunate that in spite of Christ's example, Christianity has not been immune to sexism.

In an article published in the *Bangkok Post*, Mettanando Bhikkhu, a Thai Buddhist monk, concluded that, in spite of quite extensive evidence that Buddhism throughout history has discriminated against women, that "the Lord Buddha...was not a sexist."[33] The background provided by this article is highly informative. However, I have not quoted other excerpts from it because of my stated goal of trying to view Buddhism in a positive, objective light.

If ethics was all that mattered, then one could simultaneously be both a Buddhist and a Christian. However, for anyone seeking a deeper identification with either religion, each of the differences between Buddhism and Christianity delineated in this chapter would be sources of considerable tension and likely disagreement. True reconciliation between the two would be quite problematic.

Given these dramatic differences, sincere efforts to follow both religions simultaneously are not feasible. If they are true to their beliefs, however, both Buddhists and Christians should treat one another as the Golden Rule would dictate: as each would prefer to be treated themselves—with mutual respect, empathy, and compassion.

In the next chapter, which provides answers to frequently asked questions, there is some discussion of the ways that liberal Christians differ from Buddhists.

While both religions teach love and compassion for those with different beliefs, these ideals can, in practice, be difficult to achieve, given the substantial differences between Buddhism and Christianity. What typically occurs is avoidance of contact and dialogue. Cooperation is even more rare. Buddhist/Christian dialogue, collaborative projects, and cooperative efforts to reach common goals should all be pursued in a spirit of deepening understanding between the two groups.

---

[1] In preparing this comparison I had a Buddhist lama (who shall remain anonymous) review the bulk of the commentary about Buddhism for its fairness and accuracy. His assistance was invaluable and much appreciated.

[2] See, for example, Romans 8:28 and James 1:3–4 in the New Testament.

[3] Huston Smith, *The Religions of Man* (New York: Harper & Row, 1958), 106. Smith noted, "I have paraphrased slightly the discourse as it appears in Majjhima Nikaya, Sutta 63, as translated by E. J. Thomas in Early Buddhist Scriptures (London: K. Pau, Trench, Trubner & Co., 1935), pp, 64–67."

[4] Matthew 5:11–12 (NIV).

[5] Lit-Sen Chang, *Asia's Religions: Christianity's Momentous Encounter with Paganism* (Vancouver, Canada: China Horizon, 1999), 124. Source cited as Hardy, Robert Spence. *The Legends and Theories of the Buddhists Compared with History and Science with Introductory Notices of the Life and System of Gotama Buddha*, 2d ed. (London: F. Norgate, 1881), and *A Manual of Buddhism in its Modern Development*, 2d ed. (London: Williams and Norgate, 1880).

[6] Luke 23:40–43.

[7] Psalm 37:4 (NKJV).

[8] 2 Thessalonians 5:16–18.

[9] John 16:33b (NASB).

[10] James 1:3–4.

[11] Dhammapada 160 (emphasis added).

[12] John 15:5b (NIV) (emphasis added).

[13] *Gîtassara Sutta* (A.iii.250) from "Association for Insight Meditation," www.aimwell.org/Books/Suttas/Ghitassara/ghitassara.html, as cited in "Buddhist Chant," Wikipedia, http://en.wikipedia.org/wiki/Buddhist_chant, retrieved October 30, 2010.

[14] John 14:6 (NIV).

[15] See, for example, Ephesians 6:12.

[16] John 1:3 (English Standard Version).

[17] John 12:31 (NIV): "Now is the time for judgment on this world; now the prince of this world will be driven out."

[18] Ephesians 5:23–32.

[19] Dhammapada 284.

[20] Luke 8:3.

[21] "Patimokkha," Wikisource, http://en.wikisource.org/wiki/Patimokkha, retrieved May 23, 2011.

[22] Steve Cioccolanti, *From Buddha to Jesus: An Insider's View of Buddhism and Christianity.* (Oxford: Lion Hudson, Monarch, 2007), 119.

[23] Galatians 3:28, NKJV.

[24] Cioccolanti, *From Buddha to Jesus,* 119.

[25] Luke 8:1–3 (NIV).

[26] John 20:11–18.

[27] John 4:1–30; John 8:1–11; Luke 7:36–50.

[28] Mark 1:29–31; Mark 5:25–34; Luke 13:10–17.

[29] Luke 7:11–17; Matthew 15:21–28.

[30] Mark 5:21–43.

[31] John 11:1–44.

[32] Luke 18:1–14; Mark 21:1–4.

[33] Mettanando Bhikkhu, "Was the Lord Buddha a Sexist?" *Bangkok Post,* www.buddhistchannel.tv/index.php?id=8,2666,0,0,1,0, retrieved May 24, 2011.

Chapter Thirteen
Frequently Asked Questions

There is so much to cover when comparing Buddhism and Christianity. In this chapter we cover a wide range of key topics by means of a question-and-answer format. In doing so, we will look at: (1) a broad range of similarities and differences beyond those highlighted the two previous chapters, (2) what Christians and Buddhists could stand to learn from the other, (3) the nature of major divisions within each religion, (4) how each religion struggles with the stubborn blight of hypocrisy, and (5) the feasibility of trying to be some kind of Buddhist and some type of Christian at the same time.

Q: *What elements of Christianity are similar to Buddhism's Four Noble Truths and Noble Eightfold Path?*

The Four Noble Truths	Counterparts in Christianity
Life is suffering.	"In the world you will have tribulation . . ."[1]
The origin of suffering is desire.	Do not covet (wanting what others have).[2]
Ceasing to desire will end suffering.	Coveting naturally produces suffering. However, many kinds of suffering are not the result of desire (e.g., cancer, accidents).
The Noble Eightfold Path will lead to a cessation of suffering.	See next chart.

The Noble Eightfold Path	Counterparts in Christianity
Right View: Realize the Four Noble Truths.	See previous chart.

Right Intention: Intend to renounce desire, have goodwill toward others, and develop compassion.

Jesus said to him, "'You shall love the LORD your God with all your heart, with all your soul, and with all your mind.' This is the first and greatest commandment. And the second is like it: 'You shall love your neighbor as yourself.' On these two commandments hang all the Law and the Prophets."[3]

Right Speech: Do not lie or bear false witness. Do not use harsh or idle words.

Do not lie or bear false witness.[4]

He who calls his brother a fool is a murderer of him in his heart.[5]

"And when you pray, do not use vain repetitions as the heathen *do*. For they think that they will be heard for their many words. Therefore do not be like them."[6]

Right Action: Do not harm any conscious beings (i.e., people and animals). Do not steal. Abstain from sexual misconduct.

Do not hurt other people.[7]

Do not steal.[8]

Abstain from sexual misconduct.[9]

Right Livelihood: Only engage in legal and peaceful ways of making a living. Do not be associated with making weapons, butchering animals, prostitution, selling intoxicants/poisons.

"Whether, then, you eat or drink or whatever you do, do all to the glory of God."[10]

Right Effort: Devote your mental energy to wholesome goals and activities.

"Finally, brothers, whatever is true, whatever is noble, whatever is right, whatever is pure, whatever is lovely, whatever is admirable—if anything is excellent or praiseworthy—think about such things. Whatever you have learned or received or heard from me, or seen in me—put it into practice. And the God of peace will be with you."[11]

Right Mindfulness: Try to see things objectively without jumping to conclusions.	"And why do you look at the speck in your brother's eye, but do not consider the plank in your own eye? Or how can you say to your brother, 'Let me remove the speck from your eye'; and look, a plank is in your own eye? Hypocrite! First remove the plank from your own eye, and then you will see clearly to remove the speck from your brother's eye."[12]
Right Concentration: Be single-minded. Practice meditation.	"No one can serve two masters."[13] "But if any of you lacks wisdom, let him ask of God, who gives to all generously and without reproach, and it will be given to him. But he must ask in faith without any doubting, for the one who doubts is like the surf of the sea, driven and tossed by the wind. For that man ought not to expect that he will receive anything from the Lord, being a double-minded man, unstable in all his ways."[14]

Q: Other than the Ten Major Differences between Buddhism and Christianity presented in Chapter Twelve, are there other miscellaneous notable contrasts?

Miscellaneous Notable Contrasts

Buddhism	Christianity
All sentient (i.e., aware) beings must be treated with compassion and respect. Killing any animal is wrong.	Killing of many animals for food is acceptable. Human beings were given authority over animals by God.

In having compassion for others, one must not become emotionally attached to them, for that would be a desire, and all desire must be eliminated, because desire causes suffering.

Desiring the good of others above our own is one of the greatest virtues. The extent of such desire can be great, and yet still be very healthy and moral. Having this desire for one's spouse, for example, would be highly virtuous.

Ethics regarding marriage are comparatively liberal.

Ethics regarding marriage are demanding and conservative.

Buddha taught that all language is inherently inadequate.

Jesus emphasized that the Word of God is powerfully relevant to all aspects of life.

Q: How do Buddhists typically view Christians, and vice versa?

Buddhist Views of Christians	Christian Views of Buddhists
There are many paths to transcending the self. Christianity is an inferior way of accomplishing that because: (1) It is dualistic. (2) It is often intolerant, claiming that it is the only true way. (3) It encourages emotional attachments if they are ostensibly good. (4) It cultivates the belief in the eternal existence of the soul as a unique personality. (5) It has often tolerated violence as a means to achieving various objectives.	Christ is the only way of salvation; Buddhism does not concur with this and is therefore misleading. A relevant quotation from the epistles of the New Testament is: "See to it that no one takes you captive through hollow and deceptive philosophy, which depends on human tradition and the basic principles of this world rather than on Christ. For in Christ all the fullness of the Deity lives in bodily form, and you have been given fullness in Christ, who is the head over every power and authority."[15]

Jesus was only one of many bodhisattvas, or manifestations of enlightenment.

Buddhism's openness to a variety of bodhisattvas is misleading because Christ is the only way of salvation (see above). Jesus said: "Watch out that no one deceives you. For many will come in my name, claiming, 'I am the Christ', and will deceive many."[16]

By retaining part of the self, under the illusion that each person has a unique, eternal soul, rather than transcending the self, Christians are prone to trying to make God a being who serves their own desires and dreams. Christians should heed Christ's call to deny one's self, take up their cross, and follow him.[17]

Buddhism relies on the self to make a way of salvation instead of looking to the grace of God through Jesus Christ. As Christian thinker Oswald Chambers wrote: "The *disposition of sin* is not immorality and wrong-doing, but *the disposition of self-realization—I am my own god*. This disposition may work out in decorous morality or in indecorous immorality, but it has the one basis, my claim to my right to myself."[18]

Buddha seekers have trouble relating to:

1. The value of a substitutionary blood sacrifice.

2. God's mercy and grace, which seem too easy.

3. Lack of meditation.

4. Narrow-minded, judgmental, and/or materialistic attitudes.

5. The idea of a Creator and one true God.

Christians have trouble relating to:

1. Seemingly endless stints of meditation in solitude.

2. An absence of awareness of the power and presence of God.

3. An absence of the concepts of mercy, grace, and forgiveness.

4. The idea that one's words and thoughts can directly change reality.

5. Buddhism's ready willingness to blend occult beliefs and practices into Buddhist meditation and life.

Q: *What differences are there between how Buddhists and Christians view Jesus?*

Buddhists	Christians
Jesus was a perfect example of what any human can achieve, i.e., becoming a guru, bodhisattva, or enlightened master.	Jesus is uniquely the Son of God, being one with God as part of the Trinity.
Jesus' crucifixion has relevance only as an example of great compassion and of dying to self. People can escape their karma and find liberation only by their own efforts.	Jesus' death on the cross was essential as the one way to atone for the sins of all mankind.
If Jesus was resurrected in a physical body, he would not have progressed spiritually to a higher state of existence.	Jesus was resurrected in a physical body and appeared to hundreds as proof of his divinity and the sufficiency of his sacrifice as an atonement for the sins of all mankind.

Q: *What are some ways that Christians could stand to learn from Buddhists, and vice versa?*

Buddhism and Christianity are both deep and comprehensive religions, and followers of each could stand to learn much from one another, regardless of whether or not they are trying to somehow merge the two in practice. For example, most Christians could stand to benefit from the example of Buddhists in terms of:

1. A more tolerant, respectful attitude toward those with different beliefs.

2. A range of proven practices in meditation.

3. A deeper respect for the environment.

4. A commitment to practicing self-denial.

Correspondingly, most Buddhists could benefit from the example of many Christians in:

1. Being more liberal in actively helping people in need.

2. Going beyond adhering to nonviolence and forbearance to giving and receiving mercy, grace, and forgiveness.

3. Drawing upon empowerment provided by an all-powerful God who loves them and desires to bless them.

Can Someone Be a Buddhist and a Christian at the Same Time?

Chapters Eleven and Twelve compared the beliefs of conservative Buddhists and conservative Christians. From that analysis, we concluded that it really is not possible to be both at the same time. But what about other pairings, such as:

...A liberal Christian and a liberal Buddhist?

...A liberal Christian and a conservative Buddhist?

...A New Age believer in "Christ consciousness" and a Buddhist?

By considering possible answers to frequently asked questions, we will explore the degree of compatibility (or incompatibility) of each of these pairings.

What of liberals from both religions? There is a wide spectrum of beliefs and practices among liberals in Buddhism and Christianity, making comparisons uncertain. Nevertheless, an analysis is attempted below.

Q: *What are the primary differences between conservative and liberal Buddhists?*

Huston Smith[19] summarized the two great branches of Buddhism by making a series of comparisons.

A Theravada (Conservative) Buddhist is quite existentialist, focusing on the individual self being alone in the universe and seeking emancipation by self-effort. A Mahayana (Liberal) Buddhist is much more relational in his or her thinking and acting. For the Theravada Buddhist, religion is a full-time preoccupation, typically as a monk, and the key focus is wisdom. For the Mahayana Buddhist, religion is very applicable to life in this world and is helpful not only to the monk but also to the common person.

For the Theravada Buddhist, Buddha was a saint, while to the Mahayana Buddhist, Buddha was a mystical being. The Theravada Buddhist avoids focusing on metaphysics (i.e., the nature of reality) and downplays ritual, confining prayer to meditation. The Mahayana Buddhist focuses quite a bit on metaphysics and rituals and includes prayers for various personal concerns as part of his or her practice.

Clearly, Mahayana Buddhists are much more similar to Christians than are Theravada Buddhists.

Q: *What are the primary differences between conservative and liberal Christians?*

Christians also tend to fall into two categories: conservative and liberal. From the chart below, it is obvious that there are major differences between them.

Conservative	Liberal
The Bible is to be taken literally whenever possible.	Much of the Bible should be taken figuratively.

The Bible provides us with a completely accurate, representative account of Jesus, his life, and his divinity.	We can only guess at what the real Jesus was like, since the early Church fathers may have changed the accounts of Jesus' life to suit their purposes.
Jesus was fully God and fully man.	Jesus was a great prophet and teacher, but he was not divine.
Jesus was crucified, died, and rose from the dead.	Jesus was crucified and died, but he did not rise from the dead.
Salvation is by faith in Christ, not good works. Good works follow as a natural byproduct of faith.	Although faith is involved in salvation, it must be proven by good works and compassion.
Jesus judges each person on the basis of the extent and quality of their faith in him as their Savior.	God judges each person in terms of their works. If the good works outweigh the bad, their fate in the afterlife will be favorably affected.
Emphasis is on correct doctrine and spreading the Gospel. Other religions are viewed as being incorrect.	Emphasis is on compassion, social action, and tolerance. God is far more interested in the sincerity of a person's beliefs than in their correctness.
Every book in the Bible was directly inspired by God, even though these books were written by many authors, often many centuries apart.	The Bible was written by many authors, all of whom were spiritual men, over many centuries, at the prompting of general inspiration from God. It contains many errors and contradictions, so we must use our own judgment in deciding whether or not to accept any of its statements as being true.
Meditation is rarely practiced.	Meditation is not an uncommon practice.
Correct metaphysics is important.	Metaphysics is not important.

Q: *Can a liberal Christian also be a Buddhist?*

Given the very broad range of beliefs of liberal Christians, it would be very difficult to offer any answers to this question without making some assumptions as to what the liberal Christians in question believed. In the chart below, several common beliefs of liberal Christians are listed, along with how those beliefs would need to change, at least significantly, in order for the liberal Christian to also be a Buddhist.

Typical Belief of a Liberal Christian	Change in Belief Required to Also Be a Buddhist
I have a soul and a personality that will continue to exist eternally.	Realize that such beliefs are an illusion.
I am, at least to some extent, a self-made person.	Realize that the present self has been tightly determined by karma from past lives.
I am motivated by compassion for the less fortunate.	Come to regard such compassion as improper because it is a desire, and desire causes suffering.
I see the highest value as being energetically involved in helping the poor and less fortunate.	Be willing to see the great value of completely withdrawing from the world to meditate in solitude in hopes of gaining enlightenment.
Though I appreciate that suffering is commonplace, I believe that many parts of life can be filled with joy, and this joy is not an illusion, if you are thankful to God for them.	Realize that life on earth inherently involves suffering, and that the only kind of joy possible is the cessation of personal desire.
It is important to have some kind of strong belief in God.	Be willing to regard the question of the existence of God as irrelevant to one's own spiritual journey toward enlightenment.
It is more effective to fill one's mind and spirit with the positive presence of God than to look within.	It is more effective to meditate, focusing on emptying one's mind of negative and selfish thoughts and desires.

Jesus Christ was the greatest spiritual leader and teacher in the history of the world.	Christ was just one of many enlightened ones, or buddhas, who have served as examples and guides to mankind in the quest for enlightenment.
By pure, simple faith, one can be quickly and radically transformed, because such faith results in the powerful indwelling of the Holy Spirit, who takes control as long as the believer is willing to yield to the leading of the Spirit.	Attaining enlightenment requires many years (or many lifetimes) of devoted meditation under the direction of a spiritual master.
Buddhist chanting has a droning aspect that is hard for westerners to appreciate and find inspiration from.	Be willing to regard such chanting as comparable to the broad and deep range of Christian music, hymns, and classical religious masterpieces.
It is acceptable to eat meat.	Become a vegetarian out of respect for animals that are reincarnations of people.

It is clear that any liberal Christian who also wants to be a Buddhist would have to make very substantial changes to their beliefs, often to the extent of contradicting their former views.

Q: In what ways is hypocrisy a problem for Buddhists and Christians?

Hypocrisy is a troublesome problem for all religions, but especially those that espouse clearly defined standards of conduct. Certainly, Buddhism and Christianity would fall under that description. Below we compare what hypocrisy looks like in each religion.

Buddhists	Christians
Shallow Buddhists don't meditate much and try to use "spirituality" to serve their selfish needs. They believe that somehow, the impersonal God (or principle) that is in everything will cause life to work out just as they selfishly wish it would.	Shallow Christians try to use God to further their own personal agendas. They pray, asking God to be their personal servant. Genuine Christians have surrendered their lives to follow Jesus in gratitude and obedience.
Shallow Buddhists have not renounced their selfish desires.	Shallow Christians have not surrendered to Christ's authority and active direction.
Buddhism is a religion that requires a substantial amount of discipline in the regular practice of meditation. It would be difficult for someone to simply be a nominal Buddhist.	Because Christianity is universally accessible and quickly available to those who make a faith-based decision, a greater percentage of its adherents are shallow (or nominal) in their practice of it.
No one is motivated to quickly report or seize upon examples of hypocritical Buddhists. There has been much sympathy toward Buddhists because of the repression of Tibet by China.	People upset by Christianity's "one way" claim are quick to report and seize upon examples of hypocritical Christians as a basis for discrediting their beliefs.
Hypocrisy is hard to identify relative to a subjective set of ethics and beliefs. It could be dismissed as just being a different path.	Hypocrisy is easy to identify relative to a well-known, objective set of demanding ethics.
If one is finding one's own path, one can make up one's own rules, at least in grey areas. People will naturally make up rules that would be easy to live up to.	Christ espoused ethics that are extremely difficult to live up to, even if one is wholeheartedly devoted to following him. This is fundamentally true, because the Evil One is in charge of this world, and the primal tendencies of people (i.e., "the flesh") are at odds with the holy nature of God.

High achievers are likely to feel that truth can be found within, when their strengths or successes may be due to caring parents and a prior Judeo/Christian or other religious background.	Big sinners know that truth and goodness are not within. When becoming Christian many people experience a radical conversion from a life of obvious, habitual sin and change dramatically from who they previously were. But such people often have not had caring parents or a religious background and may be prone to reverting back to prior sins.

Although everyone has heard about notable sex scandals in the Roman Catholic Church[20] and among televangelists,[21] the press has generally been very slow to cover similar problems among Buddhist leaders. However, an August 20, 2010, article in the *New York Times*, "Sex Scandal Has U.S. Buddhists Looking Within,"[22] chronicled a shocking account of the excessive tolerance of sexual immorality between a married spiritual teacher of the Zen Studies Society and numerous students and other women over a period of fifty-five years. The article made the following points:

- Because the student/teacher "relationship is considered sacrosanct, affairs were not always condemned, or even disapproved of."
- "There has also been a cultural aversion among Zen Buddhists to seeming censorious about sexuality."
- Of "Richard Baker, the abbot of the San Francisco Zen Center in the 1970s and '80s, Frederick Crews wrote that Mr. Baker's 'serial liaisons, hardly unique in the world of high-level American Buddhism, could have been forgiven, but his chronic untruthfulness about them could not.'"
- "Sex, alcoholism and drug abuse by major Buddhist leaders have all been tolerated over the years, by followers who look the other way, or even looked right at it and pretend not to care."

Two books, *Rogues in Robes: An Inside Chronicle of a Recent Chinese-Tibetan Intrigue in the Karma Kagyu Lineage of Diamond Way Buddhism*[23] and *Buddha's Not Smiling: Uncovering Corruption at the Heart of Tibetan Buddhism Today*,[24] have also documented major political scandals within the higher ranks of Tibetan Buddhism. In an opening quotation to the second book, we have this assessment:

> If the truth be told, the Buddha has not been smiling for a very long time. In the same way the Catholic Church transformed Jesus' simple message of peace and love into Crusades and Inquisitions, the Buddha's clear message of yoga and asceticism was largely ignored while rival schools developed throughout East Asia. . . . *Buddha's Not Smiling* is a stark reminder that when false teachings are introduced for political gain . . . only more ignorance, and ultimately violence will result.[25]

Q: The type of Christianity described in this comparison is quite different from what I have experienced, which is a religion based on rules and guilt. Have I missed something?

There is a reason this question follows the discussion on hypocrisy, because hypocrisy is quite common in rules- and guilt-based churchianity. The next chart provides some contrasts between churchianity based on legalism and biblical Christianity based on grace and faith in Christ.

Churchianity Based on Guilt and Obeying Rules	Christianity as a Personal Relationship with Jesus
Obedience to Do's and Don'ts is the highest priority.	Developing a growing and interactive relationship directly with Jesus is the highest priority.
Characterized by tedious memorization of Do's and Don'ts and some Bible verses.	Characterized by interaction through prayer and personal Bible study and reflection.
Referring to publicized list of Do's and Don'ts, or to priests/clergy, to decide how to act.	Looking to Jesus, and relevant biblical passages, for specific guidance in each situation.
Guilt over past sins creates an obligation to submit to priests/clergy to confess and atone.	Submission is directly to God instead of to clergy.
Fearing God and submitting to church leaders are both critical.	Worshipping God and giving him glory are critical. The focus is on the love and grace of God.
Main motivators are guilt and fear of punishment.	Main motivation is gratitude toward God that he took the initiative in seeking to rescue mankind from the penalty for sin (i.e., death and condemnation).
The ability to behave is based on self-discipline, with little or no help from God.	People are enabled by the filling of the Holy Spirit and being inspired by the love of God (in spite of our unworthiness).
The church is a building.	The church is an interconnected group of believers who worship and study the Bible together and pray for one another.
People focus on maintaining a façade of correct conduct and language, but there is little caring for one another, and a tendency to quickly judge others.	People share their real hurts and weaknesses in small groups and support one another in prayer, compassion, and forgiveness.

Q: How does "Christ Consciousness" differ from the Jesus portrayed in the Bible? Is it compatible with Buddhism?

How is "Christ consciousness" different from Jesus Christ? The first is a principle, office, or position that has been and will be held by many different people, while the latter is a single, historical person, Jesus of Nazareth. In the New Age, not only Buddha and Jesus have held this position, but also many other avatars, who are manifestations, or incarnations, of this exalted office, or position. In this sense, Christ consciousness and Buddha are quite compatible, and indeed related.

Christ Consciousness	The Biblical Jesus
Jesus was overshadowed at age thirty by a spirit of Christ consciousness when his public ministry began.	Jesus coexisted with God the Father and the Holy Spirit as the Trinity before he shed much of his divinity to come to earth and become both God and man on earth during his lifetime.
After Jesus' crucifixion, he did not rise from the dead, or if he did, he did not rise in a physical body.	After Jesus' crucifixion, he rose from the dead, appeared to hundreds, and then ascended into heaven to sit at the right hand of the Father. He will return at the Second Coming to establish his kingdom with a new heaven and a new earth.
Jesus was a "way-shower," but not a savior to all mankind.	Jesus is Savior to all who accept and follow him.
Christ is the pattern that connects, a prerunner for all who follow the path.	"For in Christ all the fullness of the Deity lives in bodily form, and you have been given fullness in Christ, who is the head over every power and authority."[26]

It should be noted that the Jesus portrayed by New Agers has been constructed from a very selective extraction of scattered quotations of Jesus from the Gospels. In addition, many of the key words in these selected quotations have been given very different meanings by New Agers than those ascribed to them by traditional Christianity. It is not the purpose of this article to survey these matters, which could be the subject of an entire chapter.

Q: What does God think about someone being a Buddhist and a Christian at the same time?

While it seems possible that a very liberal Christian could also be a liberal Buddhist, one would have to pause and ask at what point God's opinion about all of this is important. At what point would a Christian become so liberal as to be rejected by God? On more than one occasion Jesus made it clear that he would reject some of those who claimed to follow him.

> "Not everyone who says to me, 'Lord, Lord,' will enter the kingdom of heaven, but only he who does the will of my Father who is in heaven. Many will say to me on that day, 'Lord, Lord, did we not prophesy in your name, and in your name drive out demons and perform many miracles?' Then I will tell them plainly, 'I never knew you. Away from me, you evildoers!'"[27]

> "I know your deeds, that you are neither cold nor hot. I wish you were either one or the other! So, because you are lukewarm—neither hot nor cold—I am about to spit you out of my mouth."[28]

We can also ask at what point a Buddhist would become so liberal that Buddha himself would disavow him or her as a follower? If Buddha were in nirvana now, would it matter to him what his self-proclaimed followers were doing or saying?

---

[1] John 16:33b (NKJV).

[2] Exodus 20:17.

[3] Matthew 22:37–40 (NKJV).

[4] Exodus 20:16.

[5] Matthew 5:21–22.

[6] Matthew 6:7–8a (NKJV).

[7] Matthew 5:21–22.

[8] Exodus 20:15.

[9] Exodus 20:14.

[10] 1 Corinthians 10:31 (NASB).

[11] Philippians 4:8–9 (NIV).

[12] Matthew 7:3–5 (NKJV).

[13] Matthew 6:24a (NIV).

[14] James 1:5–8 (NASB).

[15] Colossians 2:8–10 (NIV).

[16] Matthew 24:4–5 (NIV).

[17] Matthew 16:24.

[18] Oswald Chambers, *My Utmost for His Highest*, excerpt at www.myutmost.org/10/1005.html, (emphasis added).

[19] Huston Smith, *The Religions of Man* (New York: Harper and Row, 1965), 138.

[20] "Child Sex Abuse Cases," Wikipedia, http://en.wikipedia.org/wiki/Catholic_sex_abuse_cases, is an extensive, detailed reporting, retrieved February 23, 2011.

[21] "Christian Evangelist Scandals," Wikipedia, http://en.wikipedia.org/wiki/Christian_evangelist_scandals, provides a lengthy list, retrieved February 23, 2011.

[22] Mark Oppenheimer, "Sex Scandal Has U.S. Buddhists Looking Within" *New York Times*, (August 20, 2010), www.nytimes.com/2010/08/21/us/21beliefs.html?pagewanted=1&sq=Frederick%20Crews&st=cse&scp=4, retrieved February 23, 2011.

[23] Tomek Lehnert, *Rogues in Robes* (Nevada City, CA: Blue Dolphin, 1998).

[24] Erik Curren, *Buddha's Not Smiling* (Staunton, VA. Alaya Press, 2006).

[25] Sankara Saranam, author of *God Without Religion*, in an introductory quotation to Curren, *Buddha's Not Smiling*.

[26] Colossians 2:9–10 (NIV).

[27] Matthew 7:21–23 (NIV).

[28] Revelation 3:15–16 (NIV).

Chapter Fourteen
Common Roots in Judaism?

Some have asserted that similarities between the ethical teachings of Buddha and Jesus provide evidence that Jesus may have traveled to India.[1] The argument usually points out that the Bible makes no reference to events in Jesus' life when he was between the ages of twelve and thirty, providing ample time for these travels to have taken place. In this book, we set forth an alternative explanation: Buddha and Jesus were both significantly influenced by Judaism, in general, and the proverbs of Solomon, in particular.

Buddha/Jesus Similarities to the Books of Moses

The five books of Moses (the Torah) were first written around 1380 B.C., more than nine hundred years before Buddha lived and taught. In light of that fact, it is not unreasonable to suppose, when one of Buddha's key teachings is virtually the same as a key verse of Moses', that Buddha could have been echoing Moses' words. This likely was also the case with Jesus. The following diagram provides a key example.

Love Your Neighbor

Moses (1300 B.C.)

"Love your neighbor as yourself."[2]

Buddha (525 B.C.)   **Christ (A.D. 30)**

Buddha (525 B.C.)

"Consider others as yourself."[3]

Christ (A.D. 30)

"You shall love your neighbor as yourself."[4]

"Do to others as you would have them do to you."[5]

Given the close similarities of these sayings, would it be more reasonable to presume that Jesus was quoting Buddha or that he was quoting Moses? Jesus was a Jewish rabbi who often quoted Moses and other Old Testament authors. The Torah was very widely known in Israel for almost 1,400 years before Jesus quoted it. So, Jesus was probably quoting Moses.

Love Strangers

Let's look at another example. In the same chapter of Leviticus in which Moses exhorted his people to love their neighbors as themselves, he urged them to also love strangers from other cultures and peoples. Jesus taught that God loved men and women from every culture so much that God sent him to make salvation available to all people. In this, we again see the inclusion of every manner of stranger within the scope of God's love. It is much more natural to assume that Jesus inherited this "love strangers" principle from Moses than that he traveled to India and picked it up from Buddhism.

Moses (1300 B.C.)

"The stranger who dwells among you shall be to you as one born among you, and you shall love him as yourself; for you were strangers in the land of Egypt: I am the Lord your God." [6]

Buddha (525 B.C.)	Christ (A.D. 30)
"Just as a mother would protect her only child at the risk of her own life, even so, cultivate a boundless heart towards all beings. Let your thoughts of boundless love pervade the whole world." [7]	"This is My commandment, that you love one another as I have loved you. Greater love has no one than this, than to lay down one's life for his friends." [8,] "For God so loved the world that He gave His only begotten Son, that whoever believes in Him should not perish but have everlasting life." [9]

Buddha's exhortation to love people everywhere reiterates the same theme that was sounded by Moses nine hundred years earlier.

Buddha's example of caring for anyone anywhere as a mother would her only child is echoed in Jesus' exhortation to lay down one's life for one's friends. It differs in that Jesus' exhortation is tighter in scope; however, this scope is widened to the whole world in the second quotation from Jesus.

Buddha/Jesus Similarities to Solomon's Proverbs

There are many examples of the words of Buddha (and of Christ) echoing the writings of Solomon. Often, the similarities are so striking that one can only wonder whether Solomon's influence was direct. This chapter provides numerous examples of this, but it is not intended to be a comprehensive collection, which would be much more extensive. The similarities between Buddha and Solomon were covered in great detail in Chapters Three through Nine.

Love Your Enemies

Solomon (950 B.C.)

"If your enemy is hungry, give him bread to eat; and if he is thirsty, give him water to drink." [10]

Buddha (525 B.C.)

"For hatred does not cease by hatred at any time: hatred ceases by love, this is an old rule." [11]

"Let a man overcome anger by love, let him overcome evil by good; let him overcome the greedy by liberality, the liar by truth!" [12]

Christ (A.D. 30)

"Love your enemies, do good to those who hate you, bless those who curse you, and pray for those who mistreat you." [13,]

"You have heard that it was said, 'Eye for eye, and tooth for tooth.' But I tell you, Do not resist an evil person. If someone strikes you on the right cheek, turn to him the other also. And if someone wants to sue you and take your tunic, let him have your cloak as well. If someone forces you to go one mile, go with him two miles. Give to the one who asks you, and do not turn away from the one who wants to borrow from you." [14]

Note that Buddha's first proverb above ends with the words, "This is an old rule." This is direct evidence that at least one of the proverbs in the Dhammapada came from an earlier source than Buddha himself.

Solomon's proverb may have had its roots in these words of Moses, who in this verse is recording a portion of the commandments to the Israelites as given to him by God:

The stranger who dwells among you shall be to you as one born among you, and you shall love him as yourself; for you were strangers in the land of Egypt: I am the Lord your God.[15]

The natural tendency of people to distrust and even to hate people of a different race or culture is very common. Why should you feed your enemy if he is hungry, and give him water if he is thirsty? Isn't it to melt your enemy's animosity, so that he will be persuaded to be kind and caring? Buddha's teachings closely parallel Solomon's proverb, and his exhortation to love echoes Moses' teaching.

Jesus expanded on Solomon's proverb. He starts with doing good, and then adds spiritual ways of loving your enemy—by blessing them and praying for them. In Jesus' second quotation above, additional examples are provided.

Care for Your Companions

The concept of caring for others as one would within a close-knit family was expressed by Solomon centuries before Buddha.

Solomon (950 B.C.)

"Two are better than one because they have a good return for their labor. For if either of them falls, the one will lift up his companion."[16]

". . . there is a friend who sticks closer than a brother."[17]

"Do not withhold good from those who deserve it, when it is in your power to act. Do not say to your neighbor, 'Come back later, I'll give it tomorrow'—when you now have it with you."[18]

Buddha (525 B.C.)   **Christ (A.D. 30)**

Buddha (525 B.C.)	**Christ (A.D. 30)**
"If you do not tend to one another then who is there to tend to you? Whoever would tend me, he should tend the sick."[19]	"Truly I say to you, to the extent that you did it to one of these brothers of Mine, even the least of them, you did it to Me."[20]

Buddha's wisdom and Jesus' teaching echo Solomon's emphasis on caring for one another. Buddha equates tending to the sick and suffering with tending to him personally. In the following explanation of what will happen at the last judgment, Jesus made the same comparison much more clearly:

When the Son of Man comes in his glory, and all the angels with him, he will sit on his throne in heavenly glory. All the nations will be gathered before him, and he will separate the people one from another as a shepherd separates the sheep from the goats. He will put the sheep on his right and the goats on his left.

Then the King will say to those on his right, "Come, you who are blessed by my Father; take your inheritance, the kingdom prepared for you since the creation of the world. For I was hungry and you gave me something to eat, I was thirsty and you gave me something to drink, I was a stranger and you invited me in, I needed clothes and you clothed me, *I was sick and you looked after me*, I was in prison and you came to visit me."

Then the righteous will answer him, "Lord, when did we see you hungry and feed you, or thirsty and give you something to drink? When did we see you a stranger and invite you in, or needing clothes and clothe you? When did we see you sick or in prison and go to visit you?"

The King will reply, "I tell you the truth, whatever you did for one of the least of these brothers of mine, you did for me."[21]

The italicized passages above directly mirror Buddha's teaching, and the meaning is reinforced by the entire passage.

Buddha's and Jesus' words above are much more similar to one another than they are to Solomon's proverbs. At first this might be taken as evidence that Buddha influenced Jesus. However, it should be remembered that Solomon was the wealthiest and most powerful king of his time, so the notion of someone caring for him out of compassion for his needy state would have been ludicrous. On the other hand, both Buddha and Jesus were very poor, and doing something to care for them personally would have been a very natural thing to do.

Generosity

Solomon (950 B.C.)

"One man gives freely, yet gains even more; another withholds unduly, but comes to poverty. A generous man will prosper; he who refreshes others will himself be refreshed."[22]

"He who pursues righteousness and love finds life, righteousness and honor."[23]

Buddha (525 B.C.)

Christ (A.D. 30)

Buddha (525 B.C.)	**Christ (A.D. 30)**
"Hard it is to understand: By giving away our *food*, we get more strength; by bestowing *clothing* on others, we gain more beauty."[24]	"Give and it will be given to you. A good measure, pressed down, shaken together and running over, will be poured into your lap. For with the measure you use, it will be measured to you."[26]
"With generosity and kind words, always doing to others what is good, he treats all people as the same. His compassion for the world is like the hub that makes the wheel go round."[25]	". . . you must help the weak and remember the words of the Lord Jesus, that He Himself said, 'It is more blessed to give than to receive.'"[27]

Buddha's words here carry the same essence as Solomon's two verses, as do the words of Jesus. Again, there is no reason to posit a direct relationship between Buddha and Jesus, because Jesus clearly was echoing Solomon, and Buddha may well have been echoing Solomon as well.

Further, the following excerpt from Jesus' Sermon on the Mount is reminiscent of Solomon's teachings on generosity:

Therefore I tell you, do not worry about your life, *what you will eat or drink; or about your body, what you will wear*. Is not life more important than *food*, and the body more important than *clothes*? Look at the birds of the air; they do not sow or reap or store away in barns, and yet your heavenly Father *feeds* them. Are you not much more valuable than they? Who of you by worrying can add a single hour to his life?

And why do you worry about *clothes*? See how the lilies of the field grow. They do not labor or spin. Yet I tell you that not even Solomon in all his splendor was *dressed* like one of these. If that is how God *clothes* the grass of the field, which is here today and tomorrow is thrown into the fire, will he not much more *clothe* you, O you of little faith? So do not worry, saying, *"What shall we* eat?" or "What shall we drink?" or "*What shall we wear?*" For the pagans run after all these things, and your heavenly Father knows that you need them. But *seek first his kingdom and his righteousness, and all these things will be given to you as well.* Therefore do not worry about tomorrow, for tomorrow will worry about itself. Each day has enough trouble of its own.[28]

In this passage Jesus even mentions Solomon by name, providing further evidence that he had Solomon in mind as he was speaking. Solomon, too, taught the great importance of pursuing, or "treasuring," righteousness and love.

Practice Charity

Solomon (950 B.C.)

"There is one who makes himself rich, yet has nothing; and one who makes himself poor, yet has great riches."[29]

"Cast your bread upon the waters, for you will find it after many days. Give a serving to seven, and also to eight, for you do not know what evil will be on the earth."[30]

"Honor the Lord with your wealth, with the first fruits of all your crops; then your barns will be filled to overflowing, and your vats will brim over with new wine."[31]

Buddha (525 B.C.)   **Christ (A.D. 30)**

Buddha (525 B.C.)

"The greatest reward in the world is to provide for others."[32]

"Because he gives a gift at the right time, wherever the result of that gift ripens he becomes rich, affluent, and wealthy, and benefits come to him at the right time, in abundant measure."[33]

Christ (A.D. 30)

". . . you must help the weak and remember the words of the Lord Jesus, that He Himself said, 'It is more blessed to give than to receive.'"[34]

"Give and it will be given to you. A good measure, pressed down, shaken together and running over, will be poured into your lap. For with the measure you use, it will be measured to you."[35]

Buddha's quote draws an analogy from farming—the planting of trees that will "ripen" to provide shade, flowers, and fruit. His imagery is similar to Solomon's third quotation, which refers to fruits, crops, and vats of wine. As usual, Buddha leaves out any reference to God, implying that the universe (via karma) will naturally bring blessings to those who are generous toward the needy. In contrast, Solomon and Jesus saw a personal God as the one who provided blessings to those who were charitable toward others in need.

False Sacrifices and Generosity

Solomon (950 B.C.)

"The sacrifice of the wicked is exceedingly disgusting and abhorrent [to the Lord]—how much more when he brings it with evil intention?"[36]

Buddha (525 B.C.)

"The world gives according to their faith or according to their pleasure: if a man frets about the food and the drink given to others, he will find no rest either by day or by night."[37]

Christ (A.D. 30)

"Take heed that you do not do your charitable deeds before men, to be seen by them. Otherwise you have no reward from your Father in heaven. Therefore, when you do a charitable deed, do not sound a trumpet before you as the hypocrites do in the synagogues and in the streets, that they may have glory from men. Assuredly, I say to you, they have their reward. But when you do a charitable deed, do not let your left hand know what your right hand is doing, that your charitable deed may be in secret; and your Father who sees in secret will Himself reward you openly."[38]

Buddha's saying is secular, whereas Solomon and Jesus make specific reference to God. Underlying the words of both Solomon and Jesus is the idea that a charitable giver should be attempting to please God, not man. Ultimately, God is the one who will reward good deeds. Jesus' quotation therefore has a clear precedent in Solomon rather than in Buddha.

Lay Up Treasures

Solomon (950 B.C.)

"He who pursues righteousness and love finds life, righteousness and honor."[39]

Buddha (525 B.C.)	**Christ (A.D. 30)**
"Let the wise man do righteousness: A treasure that others cannot share, which no thief can steal; a treasure which does not pass away."[40]	"Blessed are the pure in heart, for they shall see God."[41] ". . . lay up for yourselves treasures in heaven. . . ."[42]

Solomon's teaching about the rewards of pursuing righteousness is echoed by both Buddha and Jesus. Jesus further warned against trying to amass worldly riches:

> Do not store up for yourselves treasures on earth, where moth and rust destroy, and where thieves break in and steal. But store up for yourselves treasures in heaven, where moth and rust do not destroy, and where thieves do not break in and steal. For where your treasure is, there your heart will be also. . . . No one can serve two masters. Either he will hate the one and love the other, or he will be devoted to the one and despise the other. You cannot serve both God and Money.[43]

Both Buddha and Jesus therefore discussed storing up treasure that was permanent rather than temporary. But Jesus also emphasized having a pure heart that could only come from serving God. For Jesus, the treasure would be in heaven, where God would give rewards to those who did good deeds on earth. For Buddha, the treasure would be in the form of positive karma and progress toward enlightenment. Jesus, we can conclude, was drawing from Solomon directly, as Buddha may have been.

There is further precedent in Solomon for comparing wisdom and righteousness with precious treasure. For example:

> How blessed is the man who finds wisdom and the man who gains understanding. For her profit is better than the profit of silver and her gain better than fine gold. She is more precious than jewels; and nothing you desire compares with her.[44]

Failure to See Your Own Faults

Solomon (950 B.C.)

"Every man's way is right in his own eyes, but the LORD weighs the hearts."[45]

"He who is of a proud heart stirs up strife..."[46]

Buddha (525 B.C.)

"It is easy to see the fault of others, but much harder to see your own faults. You can point out other people's faults as easily as pointing out chaff blowing in the wind. But you are liable to conceal your own faults as a cunning gambler conceals his dice."

"The fault of others is easily perceived, but that of oneself is difficult to perceive; a man winnows his neighbour's faults like chaff, but his own fault he hides, as a cheat hides the bad die from the gambler."[47]

Christ (A.D. 30)

"Judge not, that you be not judged. For with what judgment you judge, you will be judged; and with the measure you use, it will be measured back to you. And why do you look at the speck in your brother's eye, but do not consider the plank in your own eye? Or how can you say to your brother, 'Let me remove the speck from your eye'; and look, a plank is in your own eye? Hypocrite! First remove the plank from your own eye, and then you will see clearly to remove the speck from your brother's eye."[48]

Solomon was so right in pointing out the tremendous powers of self-rationalization that all human beings have. One way or another, we will find a way to justify what we really want to do. He repeatedly warns against self-pride, on one hand, and speaking critically of others, on the other. Both Buddha and Jesus add vivid and dramatic imagery to contrast the relative ease of finding fault with others (chaff vs. dice for Buddha; a fine speck in the eye vs. a log for Jesus). There is no reason to suspect that Jesus must have gotten this idea from Buddha, however, since it is fully expressed in Solomon.

Life Is Full of Trouble

Solomon (950 B.C.)

"So I hated life, because the work that is done under the sun was grievous to me. All of it is meaningless, a chasing after the wind."

"What does a man get for all the toil and anxious striving with which he labors under the sun? All his days his work is pain and grief; even at night his mind does not rest. This too is meaningless."[49]

Buddha (525 B.C.)

"'All created things perish,' he who knows and sees this becomes passive in pain; this is the way to purity."[50]

"'All created things are grief and pain,' he who knows and sees this becomes passive in pain; this is the way that leads to purity."[51]

Christ (A.D. 30)

"In this world you will have trouble."[52]

"Do not store up for yourselves treasures on earth, where moth and rust destroy, and where thieves break in and steal."[53]

"Everyone who hears these words of mine and does not put them into practice is like a foolish man who built his house on sand. The rain came down, the streams rose, and the winds blew and beat against that house, and it fell with a great crash."[54]

In the first book of Moses (Genesis), God speaks sternly to Adam after the fall:

To Adam he said, "Because you listened to your wife and ate from the tree about which I commanded you, 'You must not eat of it,' cursed is the ground because of you; through painful toil you will eat of it all the days of your life. It will produce thorns and thistles for you, and you will eat the plants of the field. By the sweat of your brow you will eat your food until you return to the ground, since from it you were taken; for dust you are and to dust you will return."[55]

This sounds a bit like Buddha's dictum that life is suffering. And then there is this excerpt from the Book of Job:

For hardship does not spring from the soil, nor does trouble sprout from the ground. Man is born to trouble as surely as sparks fly upward.[56]

Thus, when Jesus spoke of tribulation in this world, he was firmly in the tradition of Judaic doctrine.

Good and Bad Things Happen to Every Kind of Person

Solomon, Buddha, and Christ all believed that each person would reap as they had sown. How, then, could it be true that some things, such as sunlight, rain, death, and not being remembered after dying, were common both to wise men and to fools, and to good and bad people alike? How fair is that? They made similar observations about this conundrum.

Solomon (950 B.C.)

"The wise man has eyes in his head, while the fool walks in the darkness; but I came to realize that the same fate overtakes them both. Then I thought in my heart, 'The fate of the fool will overtake me also. What then do I gain by being wise?' I said in my heart, 'This too is meaningless.' For the wise man, like the fool, will not be long remembered; in days to come both will be forgotten. Like the fool, the wise man too must die!"[57]

Buddha (525 B.C.)

"That great cloud rains down on all whether their nature is superior or inferior. The light of the sun and the moon illuminates the whole world, both him who does well and him who does ill, both him who stands high and him who stands low."[58]

Christ (A.D. 30)

". . . love your enemies and pray for those who persecute you, that you may be sons of your Father in heaven. He causes his sun to rise on the evil and the good, and sends rain on the righteous and the unrighteous."[59]

Solomon's quotation emphasizes that death (and being forgotten after death) come to both the just and the unjust. Buddha and Christ point out that naturally good things, such as sunlight and rain, happen to both the just and the unjust. So, is this an example of an area where Jesus' view is closer to Buddha's than to Solomon's? If you only look at one aspect of this comparison (nature bringing good to all kinds of people), Jesus would be closer to Buddha. On the other hand, there is a striking difference, even within the short excerpts quoted above. For Buddha, this is just the way things are, whereas for Jesus, it is a result of God's lovingkindness and compassion for everyone.

Still, you might object that Solomon's example deals with negative events happening to every kind of person, while Jesus' illustration only cites positive events. While the immediate context of Jesus' words clearly refers to positive events, the same Sermon on the Mount that Jesus' words come from dramatically ends with an example of rain having very negative consequences:

Therefore everyone who hears these words of Mine and acts on them, may be compared to a wise man who built his house on the rock. And the rain fell, and the floods came, and the winds blew and slammed against that house; and yet it did not fall, for it had been founded on the rock. Everyone who hears these words of Mine and does not act on them, will be like a foolish man who built his house on the sand. The rain fell, and the floods came, and the winds blew and slammed against that house; and it fell—and great was its fall.[60]

Speak Little, But Wisely

Solomon (950 B.C.)

"Do not be quick with your mouth, do not be hasty in your heart to utter anything before God. God is in heaven and you are on earth, so let your words be few."[61]

"When words are many, sin is not absent, but he who holds his tongue is wise."[62]

"A man of knowledge uses words with restraint, and a man of understanding is even-tempered. Even a fool is thought wise if he keeps silent, and discerning if he holds his tongue."[63]

"A fool finds no pleasure in understanding but delights in airing his own opinions."[64]

Buddha (525 B.C.)   **Christ (A.D. 30)**

Buddha (525 B.C.)

"If a man for a hundred years sacrifice month after month with a thousand, and if he but for one moment pay homage to a man whose soul is grounded (in true knowledge), better is that homage than sacrifice for a hundred years."[65]

"But he who lives a hundred years, vicious and unrestrained, a life of one day is better if a man is virtuous and reflecting."[66]

"As the impurity which springs from the iron, when it springs from it, destroys it; thus do a transgressor's own works lead him to the evil path."[67]

Christ (A.D. 30)

"And when you pray, do not be like the hypocrites, for they love to pray standing in the synagogues and on the street corners to be seen by men. I tell you the truth, they have received their reward in full. But when you pray, go into your room, close the door and pray to your Father, who is unseen. Then your Father, who sees what is done in secret, will reward you. And when you pray, do not keep on babbling like pagans, for they think they will be heard because of their many words. Do not be like them, for your Father knows what you need before you ask him."[68]

All of the above quotations emphasize the great value of a few meaningful words in contrast to the worthlessness of volumes of empty chatter or large quantities of pointless actions. But again, there is no evidence for an exclusive connection between Buddha and Jesus, since Buddha could have known Solomon's writings, and Jesus definitely knew them.

Beautiful Outside, Rotten Inside

Solomon (950 B.C.)

"Like a gold ring in a pig's snout is a beautiful woman who shows no discretion."[69]

Buddha (525 B.C.)

"What good is hide clothing? While your inward state is a tangle, you polish your exterior."[70]

Christ (A.D. 30)

"Beware of false prophets, who come to you in sheep's clothing, but inwardly they are ravenous wolves."[71]

Outwardly, the woman Solomon refers to is unusually attractive, but inside she lacks sound judgment and discernment. With her, first appearances are completely deceptive. Her looks can be likened to a gold ring, yet inside she has no discretion about what she takes in, much as a pig will eat anything heartily. As Buddha's proverb states, it is not unusual that those who are messed up inside devote much effort to putting on a good front. Jesus touched on a similar theme, where showy religiosity is a cover-up for spiritual wantonness. The analogies between the different quotations for this topic are not as strong as for previous issues, but are nevertheless interesting. Again, we find no direct relationship between Buddha and Jesus that could not be explained by the connection both may have had to Solomon.

Protection Against Bad Outside Influences

Solomon (950 B.C.)

"If a man is lazy, the rafters sag; if his hands are idle, the house leaks."[72]

"The wise woman builds her house, but with her own hands the foolish one tears hers down."[73]

"The integrity of the upright will guide them, but the perversity of the unfaithful will destroy them."[74]

Buddha (525 B.C.

"As rain leaks into a poorly roofed house, so does passion invade an uncultivated mind. As no rain leaks into a well-roofed house, passion does not invade a cultivated mind."[75]

Christ (A.D. 30)

"Everyone who comes to Me and hears My words and acts on them, I will show you whom he is like: he is like a man building a house, who dug deep and laid a foundation on the rock; and when a flood occurred, the torrent burst against that house and could not shake it, because it had been well built. But the one who has heard and has not acted accordingly, is like a man who built a house on the ground without any foundation; and the torrent burst against it and immediately it collapsed, and the ruin of that house was great."[76]

Except for the third of Solomon's proverbs above, all of the above proverbs use an analogy involving a house. The first Solomon proverb and the Buddha proverb both allude to a house that leaks. Jesus' parable involves a house assaulted by floodwaters, so it is a bit different from Solomon's first proverb and Buddha's proverb.

All three of Solomon's proverbs credit human effort and character to preserving a good house or a good life, while Jesus' parable pointedly asserts that what is truly important is listening to him and acting on his words, which involves at least some element of faith. The similarities between Solomon and Buddha are much clearer than the similarities between Buddha and Jesus.

Bad Desires Lead to Ruin

These quotes focus on what happens to people controlled by their desires rather than their good sense. They are ruined, snared and enslaved.

Solomon (950 B.C.)

"The desires of lazy people will be their ruin, for their hands refuse to work. They are always greedy for more, while the godly love to give!"[77]

Buddha (525 B.C.)

"People compelled by craving crawl like snared rabbits."[78]

Christ (A.D. 30)

". . . everyone who commits sin is a slave to sin."[79]

Though all three quotes point out the power of sin to ensnare, Jesus spoke in the context of a discussion about being set free by becoming his follower. A couple of lines later, he says: "So if the Son makes you free, you will be free indeed."[80] In the overall context for each, Solomon and Buddha were talking about making diligent, personal efforts to do good deeds and avoid sin in order to overcome evil, while Jesus was talking about being set free simply through faith in him. Thus, it would not make sense to assert that Jesus had taken his ideas from Buddha in this case.

Truth (Wisdom) Liberates

So what do Solomon, Buddha, and Christ have to say about the relationship between truth (or wisdom) and freedom? What is the source of freedom for each?

Solomon (950 B.C.)

"Happy is the man who finds wisdom, and the man who gains understanding; For her proceeds are better than the profits of silver, and her gain than fine gold. She is more precious than rubies, and all the things you may desire cannot compare with her."[81]

Buddha (525 B.C.)

"One who acts on truth is happy in this world and beyond."[82]

Christ (A.D. 30)

"Then you will know the truth, and the truth will set you free."[83]

Buddha's proverb is closer to Solomon's than Jesus' saying is. The first two see happiness as the direct result of acting on the basis of truth (or alternatively, wisdom and understanding), whereas Jesus depicts freedom as the result of knowing truth. In the case of both Solomon and Jesus, truth is a person (the woman Wisdom for Solomon, and Jesus himself for Jesus). Jesus said, "I am the way, the truth and the life."[84] Nevertheless, liberation was an important theme for Buddha, since the point of seeking enlightenment was to be freed from the cycle of birth and death (reincarnation), an arduous process. Jesus, in contrast to Buddha, was talking about freedom from sin and death and being reborn spiritually to eternal life, something available immediately to all who believe. There is no indication of a link from Jesus to Buddha here.

We have looked at parallel sayings on sixteen different topics in this chapter. Further research would undoubtedly yield additional parallels of thought. There is much to suggest that similarities between the sayings of Buddha and Jesus may be due to each being influenced by Judaism in general and Solomon in particular. Jesus readily acknowledged that his teachings were in line with Jewish writings and traditions, saying:

> Do not think that I have come to abolish the Law or the Prophets; I have not come to abolish them but to fulfill them. I tell you the truth, until heaven and earth disappear, not the smallest letter, not the least stroke of a pen, will by any means disappear from the Law until everything is accomplished. Anyone who breaks one of the least of these commandments and teaches others to do the same will be called least in the kingdom of heaven, but whoever practices and teaches these commands will be called great in the kingdom of heaven.[85]

Indeed, Christians believe that everything that happened to the Jewish people before the coming of Christ was part of God's plan of salvation for humanity that was fulfilled in Jesus' death on the cross. Many Old Testament events thus foreshadowed the events of the New Testament. In this light, it makes sense for Jesus to reiterate and confirm Old Testament teachings. There would be no reason to add a trip to India on Jesus' part or a desire to teach something brand new.

In fact, from the collection in this chapter, one is left contemplating the plausibility of an assertion of Solomon's: "What has been will be again, what has been done will be done again; there is nothing new under the sun."[86] Buddhism claims that Buddha came up with the fundamentals of his new religion by meditating nonstop for forty-nine days under a bodhi tree, and that somehow from this experience he divulged from deep within himself a compendium of life-transforming revelations. Can this view of Buddha be correct? The idea that he may have had contact with Solomon's ideas and drawn from them in his teachings would suggest otherwise. Perhaps Buddha's sudden enlightenment was more down to earth: He suddenly realized that by melding together the wisdom of Solomon and parts of the Jain religion, he would have a profound new religion to offer to mankind.

[1] Swami Abhedananda, *Journey into Kashmir and Tibet (the English translation of Kashmiri 0 Tibbate)* (Calcutta: Ramakrishna Vivekananda Math, 1987).

[2] Leviticus 19:18b (NIV).

[3] Dhammapada 10:1, in Marcus Borg, ed., with coeditor Ray Riegert and an Introduction by Jack Kornfield, *Jesus and Buddha: The Parallel Sayings* (Berkeley: Ulysses Press, 1997), 15.

[4] Mark 12:31b (NKJV).

[5] Luke 6:31 (NIV).

[6] Leviticus 19:34 (NKJV).

[7] Buddha, Sutta Nipata 149–150, in Borg, *Jesus and Buddha*, 25.

[8] John 15:12–13 (NKJV).

[9] John 3:16 (NKJV).

[10] Proverbs 25:21 (NKJV).

[11] Dhammapada 5.

[12] Ibid., 223.

[13] Luke 6:27b–28 (NKJV).

[14] Matthew 5:38–42 (NIV).

[15] Leviticus 19:34 (NKJV).

[16] Ecclesiastes 4:9–10 (NASB).

[17] Proverbs 18:24b (NASB).

[18] Proverbs 3:27–28 (NIV).

[19] Buddha, Vinaya, Mahavagga 8.26.3, in Borg, *Jesus and Buddha*, 21.

[20] Matthew 25:40b (NASB).

[21] Matthew 25:31–40 (NIV) (emphasis added).

[22] Proverbs 11:24–25 (NIV).

[23] Proverbs 21:21 (NIV).

[24] Nitin Kumar "Buddha and Christ: Two Gods on the Path to Humanity," Exotic India, November 2003, www.exoticindiaart.com/article/buddhaandchrist, retrieved February 3, 2011.

[25] Richard Hooper, *Jesus Buddha Krishna Lao Tzu: The Parallel Sayings* (Sedona, AZ: Sanctuary Publications, 2007), 117.

[26] Luke 6:38 (NIV).

[27] Acts 20:35b (NASB).

[28] Matthew 6:25–34 (NIV) (emphasis added).

[29] Proverbs 13:7 (NKJV).

[30] Ecclesiastes 11:1–2 (NKJV).

[31] Proverbs 3:9–10 (NIV).

[32] Hooper, *Jesus Buddha Krishna Lao Tzu*, 120.

[33] Bhikkhu Bodhi, ed. *In the Buddha's Words: An Anthology of Discourses from the Pali Canon* (Somerville, MA: Wisdom Publications, 2005), 170–171.

[34] Acts 20:35b (NASB).

[35] Luke 6:38 (NIV).

[36] Proverbs 21:27 (AMP).

[37] Dhammapada 249.

[38] Matthew 6:1–4 (NKJV).

[39] Proverbs 21:21 (NIV).

[40] Buddha, Khuddakapatha 8.9, in Borg, *Jesus and Buddha*, 69.

[41] Matthew 5:8 (NKJV).

[42] Matthew 6:20a (NKJV).

[43] Matthew 6:19–21, 24 (NIV).

[44] Proverbs 3:13–15 (NASB).

[45] Proverbs 21:2 (NASB).

[46] Proverbs 28:25 (NKJV).

[47] Dhammapada 252.

[48] Matthew 7:1–5 (NKJV).

[49] Ecclesiastes 2:17, 22–23 (NIV).

[50] Dhammapada 277.

[51] Ibid., 278.

[52] John 16:33b (NIV).

[53] Matthew 6:19 (NIV).

[54] Matthew 7:26–27 (NIV).

[55] Genesis 3:17–19 (NIV).

[56] Job 5:6–7 (NIV).

[57] Ecclesiastes 2:14–16 (NIV).

[58] Buddha, Sadharmapundarika Sutra 5, in Borg, *Jesus and Buddha*, 45.

[59] Matthew 5:44b–45 (NIV).

[60] Matthew 7:24–27 (NASB).

[61] Ecclesiastes 5:2 (NIV).

[62] Proverbs 10:19 (NIV).

[63] Proverbs 17:27–28 (NIV).

[64] Proverbs 18:2 (NIV).

[65] Dhammapada 106.

[66] Ibid., 110.

[67] Ibid., 240.

[68] Matthew 6:5–8 (NIV).

[69] Proverbs 11:22 (NIV).

[70] Buddha, Dhammapada 26.12, in Borg, *Jesus and Buddha*, 75.

[71] Matthew 7:15 (NKJV).

[72] Ecclesiastes 10:18 (NIV).

[73] Proverbs 14:1 (NIV).

[74] Proverbs 11:3 (NKJV).

[75] Buddha, Dhammapada 1.13–14, in Borg, *Jesus and Buddha*, 77.

[76] Luke 6:47–49 (NASB).

[77] Paraphrased from Proverbs 21:25–26.

[78] Buddha, Dhammapada 24.9, in Borg, *Jesus and Buddha*, 89.

[79] John 8:34b (NASB).

[80] John 8:36 (NASB).

[81] Proverbs 3:13–15 (NKJV).

[82] Buddha, Dhammapada 13.2, in Borg, *Jesus and Buddha*, 113.

[83] John 8:32 (NIV).

[84] John 14:6 (NKJV).

[85] Matthew 5:17–19 (NIV).

[86] Ecclesiastes 1:9 (NIV).

Chapter Fifteen
Realizing Liberation

As we saw in Chapters Three through Eleven, there are sweeping similarities between Buddhism and Judeo-Christian teachings. In those chapters we reviewed extensive precursors from Solomon's writings that tightly covered every detail of Buddha's Four Noble Truths and his Noble Eightfold Path. Those writings pre-dated Buddha's public teachings by four hundred years. It is as if Buddha grafted Solomon's teachings into the framework of his contemporaries, the detractors from Hinduism, to formulate his new religion. When Buddha realized how revolutionary that infusion of West into East might be, that may have been the crux of his enlightenment. We saw in Chapters One and Two that this may have been what actually happened.

Realizing Liberation

Buddhism and Christianity share a common goal: realizing liberation. Yet their paths to liberation are radically different, as are the envisioned ultimate destinations. The Sanskrit word for liberation is *moksha*, which also means "enlightenment" or "nirvana." Whatever nirvana is, it is not the heaven of Christians. For all of the Western elements present in Buddhism, its Eastern tilt prevails.

Each path, both Buddhist and Christian, is littered with hazards. Dramatic differences in the nature of these hazards reveal sharp contrasts in the true nature of each religion. Buddhism appeals to intelligent, highly educated, free-thinking, very disciplined, self-directed people. It offers down-to-earth methodologies for self-improvement: right living and meditation. However, the possibility of liberation is limited to the elite few who have the mental discipline and the intense commitment to consistently meditate for prolonged periods for many years, and possibly many lifetimes.

Liberation through Buddhism is restricted to those who have maintained a very high standard of ethical conduct throughout their life. Otherwise, the weight of bad karma from past misdeeds is too

debilitating to allow a sincere seeker to progress toward enlightenment. Since Buddhists do not have access to the mercy and forgiveness of God to clear them of the weight of past bad karma, they
must struggle against its daunting consequences.

The Buddhist path is so demanding and unnatural to westerners
that it will quickly demoralize them—if they seriously try to follow
it. Nirvana is as unreachable spiritually as the top of Mt. Everest.
As noted in the "Invitation to the Reader" at the beginning of this
book, the Dalai Lama had this to say: "In the West, I do not think it
advisable to follow Buddhism. Changing religions is not like
changing professions. Excitement lessens over the years, and soon
you are not excited, and then where are you? Homeless inside
yourself."[1]

Westerners are initially attracted to the parts of Buddhism that
may have originated from the West, as described in Chapters Three
through Nine. But then they become estranged from it as they
encounter and try to adapt to its truly Eastern elements, such as
homelessness and utter solitude. These were extolled by Buddha:

> A wise man should leave the dark state (of ordinary life), and
> follow the bright state (of the Bhikshu). After going from his
> home to a homeless state, he should in his retirement look for
> enjoyment [the bliss of solitude] where there seemed to be no
> enjoyment.[2]

While Buddhism is largely restricted to highly intelligent,
disciplined people, Christianity, and its heaven, are wide open to
people of virtually every level of intelligence and ability to exert
self-discipline. If anything, pride, exceptional intelligence, good
self-discipline, and worldly success are obstacles to becoming a
Christian, though they are not insurmountable. Each of these
admirable qualities can be serious obstacles to understanding that
one is in need of a savior, of accepting the notion of grace through
faith alone, and of following the leading and direction of the Holy
Spirit. While the Buddhist path is slow and arduous, conversion to
Christianity and entering a state of salvation can be rapid, causing a
radical upgrade in moral behavior almost overnight.

The Christian author and apologist C. S. Lewis[3] observed that the spiritual life of a Christian is like the opportunities and risks available to an egg. If an egg never advances beyond just being an egg, it will rot and decay. It is designed to hatch, become a bird, and take flight. A major problem with Christianity is that too many of its followers:

1. never really break out of their shell, or

2. if they do, they don't spread their wings, or

3. if they do, they try to fly by relying on their own power and direction.

The third option is much like a bird leaping from a tree branch without spreading its wings. It will plummet even though it wants to fly. The opportunity to receive the uplifting wind of the Holy Spirit is always available, but it requires not only an initial leap of faith but also the ongoing, moment-by-moment surrender of one's life to God. Without that surrender, the believer's behavior can easily become a blight on the reputation of Christianity.

Practicing Buddhism is much like swimming,[4] while attempting to be a Christian is like flying. If a way can be found to fly, it is a more efficient way of getting around. Yet an air crash draws much more attention than a drowning. Like meditation, swimming is incredibly repetitive and inward focused. Like seeking the direction in which the spirit of God is leading you as a Christian, the flying bird can easily be blown this way or that by puffs of wind.

How Feasible Is Liberation?

Buddha's Noble Eightfold Path is a very demanding way to become a better person. It is so challenging we must ask how feasible it is as a path to true liberation. Consider Buddha's own spiritual journey. As the Dalai Lama noted, Buddhist "texts speak of the Buddha as having practiced life after life over three periods of countless eons to complete the requisite stores of merit and wisdom, and bring his development to perfection."[5]

It is only fair to ask, if achieving enlightenment took Buddha close to forever, how much longer would it take seekers today? Were eons required because Buddha was a trailblazer, having to wrestle endlessly with Mara, the Evil One, as he explored different possible avenues for advancing spiritually? Or was it because there is something inherent in human nature that would cause the path to enlightenment to be imperceptibly slow?

A sacred Buddhist text tells the story about an old Brahman who asked Buddha, "How can . . . a priest follow all the commandments and escape from all his sins?" Buddha answered that even if he were to do all manner of good deeds and keep all the commandments every day,

> your good deeds would be worth no more than a strand of baby hair still in its mother's womb for 8 months. It is not even good enough to get close to the gates of Heaven. . . . I myself have left all my princely inheritance, abandoned lust and became a monk. I esteem that my good deeds are not few. I hold onto the 8 commandments, even up to 100,000. If I could do this and give away everything I have for 10 lives, *yet I still cannot get over one of my sins.*

> The Brahman pressed on, "If this be the case, what must I do to get over all my sins?"

> Buddha told him, "Let all of you do a good deed and seek for *another* Holy One who will come and save the world."[6]

Did Buddha say this because he realized that he had not found a feasible way to true liberation? How long are three eons? According to scientists, they would amount to about 13,500,000,000 years.[7] We don't know what an "eon" meant to Buddha, but it is clear that the prospects of any one person reaching enlightenment and liberation from suffering through Buddhism are very remote, or at least very far in the future.

Initially, the Buddhist aspirant is hopeful of experiencing substantive empowerment and freedom from suffering. Practicing deep, prolonged meditation can noticeably reduce stress levels and have a calming effect. So far, so good. After a while, another reality begins to set in. Making progress spiritually as a Buddhist is amazingly slow—to the point where the feasibility of achieving liberation comes into question. To use the swimming analogy, it is often refreshing initially to dive into the water and begin swimming. However, attaining enlightenment is much like swimming the 26 miles from Long Beach to Catalina Island. Most can swim out from the shoreline and make progress for a while, but only a very select few have trained to the point where they can go the distance. And so it is that while Buddhism has its appeal initially, over the long run it delivers what it promises to at most a select few seekers who somehow endure to the end.

Christians would argue that receiving salvation by sheer human effort is not possible. It would be like swimming from California to Hawaii. No one, by good works, can traverse the 2,400 miles of ocean to get there. Rather, becoming saved is like entrusting yourself to a ship or jet to transport you there. You have to board, committing yourself to the entire journey. You can't wander out on the wings during flight, or dive into the ocean for a bit to swim part of the way.

The reality is that each human lifetime is fraught with billions of opportunities to commit bad deeds or think bad thoughts, and that each stumbling takes untold human effort to work off the bad karma it creates. Given such a dynamic, the likely path of virtually every Buddhist is to become more and more deeply mired in the thickening swamp of bad karma generated by past misdeeds. Furthermore, Buddhists believe that their present lives are very largely predetermined by the effects of good and bad karma generated during this and prior lives. So if your past is marred by chronic sins, there is little freedom to seize a moral initiative to become a much better person from this point forward. This is a formula for enduring despair. It is like trying to swim upstream in a beautiful river that is flowing down almost as fast as you can swim up it. Sooner or later fatigue sets in and the downward flow of the river gains the upper hand. As Buddha said, "an illuminated person (a Buddha) is indeed very rare."

A supernatural person (a Buddha) is not easily found, he is not born everywhere.[8]

Is there any solution? As Christian author and pastor Steve Cioccolanti, who was born in Thailand in a family that included Buddhists, Muslims, Catholics, and Methodists, wrote, "it is common knowledge among Buddhists that Buddha prophesied the coming of a Savior after him. He is called the Maitreya in Sanskrit. . . . He is expected to be a world teacher and a world ruler who will end death.[9]

Who is this other "Holy One who will come and save the world" that Buddha told the old Brahman to seek? Cioccolanti retold the story of this amazing conversation in this way:

The old Brahman asked, "This Holy One who will come and rescue the world in the near future, what does he look like?" Buddha replied, "The Holy One who will rescue the world in the near future will have scars in his hands and scars in his feet like the shape of a gongjak [defined below]. In His side, there is a stab wound. His forehead is full of blemish and scars. The Holy Person will be like a golden vessel, a very large one, that will carry you across the cycle of suffering until you pass over to Heaven Nippan."[10]

A *gongjak*, noted Cioccolanti, is a "sharp cutting wheel with jagged edges, an ancient weapon." The sacred text Cioccolanti quoted was found by former monk Tongsuk Siriruk in Kampee Khom, the Cambodian or Khmer Canon, in 1954. This version does not appear in most other Buddhist texts. That would leave us to wonder whether it was removed from those texts or inserted uniquely in that text. We shall never know. If it was formerly in other sacred Buddhist texts, however, it would not be surprising for it to have been extracted at some point during the Christian era, because the

person Buddha described may have looked too much like the
crucified Jesus for the comfort of those charged with preserving the
Buddhist manuscripts.

Regardless of whether or not Buddha said something like this,
the reality is that making progress spiritually through Buddhism is
painfully slow. Consider these comments from a popular guide to
Buddhism:

- "Through his intense devotion to his guru Marpa and his
  unwavering practice, [Tibet's beloved yogi Milarepa]
  achieved Buddhahood during his lifetime."[11]
- "Though the approach of Dzogchen-Mahamudra may be
  considered direct, mastering it is extremely difficult and
  may take a lifetime—at least."[12]
- "An understanding of emptiness is the culmination of
  the Mahayana path and can take many years to
  accomplish!"[13]
- "Navigating the path from beginning to end requires a
  qualified teacher, diligent practice, wholehearted
  dedication, and numerous intensive retreats."[14]

One major branch of Buddhism, Vajrayana, claims that its practices
can greatly accelerate progress toward enlightenment. Whether or
not this is true, the intensity of its practices is truly inhuman.
Vajrayana monks undergo extremely grueling training in meditative practices.[15] As Richard A. Gard, lecturer in Buddhist studies at
Yale University, noted, training in the meditation house "lasts three
years, three months, and three days. Anyone who enters the
Meditation House must be prepared to be a 'voluntary prisoner,'
observing silence most of the time, and meditating continuously for
16 hours a day—for three years, three months, and three days—
without a single day's leave! He is permitted to doze, but not to
sleep lying down, for only three or four hours a day."[16]

The Dalai Lama has been practicing techniques to greatly hasten
progress toward enlightenment, and yet he is quite uncertain what
his fate will be after he dies. "The rehearsal of the processes of
death, and those of the intermediate state, and the emergence into a

future existence," he wrote, "lies at the very heart of the path in Highest Yoga Tantra. These practices are part of my daily practice also and because of this I somehow feel a sense of excitement when I think about the experience of death. At the same time, though, sometimes I do wonder whether or not I will really be able to fully utilize my own preparatory practices when the actual moment of death comes!"[17] In other words, he is spending a great deal of time training for the big swim, but he doesn't know if he will be able to make it across the channel when the time comes. And this from a man who thinks he has made that journey before—since he and his followers believe him to be the reincarnation of a bodhisattva.[18] In reality, unlike practicing for an actual swim, practicing for death is impossible.

If the Dalai Lama is uncertain about what his next life will be, he is not enlightened, for the enlightened Buddhist is supposed to know that he will enter nirvana when he dies and that he will not reincarnate as another sentient being. Furthermore, the Dalai Lama's words highlight his uncertainty, even though he describes the state of enlightenment as including: (1) omniscience, with "full comprehension of all that can be known," and (2) victory, since "you have overcome all problems and have achieved realization of all knowables."[19] Should we believe the Dalai Lama, who has written a book entitled *Becoming Enlightened*, when he himself has not become enlightened?

If the Dalai Lama has not been liberated, what hope is there for the hundreds of millions of Buddhists whose practice has been less devoted? They are mired in the swamp of karma created by past actions, most of which they had little choice about, given that those actions were largely the result of actions even more distant in the past, most likely during several past lives.

In contrast, receiving salvation from Jesus can occur very quickly. This is well illustrated by the liberation received by the thief on the cross next to Jesus.

One of the criminals who hung there hurled insults at him: "Aren't you the Christ? Save yourself and us!" But the other criminal rebuked him. "Don't you fear God," he said, "since you are under the same sentence? We are punished justly, for we are getting what our deeds deserve. But this man has done nothing wrong." Then he said, "Jesus, remember me when you come into your kingdom." Jesus answered him, "I tell you the truth, today you will be with me in paradise."[20]

It was the faith of the thief on the cross, which Jesus perceived and honored, that motivated Jesus to give him salvation. There is no mention, in this account, of the thief's good deeds possibly outweighing his bad deeds. The thief simply confessed that he was being justly put to death and that Jesus would advance to head a kingdom after he died.

In an earlier scene, Jesus had said, "My yoke is easy and my burden is light."[21] What Jesus requires is sincere admission of our unworthiness and our inability to save ourselves by good works, and submission to the indwelling and leading of the Holy Spirit. Liberation, to the Christian, should be entirely a matter of faith, while to the Buddhist, it is entirely a matter of works.

Given these major differences in the feasibility of becoming liberated, practically speaking, Buddhism is a much narrower way than Christianity. Even the best of people commit a few bad deeds interspersed among their good deeds. So with each lifetime, there is much risk that they will step backward in their progress toward enlightenment and nirvana. Furthermore, if you are reincarnated as a rat, or a snake, what opportunity is there for you to "earn" the opportunity to be a human again in some future life?

Prolonged, intense meditation is not only difficult but sometimes hazardous. In recent years, much has come to light regarding these hazards. As noted in "Invitation to the Reader" at the beginning of this book, "the Dalai Lama has said that Eastern forms of meditation have to be handled carefully. 'Westerners who proceed too quickly to deep meditation should learn more about Eastern traditions and get better training than they usually do. Otherwise, certain physical or mental difficulties appear.'"[22] As mentioned in Chapter Ten, Lorin Roche, Ph.D., a meditation instructor who has specialized over the past three-plus decades in counseling people who have engaged in prolonged, intensive meditation, has also remarked on these difficulties. In addition to describing the effects that very intense meditation can have on "one's ability to be intimate with another human being," Dr. Roche noted hazards such as: (1) depression, (2) a feeling of being lost, (3) trouble adapting to life in the city, (4) weird health problems, (5) bipolar disorders, (6) panic attacks, (7) psychosis, and (8) suicide.[23]

Dr. Roche also observed that "we have a huge literature on 'meditation techniques to suit the needs of monks living in monasteries, if they are Hindu or Buddhist,' but not much at all about how to meditate if you live in the modern West and have a family and job that you really don't want to abandon." Further, "Monks and nuns are called renunciates, because they take vows of poverty, celibacy and obedience," Dr. Roche wrote, and although these vows can "be very liberating" to the monks and nuns, who seem to "glow with an inner luminosity," they can be "radioactive" to the average person.[24]

Dr. Roche also pointed out that "monks and nuns tend to see everyday life as a disease." Their "medicine" is to tell their charges to "slow down, kill out your passion, become submissive, cultivate disgust instead of attraction, and dissolve your identity." But all these measures, Dr. Roche said, can be harmful to most of us. They not only play havoc with relationships but also can create "long term depression." Many people become alienated from their families and even become contemptuous of their own culture. When they discover that the meditative practices are ultimately not for them, as 95 percent of Western Buddhist seekers do, they end up feeling like failures. "Almost universally," Dr. Roche wrote, "they feel that there is something wrong with them, that they can't meditate. Most feel bad that they can't make their minds blank."[25]

All of these observations come from a highly educated *advocate* of meditation. Dr. Roche teaches a form of meditation that he believes circumvents these problems. What distinguishes his approach from Buddhism is that he urges people who want to meditate to "keep it simple": "You don't need to know very much in order to begin meditating," he wrote. "Just come on in. Keep it *personal*. Do it *your* way. You can't imitate someone else's meditation. You know what you love. Be brief. A few minutes of meditation is powerful. Do that then call it a day. Dive in. Ask for help when you need it. Stay in touch."[26]

Dr. Roche's big concern is that "there is almost no information about the dangers of meditation. It is taboo to even think about it. Meditation is presented as an omni-beneficial activity. We are in the odd situation that the field that is supposed to be about truth, is presented in a deceptive way. Discussion of the real obstacles and hazards of meditation is met with denial."[27]

Dr. Roche advises people to practice simple meditation within the religion they are already familiar with. He does not see any need to convert to Buddhism or Hinduism to meditate more effectively. "There is a saying," he noted: "Prayer is talking to God, meditation is listening to God."[28] As we saw in Chapter Eight, meditation was a vital practice in the Judaism of Solomon's day, and it remains so to many Jews today. It also has a long tradition within Christianity, where it is sometimes called "contemplative prayer," "infused contemplation," or "mystical union."

How Narrow Is Each Way?

Christianity has the reputation of being a narrow way, largely because of its reputed intolerance of doctrinal differences. In contrast, Buddhism is regarded as a very tolerant religion whose meditation techniques can be quite beneficial to people of almost any faith, or even to atheists. Its initial practices may calm the troubled soul. However, the reality is that in practice Buddhism is much narrower in some ways than Christianity. The percentage of people capable of seriously practicing it is very small—and the percentage of people capable of approaching or realizing enlightenment even smaller. We are talking about something like one in 10 million people.

Buddhism's demands are quite daunting. Serious practice involves:

- Daily, or at least very frequent, lengthy sessions of meditation.
- At least 108 full prostrations every day.[29]
- Right living, as defined by constant pursuit of the Noble Eightfold Path and observance of the 223 laws for monks (or 311 laws for nuns).
- Dedication to constantly performing good works and engaging in self-denial to generate positive karma.
- Arduous suffering to begin working off the onerous burdens of past negative karma.
- Abandonment of the "illusion" that you have a soul and an individual identity.

And yet, for all of this, the best result is imperceptibly slow progress toward deeper spirituality. At its core Buddhism is all about each person withdrawing internally to tap into wisdom and truth that can only be found deep within, and to thereby improve themselves. From a Christian perspective, this is inherently impossible. Man's inner nature is corrupted. How can weak, seriously flawed people bootstrap themselves into noticeably better people? Mankind needs a savior. We all need the power of God to be truly transformed. Buddha never claimed to be a savior or to be divine, though Mahayana Buddhists typically make him both. Nor did Buddha give God any audible recognition.

When it comes to what Buddhism is really about, reality conflicts with common Western perceptions. As Steve Cioccolanti noted:

> True Buddhism is much harder than Westerners make it out to be. To some Westerners who don't really understand, Buddhism may seem like an easy alternative to Christianity. For them to say, "I'm more interested in Buddhism," is often their way of rejecting Christianity. But the fact is Buddhism is not the all-accepting path for anyone to follow. It prescribes a definite set of strict rules and conditions, much like the Biblical Old Testament. It proscribes a long list of immoral behavior.

Buddhism shares much in common with the Old Testament and there are many bridges one can build between the two.[30]

In Buddhism, the negative effects of bad karma follow a person in this and future lives until they suffer enough to work it off and/or perform a long series of good deeds to generate good karma. Bad karma is like an implacable bulldog that is temporarily penned up but is sure to get out at some time in the future and sink his teeth into you. The only consolation is that his attack will only be about as damaging as the harm you have done to others. That may or may not be a comforting thought.

Will the Christian who confesses his or her sin and repents be spared from the attack of the bulldog? After all, "As you sow, so shall you reap,"[31] is a well-known verse in the New Testament. When Jesus confronted the woman caught in adultery in John 8:3–11, did he hold her to account for the bad karma of her sin? He sent away the bulldog of the angry crowd that threatened to stone her, but exacted something far more important from her. He commanded her to "Go now and leave your life of sin."[32] So, the compassionate Jesus opened the way for her to be freed from her bad karma and begin a new life, unencumbered, as long as she would actually do just that. Jesus also did what only God can do: He forgave her sins. He gave her the chance to be liberated from her old life and empowered her to begin a radically better life. He didn't force her to change, but he opened the door wide for that to happen, if she would submit to his command.

What if the woman caught in adultery had followed Jesus' command, but later fell back into her former lifestyle? Would Jesus offer her another chance? Since Jesus is full of grace,[33] he would in all likelihood have offered another chance. But how many times could she fall again and be offered a fresh start? One indication can be found in his words to the apostle Peter, who had asked him how many times he had to forgive someone who had sinned against him. Peter thought that possibly seven times was enough, but Jesus said: ""I do not say to you seven times, but seventy times seven." Since seven is the number of perfection in the Bible, he probably meant an infinite number of times, not 490.

But it would be entirely up to Jesus to decide. And he would make that decision knowing everything about what she was thinking and feeling and whether she would be able to handle the liberation he offered her. Jesus is the judge[34] of all human beings, and as such, he can pardon, or he can sentence. He can also choose something in between, such as bringing upon her a series of character-building difficulties, in order to offer her the chance to grow. Isn't that what is meant by Romans 8:28, which says, "And we know that in all things God works for the good of those who love Him, who have been called according to His purpose"?[35]

When Jesus offers forgiveness for past sins and his offer is accepted, it is enormously empowering and liberating. However, we all know that Christians fall prey to various temptations and will be repeatedly in need of the grace, mercy, and forgiveness of God. Since God is patient and loving, he will provide it, in some measure and some form or another, as long as that person has put his or her faith in Christ for the forgiveness of sins. The forgiveness is based on the work of Jesus on the cross, not our works.

Christianity's emphasis on mercy, grace, and forgiveness make it much more attractive to people who are less disciplined morally or who have troubling past sins. It offers them a chance Buddhism does not offer, for these concepts are generally absent in Buddhism, except in a truly limited way.[36] On the downside, this tendency can result in churches having a number of members who have struggled with various addictions and weaknesses. Such amazing grace might result in some Christians developing a cavalier attitude about the need for moral purity by (falsely) presuming that God will automatically forgive them of their present sins, no matter how rotten their attitude is. Forgiveness should never be presumed to be automatic.

The Nature of Empowerment: Spirit Led vs. Self-Help

Buddhists believe that positive current actions produce good karma, which will cause good things to happen in the future. Positive thoughts and expressions of positive intentions can change reality going forward. However, Buddhists also believe that virtually all of their current life circumstances are predetermined by the working out of positive and negative karma from prior actions, both in this life and previous lives. For someone with many past bad actions, the resulting negative karma can be crippling, affording them little opportunity to progress spiritually. The weight of the karma results in extensive suffering and personal limitations that must be endured while one tries to generate good karma to offset these past misdeeds. The effects of negative karma can even seriously constrain people who have some positive karma to their credit.

Buddhism appeals to those who want to pursue a solitary quest for spirituality. It is built on the premise that empowerment comes from deep within one's self. It gives the adherent the sense of charting his or her own path. Buddhists experience a sense of community while chanting, and may draw some degree of empowerment from that. However, even when Buddhists are gathered together, their primary spiritual activity, meditation, is solitary.

Christianity provides access to the enabling power of the Holy Spirit in transforming one's life. Radical conversions and dramatic upgrades in moral behavior have been commonplace in the history of the Christian church. Faith in an almighty God who rules the universe can enable believers to face great adversity and even death with peace and joy.

Rampant Hypocrisy

Sadly, believers in an almighty God can sometimes act harshly toward those of other beliefs, based on their assumption that they have been commissioned by God to chastise those with different beliefs or who engage in prohibited behaviors. Christians have difficulty appreciating the perspectives of those with different beliefs and lifestyles. The tendency to regard having "correct" beliefs as essential can easily foster a judgmental spirit toward those with different views. A dramatic example of this has been the serious persecution of Buddhists by Christians in South Korea.[37]

On the other hand, in spite of the widespread emphasis on tolerance of those with other beliefs in Buddhism, there are a number of countries with a Buddhist majority where Christians claim they are being actively and harshly persecuted by Buddhists.[38] Among them are Burma,[39] Tibet,[40] Bhutan,[41] Sri Lanka,[42] and Vietnam[43]. Perhaps the real problem is that when a majority of people in a country share a common belief, followers of contrasting minority religions may be treated poorly or harshly.

It is quite common today for Buddha seekers to applaud the great degree of tolerance of other faiths that is characteristic of Buddhism. Arguably, such tolerance is part of a subtle Buddhist strategy for expanding its influence. They will claim that what you believe isn't so important as long as you meditate, and that meditative practices can be adapted to any set of beliefs. However, Eastern-style meditation tends to subtly convert its devotee to Buddhism, or some other Eastern religion, whereas Western-style meditation is more straightforward in terms of its effects.

The prevalent image of Buddhists as passive, nonviolent people is very largely true. However, there are a few vivid counterexamples. Burma (Myanmar) is at least 90 percent Buddhist, and yet it has had a very long, bloody past of conflict with its neighbors as well as internally. Warfare and internal strife have characterized Burmese history since around A.D. 1300, and since 1962, when a military junta seized power, Burma has been ruled by one of the most oppressive, violent governments in the world.[44] Under its present government, it was ranked as the fourteenth worst country[45] in terms of human rights violations.[46]

When a Christian pastor or leader becomes embroiled in a scandal, their hypocrisy is often highlighted by anti-Christian media.[47] When a Buddhist fails to live righteously, however, it usually takes place with little notice and little or no media coverage. When Buddhist scandals are exposed, it is assumed that the individual is at fault, and not that Buddhism is somehow inadequate. One exception to this is Patrick French, author of *Tibet, Tibet*, who summarized his disillusionment with Buddhism this way:

> As I studied Buddhism more closely, some of the failings began to show, and I noticed the schisms, bigots, frauds, hypocrites and predators that you will find in any ecclesiastical system. I was put off too by the tone of many of the foreign converts, who thought they could strip the tradition of its tough ethical underpinnings. They were implausible, with their showy accoutrements of conversion, their beads and bracelets, their devotion to instant spiritual empowerment, their reliance on airport-hopping teachers who were not always taken seriously by Tibetans. Then there were the prominent blunders: the teacher and promoter Sogyal Rinpoche, served with a lawsuit for seducing a student; and the Nyingmapa monk Penor Rinpocke who, in the most dubious circumstances, identified the high-kicking Hollywood action hero Steven Seagal (*Marked for Death, Hard to Kill*) as a reincarnation of the seventeenth-century master Chungdrag Dorje.
>
> I was also cautioned by the Dalai Lama's own refusal to proselytize. After long observation, he had decided that conversion usually led to confusion, and that without the support of the prevailing culture, it was hard to maintain your spiritual practice: "In the West, I do not think it advisable to follow Buddhism. Changing religions is not like changing professions. Excitement lessens over the years, and soon you are not excited, and then where are you? Homeless inside yourself."[48]

Perhaps out of sympathy for oppressed Tibet, or out of distaste for Christianity and a desire to promote alternatives to it, or all of the above, with few exceptions the media have only projected attractive images of Buddhists. However, a February 2011 article in the *Los Angeles Times* noted that:

Tibetan Buddhism's image of placid chanting and sublime meditation belies a more edgy history, analysts say, replete with religious figures attacking each other and alliances between monasteries and brutal warlords. . . .

"We in the West tend to project all our fantasies about mystical spiritualism onto Tibetan Buddhism," said Erik Curren, author of "Buddha's Not Smiling: Uncovering Corruption at the Heart of Tibetan Buddhism Today." It's really like a civil war. There's lots of acrimony." . . .

Some analysts said some Westerners have a rosy-eyed view of Tibetan Buddhism, perhaps a reflection of their disillusionment with Western religions. . . .

"Inter-sect conflicts involving physical violence is nothing new," Curren said. "It's just like any religion. It has its share of bad apples, but that doesn't spoil the whole barrel. The sooner Westerners realize that, the better."[49]

There have also been media silences about unpopular things that the Dalai Lama has said, such as about sexuality. According to Patrick French:

In 1999 he stated: "I am a Buddhist, and, for a Buddhist, a relationship between two men is wrong. Some sexual conduct in marriage is also wrong. . . . For example, using one's mouth and the other hole." His adamant stand on sexual morality is close to that of Pope John Paul II, a fact which his Western followers tend to find embarrassing, and prefer to ignore. The Dalai Lama's US publisher even asked him to remove the injunctions against homosexuality from his book *Ethics for the New Millennium*, for fear that they would offend American readers, and the Dalai Lama acquiesced.[50]

---

[1] Patrick French, *Tibet, Tibet* (New York: Alfred A. Knopf, 2003), 27.

[2] Dhammapada 87.

[3] "Coming In Out of the Wind," July 8 reading, in C. S. Lewis, *A Year with C. S. Lewis: Daily Readings from His Classic Works*, edited by Patricia S. Klein (San Francisco: HarperSanFrancisco, 2003), 208.

[4] Buddha used this analogy when describing his path, referring to it as "entering the stream." Dhammapada 178, in Harischandra Kaviratna, trans., *Dhammapada, Wisdom of the Buddha*, 1980, Theosophical University Press Online, www.theosociety.org/pasadena/dhamma/dham-hp.htm, retrieved April 15, 2011.

[5] His Holiness the Dalai Lama, *Becoming Enlightened*, translated by Jeffrey Hopkins (New York: Simon and Schuster, Atria Books, 2009), 216.

[6] Steve Cioccolanti, *From Buddha to Jesus: An Insider's View of Buddhism and Christianity*. (Oxford: Lion Hudson, Monarch, 2007), 147–148 (emphasis added).

[7] Scientists tell us that the earth is 4.5 billion years old. If we assume a lifetime is 80 years, then the current age of the earth is 56,250,000 lifetimes. So three eons, as defined above, would be at least 168,750,000 lifetimes, or 13,500,000,000 years.

[8] Dhammapada 193a.

[9] Cioccolanti, *From Buddha to Jesus*, 146.

[10] Ibid., 150.

[11] Jonathan Landaw and Stephan Bodian, *Buddhism for Dummies* (Indianapolis: Wiley, 2003), 118.

[12] Ibid., 201.

[13] Ibid., 199.

[14] Ibid., 200.

[15] Madasamy Thirumalai, *Sharing Your Faith with a Buddhist* (Grand Rapids, MI: Baker Book House, 2003), 128.

[16] Richard A Gard, *Buddhism* (New York: George Braziller, 1961), 201.

[17] Dalai Lama, "Introductory Commentary," *The Tibetan Book of the Dead* (New York: Penguin Classics, 2005), xxviii.

[18] "A Brief Biography," His Holiness the 14th Dalai Lama of Tibet, www.dalailama.com/biography/a-brief-biography.

[19] Dalai Lama, *Becoming Enlightened*, 221.

[20] Luke 23:39–43 (NIV).

[21] Matthew 11:30 (NKJV).

[22] Mary Garden, "Can Meditation Be Bad for You?" *Humanist*, September/October 2007, www.thehumanist.org/humanist/MaryGarden.html, retrieved November 22, 2010.

[23] Lorin Roche, "The Dangers of Meditation," www.lorinroche.com/page8/page8.html, retrieved September 18, 2010.

[24] Ibid.

[25] Ibid.

[26] Roche, www.lorinroche.com/, retrieved November 18, 2010.

[27] Roche, "The Dangers of Meditation."

[28] Lorin Roche, "God and Meditation," www.lorinroche.com/page62/page62.html, retrieved November 18, 2010.

[29] Landaw and Bodian, *Buddhism for Dummies*, 172.

[30] Cioccolanti, *From Buddha to Jesus*, 65.

[31] Paraphrased from Galatians 6:7.

[32] John 8:11b (NIV).

[33] John 1:14.

[34] For example, see Acts 10:42, Colossians 1:15–20 and Philippians 2:9–11. The Nicene Creed, which is the most widely accepted creed in Christianity, states, "He suffered, and the third day he rose again, ascended into heaven; From thence he shall come to judge the quick and the dead."

[35] Romans 8:28 (NIV).

[36] In Mahayana Buddhism, bodhisattvas can transfer some of their merit to others in an effort to help them advance toward becoming enlightened. See www.essortment.com/all/whatisbodhisat_rfld.htm, retrieved July 29, 2010.

[37] According to a well-documented Wikipedia article entitled "Korean Buddhism," found at http://en.wikipedia.org/wiki/Korean_Buddhism, retrieved March 31, 2011:

> Some South Korean Buddhists have denounced what they view as discriminatory measures against them and their religion by the administration of President Lee Myung-bak, which they attribute to Lee being a Protestant. The Buddhist Jogye Order has accused the Lee government of discriminating against Buddhism by ignoring certain Buddhist temples in certain public documents. In 2006, according to the *Asia Times*, "Lee also sent a video prayer message to a Christian rally held in the southern city of Busan in which the worship leader prayed feverishly: 'Lord, let the Buddhist temples in this country crumble down!'" Further, according to an article in *Buddhist-Christian Studies*: "Over the course of the last decade a fairly large number of Buddhist temples in South Korea have been destroyed or damaged by fire by misguided Christian fundamentalists. More recently, Buddhist statues have been identified as idols, attacked and decapitated. Arrests are hard to effect, as the arsonists and vandals work by stealth of night." A 2008 incident in which police investigated protesters who had been given sanctuary in the Jogye temple in Seoul and searched a car driven by Jigwan, executive chief of the Jogye order, led to protests by some claiming police had treated Jigwan as a criminal.

Wikipedia cited "S. Korean Christians Praying for Buddhist Temple to Collapse," YouTube; Kim Rahn, "President Embarrassed over Angry Buddhists," *Korea Times*, July 30, 2008; "Buddhists Accuse Government of Favoring Christianity," *Asia Times* (date not available); and Sunny Lee, "A 'God-Given' President-Elect," *Asia Times*, February 1, 2008, www.atimes.com/atimes/Korea/JB01Dg01.html.

[38] See clickable map at "Restricted Nations," Voice of the Martyrs, www.persecution.com/public/restrictednations.aspx?clickfrom=bWFpbl9tZW51, retrieved July 28, 2010.

[39] Burma is 83 percent Buddhist and 9 percent Christian. According to Voice of the Martyrs (VOM),

> The government of Burma continues to discourage, harass and use other, more severe, forms of persecution on any group it considers harmful to the state. Christianity is high on the list, even though the government claims freedom of religion in Burma. A secret memo titled "Program to destroy the Christian religion in Burma," details instructions on how to drive out Christians. It calls for anyone caught evangelizing to be imprisoned. VOM has received widespread reports of churches being burned, *forcible conversion of Christians to Buddhism* and Christian children being barred from schools. Ethnic Christians, in particular, are singled out for repression because of the government's goal to create a uniform society of one language, one ethnicity and one religion.

Source: "Restricted Nations," Voice of the Martyrs, www.persecution.com/public/restrictednations.aspx?clickfrom=bWFpbl9tZW51 (emphasis added).

[40] Tibet is 80 percent Buddhist and 0.2 percent Christian. Voice of the Martyrs reported that

> *Most of the persecution against Christians comes from militant Tibetan Buddhists.* There may be about 1,000 evangelical and 2,000 Catholic Christians among the five million Tibetans in the world, and there are at least two groups of secret believers in Tibet. . . . Pastor Zhang Zhongxin was given two years of re-education through labor in 2008 for his crimes, one of which was preaching the gospel in Tibet."

Source: "Restricted Nations," Voice of the Martyrs, www.persecution.com/public/restrictednations.aspx?clickfrom=bWFpbl9tZW51, clickable map (emphasis added).

[41] Bhutan is 72 percent Buddhist, 23 percent Hindu, and 0.5 percent Christian. According to Voice of the Martyrs:

> Bhutan is one of the most restricted nations in the world for Christians. *All public worship and evangelism by non-Buddhists is illegal.* Churches are never permitted to evangelize. Christian family members can meet together, but they cannot meet with other Christian families. Importing printed religious material is banned, and only Buddhist religious texts are allowed in the country. Bhutanese Christians face subtle forms of discrimination from their families as well as pressure to reconvert to Buddhism.

Source: "Restricted Nations," Voice of the Martyrs, www.persecution.com/public/restrictednations.aspx?clickfrom=bWFpbl9tZW51, clickable map (emphasis added). [42] Sri Lanka is 72 percent Buddhist, 12 percent Hindu, 8 percent Muslim, and 8 percent Christian. Voice of the Martyrs reports:

> Although the constitution guarantees religious freedom, minority Protestant religions have experienced violent persecution as well as discrimination in employment and education. . . . *Much of the persecution comes from local Buddhist groups.* . . . Threats to close down churches have prevented some church members from meeting for worship.

Source: "Restricted Nations," Voice of the Martyrs, www.persecution.com/public/restrictednations.aspx?clickfrom=bWFpbl9tZW51, clickable map (emphasis added). [43] Vietnam is 54 percent Buddhist and 8 percent Christian. Voice of the Martyrs says:

> Persecution of Christians is harsh, particularly for unregistered and ethnic minority churches. Many churches have chosen to remain unregistered because of the unreasonable restrictions the government imposes on registered churches and believers. Arbitrary arrests, harassment and fines are common. Many Christians are in prison. Only a few have been released, and many have been forced to renounce their faith. Several ethnic Christians reportedly died after being released from prison or while in police custody because of injuries caused by torture.

Source: "Restricted Nations," Voice of the Martyrs, www.persecution.com/public/restrictednations.aspx?clickfrom=bWFpbl9tZW51, clickable map (emphasis added). [44] "History of Burma," Wikipedia, http://en.wikipedia.org/wiki/History_of_Burma, retrieved November 4, 2010.
[45] "The Observer Human Rights Index," www.guardian.co.uk/rightsindex/0,,201749,00.html, retrieved November 4, 2010.
[46] "Myanmar (Burma) Human Rights," Amnesty International, www.amnestyusa.org/all-countries/myanmar-burma/page.do?id=1011205, retrieved November 4, 2010.
[47] "Christian Evangelist Scandals," Wikipedia, http://en.wikipedia.org/wiki/Christian_evangelist_scandals, retrieved February 14, 2011.
[48] French, *Tibet, Tibet*, 26–27.
[49] Mark Magnier, "A Tempest in Tibetan Temples," *Los Angeles Times*, February 7, 2011, www.latimes.com/news/nationworld/world/la-fg-tibet-buddhist-tension-20110208,0,735876.story, retrieved February 9, 2011.
[50] French, *Tibet, Tibet*, 218. For the quotation from the Dalai Lama, French cited the *Daily Telegraph*, May 7, 1999, as quoted by Jeffrey Hopkins, a scholar who has translated and edited much of the Dalai Lama's work.

Chapter Sixteen
Two Different Paths

Most of the similarities between Christianity and Buddhism can be attributed to the altruism that both teach as a model of personal conduct and attitude, or to the existence and practices of monks, nuns, and monasteries among Catholics, Orthodox Christians, and Theravada Buddhists. Apart from these similarities, in many ways Buddhism and Christianity are virtual opposites. In this chapter we will look further at these contrasts.

In spite of the numerous similarities, the Christian and Buddhist paths to liberation are miles apart. At their core, they are radically different religions. The paths of Buddha and Jesus part irreparably over three key issues:

1. Are we going to seek a close, interactive relationship with a personal God, and mutually encouraging fellowship with those of the same faith, or are we going to try to zone out of this world and burrow deep within, seeking the divine within on a solo basis, apart from a personal God?

2. Will our spirituality be based on faith in God and the compassion for others that such faith can inspire, or will it be based on self-disciplined efforts to meditate, do good works, and think good thoughts?

3. Are we going to avail ourselves of God's ways of dealing with our bad karma, through his mercy, grace, and forgiveness, or are we going to try to work it off through lifetimes of stoic coping with its consequences, while taking every opportunity to generate positive karma through good deeds?

The religion someone practices is largely determined by his or her answers to these three questions. Two other critical decisions also come into play:

1. Are we going to have an attitude of arrogance or humility toward those with different beliefs?

2. Are we going to actively intervene in the lives of others or are we going to "live and let live"?

If we lay these options out in a table, we have some illuminating contrasts.

	Arrogance	*Humility*
Intervener	Christian militants	Biblical teaching
Non-intervener	Buddhist recluses	Buddha's writings

Both religions are similar in that, while humility is what was taught and modeled by their leaders,[1] arrogance is often practiced instead, resulting in two extremes of non-exemplary behavior. Since arrogant Buddhist recluses are less harmful than arrogant Christian militants, many would argue that Buddhism is the better choice. However, neither style of arrogant living is what was originally taught, which is what should really be compared.

Even though true Christianity is a religion of faith, many Christians think and act as if it were one of works, thereby living out a churchianity quite contrary to the teachings of Jesus. In addition, some Christians try to make God their personal servant rather than trying to be a servant of God. A prime example of this is someone whose prayers are mostly for selfish desires.

God

Buddhism seeks to guide people in developing spiritually without having to submit to some Higher Power. This emphasis originated with Buddha's efforts to liberate his own people from the oppressive aspects of Hinduism and its three-plus million gods. Today Buddhism continues to attract many people who for various reasons seek an alternative to religions that profess faith in a supreme being.

Regarding God as extraneous or irrelevant to the process of spiritual growth may not only be completely inaccurate, but also quite risky. Assume for the moment that a personal God exists who desires to relate to people individually, and who showers them with countless blessings, seeking to help people grow spiritually. When such a God encounters people who regard him as irrelevant, how will this supreme being react? Since a majority of mankind[2] believes in such a God, this is a very reasonable question to ask.

Initially, God may withhold a broad array of blessings he would otherwise desire to impart, because people who choose not to acknowledge him do not want to be recipients of these gifts. God is not inclined to force himself on people who don't want to have anything to do with him. So one cannot be led and guided by God if one deliberately rejects the leading and guidance of God. Further, one cannot experience being a conduit for the love of God if one rejects the love of God. The same goes for other blessings from God, such as peace, joy, and greater understanding of God's grace and mercy. Many of these blessings are avenues of rapid, substantive spiritual growth. The withdrawal of God's help and presence is crippling and debilitating spiritually.

At best, in the long run, such a God may simply grant Buddhists what they want for all of eternity: complete separation from him. The sacred texts of Jews, Christians, and Muslims characterize the fate of those who turn away from God in a myriad of ways, ranging from eternal discomfort to unending agony. So it is quite possible that the God-spurning Buddhist will be mired in the very state they have tried so hard to escape: endless suffering. This would be a very high price to pay, especially since the option of relating to such a God while also being some kind of Buddhist might be feasible, though uncommon and unnatural. Meditation can be centered on God, rather than any of the other common subjects of mantras. And the ethics of Buddha are very similar to those of Jesus. However, a more serious obstacle is that Buddhists would naturally regard a personal god who has any desires to be very inferior to an impersonal god who is identical to the entire universe.[3]

One of the biggest appeals of Christianity is that it offers an interactive relationship with a personal God who is loving, gracious, and merciful and is intimately involved in one's life. This can be very uplifting and empowering as long as one is willing to submit to such a relationship. Not uncommonly, however, people want to retain the right to engage in various pleasurable or profitable activities that are prohibited in the Bible without the specter of judgment from God. The all-too-human desire to "have it both ways" often results in hypocritical behavior by people claiming to be Christians.

Lesser Gods, Idol Worship, and the Occult

Christians believe that God created millions of angels and that many of them rebelled against God. These fallen angels became lesser "gods" (often called evil spirits or demons), and they seek to draw people away from loyalty to the one true God by attracting them to idols (i.e., anyone or anything other than God) or by harassing them. When someone receives Jesus as Lord and Savior, they also encounter subtle opposition from lesser gods, as well as persecution from opponents of Christianity. These can become serious impediments to realizing the positive benefits Christianity offers—unless the Christian willfully shuns idolatry and resists these lesser gods, commanding them to flee in the name (authority) of Jesus.

Buddhists do not look to God for protection and help. Instead, they rely on self, looking to the Buddha as an inspiring example, to his writings as a source of guidance, and/or to monks for instruction. Christians believe that people who do not turn to God will be under the subtle (or overt) influence of lesser gods and idols. This is, in fact, the case with most Buddhists, as noted by Madasamy Thirumalai, Ph.D., University of Calcutta:

- "Idol or image worship plays a prominent and approved role within scriptural or high Buddhist religion."[4]
- In most Asian countries, Buddhists regularly engage in occultic rituals, making sacrifices and offerings to spirits and following the dictates of shamans, who are "self proclaimed mediators of spirits."[5]
- "The use of magic is frequent . . . witchcraft and sorcery are also quite common."[6]
- "Buddhists go to monks and shamans seeking for the divination of their future. . . . Divination is common at all the stages of life, and fortune is often determined on the basis of astrology, which is highly respected and is considered to be lawful for monks to use."[7]
- "Buddhism started as a meditative philosophy, but . . . it rapidly adopted and assimilated the belief systems of the nations it entered. In this process, Buddhism has become an animistic religion."[8]
- Tibetan Buddhism (Vajrayana) places emphasis on occult practices as a way of greatly accelerating the adherent's progress toward enlightenment. This often involves meditating on the attributes of various lesser gods, which the Christian would label as demon worship. It can also involve very secretive rituals of a sexual nature that would be shocking to people of most other major religions.[9]
- "Neo-Buddhism, often observable in Western megacities, is mostly a reemergence of animism in the garb of refined meditative techniques."[10]

Buddhism claims to be more a technique than a religion. People of any faith, or absence of faith, it says, can benefit from the techniques of meditation it encourages. But is Buddhist meditation a universally beneficial practice, or does it presume various things spiritually? According to Mary Garden, who practiced Eastern mysticism, became disillusioned with it, and wrote about her experiences: "Eastern meditation techniques were never meant to be methods to reduce stress and bring about relaxation. They are essentially spiritual tools, designed to apparently 'cleanse' the mind of impurities and disturbances so as to progress toward *enlightenment.*"[11]

To be sure, most forms of Buddhist meditation involve extensive repetition. Jesus warned against using "vain repetitions as the heathen do. For they think that they will be heard for their many words."[12] Christians often take this as a warning against repeated Christian prayers or long, wordy prayers to God. And yet, it is interesting to note that it could also apply to repeated mantras. It seems that Jesus would have opposed the repetitive practices of Eastern meditation.

When Jesus said, "as the heathen do," perhaps he was referring to the use of heavy repetition as a way to instigate change. We might infer that from the fact that Jesus' model prayer gave no credence to selfish motives. The Lord's prayer is an expression of hopes that: (1) God will be revered, (2) God's kingdom will be established, and (3) God's will would be done. So, selfish desires are excluded.

Many heathens believe, as Buddha did, that intensive repetition of a mantra has the power to change reality. When Jesus referred to "vain repetition" he may have had in mind the confrontation between the prophet Elijah and the prophets of Baal in their efforts to bring an end to a terrible drought.[13] The prophets of Baal called on him from morning to evening in hopes that Baal would bring down fire on the bull sacrificed on an altar, yet nothing happened. When Elijah had the sacrificed bull doused with water three times, he uttered a short, pointed prayer to God, who sent lightning upon the altar and burned up the soaked offering. All of the repetitions of the prophets of Baal were worthless.

Only One Way?

Christianity is well known for its claims that Jesus is the only way to God. This claim is based on numerous biblical passages, including John 14:6b, where Jesus is quoted as saying:

> I am the way, the truth and the life. No one comes to the Father except through me.[14]

What is less known is that one of Buddha's own proverbs makes a similar assertion:

> The best of ways is the eightfold; the best of truths the four words; the best of virtues passionlessness; the best of men he who has eyes to see. This is the way, *there is no other that leads to the purifying of intelligence.* Go on this way! *Everything else* is the deceit of Mara (the tempter). If you go on this way, you will make an end of pain! The way was preached by me, when I had understood the removal of the thorns (in the flesh).[15]

In Buddhism, if you don't have purity of intelligence, then you are deluded and lost; so, in essence, Buddha was saying that his way was the only way.

Most people intuitively disagree with the notion that there is only one true way to God. Implicit in their thinking is the assumption that "good" people will go to heaven, regardless of their particular religion. That assumption feels logical and fair and helps to motivate good behavior. Yet this sensible notion is not without problems:

- First, *there is no clear standard as to what is good behavior.* Many wars have been fought where both sides claimed God was with them. Killing was viewed as being "good" by both sides. Standards of what is good change over time and between different nations and cultures. People in the American South used to think it was good to put down blacks and discriminate against them harshly. No more.

- Second, *there is no clear cutoff as to how good one has to be to get into heaven.* If you are 51 percent good and 49 percent bad, is that good enough? Wouldn't you have to be at least 90 percent good? Who knows, and who decides?
- Third, *this notion is not supported by the Bible.* For example, the following verses contradict this notion: (1) "There is not a righteous man on earth who does what is right and never sins";[16] and (2) "All of us have become like one who is unclean, and all our righteous acts are like filthy rags."[17]
- Fourth, *it makes Jesus out to be a liar.* He claimed to be the only way to God, and if people can get into heaven simply by being good, Jesus wasn't telling the truth.

There are two types of religion that include belief in some kind of heaven:

1. Those that claim that each person must earn his or her way to heaven by being a good person; and

2. Christianity, which claims that no person, except Jesus, has ever been good enough to go to heaven. The Christian path is to admit that we are incapable of being good enough, and that, to be saved, we must put our faith in Jesus, his divinity and perfect goodness, and his sacrifice on the cross as the basis for entrance into heaven.

If it is true that no person can be good enough to go to heaven on their own merits, then none of the religions in the first category provide a way to God. This then leaves Christianity as the only way to God, and its claim makes clear sense.

Many people, if pressed, might say that they are good because they obey the Ten Commandments. In other words, they don't steal, murder, or commit adultery. And they may honor their mother and father, in general, not counting their teenage years. But while there's a good chance they haven't specifically violated some

commandments, are these people aware of the other commandments? Most "good" people tell the truth, most of the time, except
for white lies, fudging on tax returns, and so forth. But have they
never "coveted," or desired someone else's spouse or possessions?
Have they never sworn? Have they always kept the Sabbath as a
holy day? Have they never sought some idol (i.e., some person or
thing other than God that they look to as their hope for happiness
and satisfaction)? Everyone today pursues some kind of idol,
whether it is money, prosperity, power, fame, or a comfortable
retirement. These are all idols. Very few "good" people have kept
more than three or four of the Ten Commandments.

The other problem many people have with Christianity's claim
to be the only way to God is the perceived behavior of Christians. If
Christianity brings people into relationship with the one true God,
it should make Christians very humble and compassionate toward
people with different beliefs. Many Christians are like that, yet they
are not the ones who are highlighted in the media. Instead, so-
called Christians who judge people with other beliefs and treat
them with disrespect are showcased by the media. A Mother Teresa
might also be showcased, but the media rarely draws attention to
common, humble Christians.

To be sure, Christianity is anything but immune from problems,
weaknesses, and divisions. But this is also the case for every other
religion. Could the difficulty here be that all religions are filled
with highly fallible, wayward people? Could it be that the real
problem is that people tend to believe their own religion provides
the one true way *while also* having an attitude of judging people of
other faiths?

How could the humble Jesus be so arrogant as to claim to be the
only way to God? This is a very troubling question, unless Jesus
was God himself and was just stating the truth succinctly. According to the Gospel accounts, Jesus claimed to be one with God many
times.[18] This precludes the option that he was just a great teacher or
prophet. He could not have been a great teacher or prophet if he
repeatedly blasphemed God by falsely claiming oneness with him.
As numerous Christian thinkers have pointed out, we are left with

two choices: Jesus was either who he said he was, or he was out of his mind. There is, actually, one other possibility: that early Christians conspired to put words into the mouth of Jesus as the New Testament was being written and when the canon was finalized at church councils. According to this view, he did not really say that he was one with God. However, those who wrote the gospel accounts were eye-witnesses of the events described. If they became co-conspirators after Jesus' death to claim he said things he did not say—and that they saw the resurrected Christ—they would not have been willing to die for their faith in the divinity of Christ. Nearly all of them were martyred.[19] And so, each person is confronted with the necessity of deciding which of these options is true.[20]

Many evangelicals insist that acceptance of Jesus and Lord and Savior is the only way to salvation. Strictly defined, this means that a high percentage of mankind has never had any opportunity to be saved. Does that strike you as the will of God?

One Way to God Available to All Mankind

If there is just one way to God, shouldn't it be available to all people at all points in time? Nevertheless, Christians have generally taken the position that the only people who will be saved are those who explicitly receive Jesus by faith as their personal Savior. This position does not provide any provision of liberation for those who have never heard the gospel. However, the Bible does imply that there is a way for such people.[21] We see this principle highlighted, though in a negative way, in the parable of the faithful and evil servants, where Jesus said:

> And that servant who knew his master's will, and did not prepare *himself* or do according to his will, shall be beaten with many *stripes*. But he who did not know, yet committed things deserving of stripes, shall be beaten with few. For everyone to whom much is given, from him much will be required; and to whom much has been committed, of him they will ask the more.[22]

While many doubt Christianity's claims in part because Christianity doesn't appear to offer salvation to those who have never heard of Jesus, no one seems to be bothered by the fact that Buddhism doesn't offer liberation to those who have never encountered it. There is, however, a Christian solution to this dilemma that is entirely consistent with biblical teachings, though it is not widely known or held.

Consider Jesus' words in John 14:6b again. He said:

> I am the way, the truth and the life, no one comes to the father except through me.[23]

It is possible that "except through me" could mean that everyone must come before Christ to be judged, and that there is no way around that. Such a belief gives Jesus the complete preeminence that evangelicals subscribe to. In fact, it gives Christ more preeminence than the standard evangelical belief. In other words, Christ is above any cut-and-dried criteria that humans think they know about who will be saved and who will not. Who will be saved? In every case, the answer is that Jesus decides.

Such an alternative belief is also completely consistent with John 3:16:

> For God so loved the world that he gave his one and only Son, that whoever believes in him shall not perish but have eternal life.[24]

That verse does not preclude Christ from granting executive pardons to any person who otherwise would be condemned because of his or her absence of belief in Christ. This would particularly be true of those who had never heard the gospel, as well as those who had never had a fair opportunity to consider and accept it. It might even include Jews who all their lives had been taught disparaging things about Jesus. Just as Jesus, dying on the cross, pled with God, saying, "Father, forgive them, for they do not know what they are doing,"[25] so Jesus may petition God for the pardon of any person who has ever lived.

Jesus is the judge of all people, including Buddha, Mohammed, and Moses. He decides the eternal destiny of every person. As stated in the New Testament book of Acts:

> He commanded us to preach to the people and to testify that He is the one whom God appointed as judge of the living and the dead.[26]

Since Jesus is "judge of the living and the dead," it could be viewed as wrong and arrogant for evangelical Christians to boldly state precisely what criteria he will use in his judgments of every person in history.

The usual interpretation of the verse where Jesus says "no one comes to the father except through me" is fraught with difficulties of application. To listen to many evangelicals, many people will be excluded from salvation who never had a chance to believe in Jesus, including those who never heard of him because of where they lived, almost everyone who lived before he was born, and even children who die young. Evangelicals claim that the basis for salvation is faith, not works, and that it is utterly critical that this faith must be in Jesus, and in no one else. Curiously, many of these evangelicals also maintain that Jesus was implicitly present in many different ways in the Old Testament. For example, Jesus was the Angel of God's Presence,[27] Commander of the Lord's Army,[28] Priest Forever,[29] Redeemer,[30] and "a witness to the peoples, a leader and commander for the peoples"[31] in different Old Testament passages that are historical accounts (and not prophecies of future events). These evangelicals also teach the Trinity, stating that God, Jesus, and the Holy Spirit are virtually interchangeable. And yet faith in God is not enough for salvation, in spite of the virtual interchangeability of God and Jesus.

Related to this issue is whether people who knew of Jesus, but never became Christians—and yet seem to have followed Christian principles, such as loving others, during their lives—can be accepted into heaven. Typically, someone who balks at the idea of these "good" people not going to heaven will say, for example, "So, will Gandhi be saved?" The truth is, we will never know for sure in this life. According to the Bible, if Gandhi is saved, it will be in spite of his Hinduism and it will truly be by the grace and pardon of Christ. Jesus will make this decision for every human being who has ever lived or who will live. In all of this Jesus is totally exalted, as is made clear in Colossians:

> He is the image of the invisible God, the firstborn over all creation. For by him all things were created: things in heaven and on earth, visible and invisible, whether thrones or powers or rulers or authorities; all things were created by him and for him. He is before all things, and in him all things hold together. And he is the head of the body, the church; he is the beginning and the firstborn from among the dead, so that in everything he might have the supremacy. For God was pleased to have all his fullness dwell in him, and through him to reconcile to himself all things, whether things on earth or things in heaven, by making peace through his blood, shed on the cross.[32]

We also see the supremacy of Jesus underscored in Philippians:

> Therefore God exalted him to the highest place and gave him the name that is above every name, that at the name of Jesus every knee should bow, in heaven and on earth and under the earth, and every tongue confess that Jesus Christ is Lord, to the glory of God the Father.[33]

Jesus also boldly proclaimed

> All authority has been given to Me in heaven and on earth.[34]

That authority includes the power to judge the eternal destiny of every person. This is not universalism, the belief that everyone will be saved. Jesus will not grant executive pardons to everyone. Furthermore, Jesus will even reject many who claim to be Christians.[35]

One reason Christians are often awkward in their sharing is that they may be overstepping the bounds of what mankind is authorized by God to do by trying to dictate what only God can decide:

who will be saved and who will not. Spiritual arrogance, whether it is really that or just appears to be that, is always awkward.

Stephen Prothero, professor of religion at Boston University, highlighted the complexity of questions such as, "Is religion toxic or tonic? Is it one of the world's greatest forces for evil, or one of the world's greatest forces for good?" His answers: "Yes and yes, which is to say that religion is a force far too powerful to ignore."[36] Buddhism has had an enormous impact on the nations where it commands large followings, and in recent decades it has drawn a sizable number of adherents in many Western nations. However, what we have seen in this and the preceding chapters is that Buddhism's most serious shortcomings are inherent and insurmountable:

- Transformation via Buddhism is very slow and is only feasible for an elite few. Because of this, in practice Buddhism is a much narrower way than Christianity.
- The absence of grace, mercy, and forgiveness in Buddhism is a crippling shortcoming. Imperfect people, no matter how good, will commit bad deeds. The process of working off the resulting bad karma is imperceptibly slow. The result is the eventual deterioration of one's spiritual condition, from one lifetime to the next, for nearly everyone. People need a savior who is gracious, merciful and forgiving, and fully divine, if they are to have a decent chance of progressing spiritually. Receiving a modest transfer of merit from a bodhisattva is not helpful enough for most people. Each person must still proceed on his or her own toward enlightenment, weighted down by bad karma and character weaknesses.
- By asserting that God is not relevant to the development of one's spirituality, Buddhists leave themselves wide open to the worship of idols and lesser gods, often

involving the slavish repetition of mantras in an effort to change reality.

The issues and problems of Christianity, though many and troublesome, are potentially resolvable. The judgmental attitude of many Christians could be neutralized if the humility and Golden Rule[37] taught by Jesus were taken more seriously. Truly encountering God should make a person humble. The problem is with so-called Christians whose arrogance prevents them from being convicted by the Holy Spirit. The need for revival is great, yet sweeping revivals have occurred many times in history. May another one begin soon!

---

[1] Buddha's life before his enlightenment was not exemplary by Western standards. While married he also had concubines. He then abandoned his wife and child to become a wandering monk. Sanderson Beck, "Buddha and Buddhism," http://san.beck.org/EC9-Buddha.html, retrieved September 18, 2010.

[2] Approximately 54 percent of the people of the world, or 3.6 billion people, are either Christians or Muslims. "Major Religions of the World, Ranked by Number of Adherents," www.adherents.com/Religions_By_Adherents.html, retrieved on September 28, 2010.

[3] Madasamy Thirumalai, *Sharing Your Faith with a Buddhist* (Grand Rapids, MI: Baker Book House, 2003), 153.

[4] Ibid., 170.

[5] Ibid., 181.

[6] Ibid., 181–182.

[7] Ibid., 193.

[8] Ibid., 179.

[9] Ibid., 123–131 (paraphrase).

[10] Ibid., 182.

[11] Mary Garden, "Can Meditation Be Bad for You?" *Humanist*, September/October 2007, www.thehumanist.org/humanist/MaryGarden.html, retrieved November 22, 2010.

[12] Matthew 6:7b (NKJV).

[13] 1 Kings 18:26–39.

[14] John 14:6b (NKJV).

[15] Dhammapada 273–275 (emphasis added).

[16] Ecclesiastes 7:20 (NIV).

[17] Isaiah 64:6a (NIV).

[18] Sample quotes appear at Matthew 11:27, John 3:16, John 5:17–23, John 8:19, John 10:30, 36–38 and John 14:1, 7–11.

[19] Steven Gertz, "How Do We Know 10 of the Disciples Were Martyred?" ChristianHistory.net, August 8, 2008, www.christianitytoday.com/ch/asktheexpert/sep23.html, retrieved May 25, 2011.

[20] C. S. Lewis popularized this argument in his BBC radio talks in the early 1940s, which were later adapted for his book *Mere Christianity*, first published in 1952. The argument is sometimes called "Lewis's trilemma." Other Christian thinkers often go back to this same argument, saying that Jesus must be "liar, lunatic, or lord." If Jesus was a liar or a lunatic, he could not have been a good teacher; furthermore, he did not seem to be a liar or a lunatic. The only option left is that he was telling the truth and is Lord. Either way, the option of calling him a good teacher is untenable. See C. S. Lewis, *Mere Christianity*, 3d ed. (San Francisco: HarperSanFrancisco, 2001).

[21] Romans 1:18–23; 2 Peter 3:9.

[22] Luke 12:47–48 (NKJV).

[23] John 14:6b (NIV).

[24] John 3:16 (NIV).

[25] Luke 23:34 (NASB).

[26] Acts 10:42 (NIV).

[27] Isaiah 63:9.

[28] Joshua 5:14–15.

[29] Psalm 110:4.

[30] Job 19:25.

[31] Isaiah 55:4b (NASB).

[32] Colossians 1:15–20 (NASB).

[33] Philippians 2:9–11 (NIV).

[34] Matthew 28:18b (NKJV).

[35] Matthew 7:21–23 and Revelation 3:14–21.

[36] Stephen Prothero, *God Is Not One: The Eight Rival Religions That Run the World—and Why Their Differences Matter* (New York: HarperOne, 2010), 10.

[37] "Treat people the same way you want them to treat you." Matthew 7:12b (NASB).

Chapter Seventeen
Reflections and Implications

This book has charted a challenging and I hope an exhilarating journey for the reader. We have entertained the hypothesis that key aspects of Eastern and Western religion are much more connected than is generally assumed, and we have seen how plausible that notion is. Appreciating potential connectedness could serve as a solid basis for greater understanding, compassion, and interchange between devout practitioners of different Eastern and Western religions.

We have also developed an appreciation for the intensity of several irreconcilable differences between Buddhism and Christianity. A spiritual marriage is out of the question. Forcing it would create spiritual schizophrenia, for which the only remedy is to join one camp and abandon the other. The choices are clear, as detailed at the beginning of Chapter Sixteen:

1. Seek an interactive relationship with a personal God and other believers, or burrow deeply into the divine within, fixating on it through marathon, self-disciplined meditation.

2. Accept God's antidote for our bad karma, his mercy, grace, and forgiveness, or tough it out, heroically accepting its ugly consequences during a succession of reincarnations.

3. Cultivate an attitude of humility — or arrogance — toward different faiths.

4. Seek to intervene in the lives of those who believe differently, or "live and let live."

If we don't make these choices, we either end up standing for nothing, or we founder, sinking into the quicksand of spiritual wishy-washiness. Jesus had words for people in that condition: "I know your deeds, that you are neither cold nor hot. I wish you were either one or the other! So, because you are lukewarm—neither hot nor cold—I am about to spit you out of my mouth."[1]

Even though I am a Christian, I have a sincere respect for Buddhists who intensely and wholeheartedly practice their religion. My thoughts toward those who dabble in Buddhism, picking and choosing what is easy and palatable, are not so kind. Nevertheless, I hold my tongue. Those thoughts are quite similar to those I have toward people who dabble in Christianity. I bite my tongue, and it hurts terribly.

The media has long presented Buddhism in glowing terms, almost as if its followers were above the foibles common to all people. We have seen in this book that Buddhists are susceptible to scandal and corruption, just as followers of Christianity, or indeed any religion, are. Comprehending that is healthy. It provides a necessary grounding in reality.

One way of wrapping up this book is to recap the strengths and weakness of Buddhism and Christianity. Each has many strengths, yet with each one is a corresponding, related weakness. We summarize all this for each religion in turn.

Buddhism: Strengths and Weaknesses

Self-Improvement. Buddhism provides a mechanism for self-improvement. However, as with all self-improvement systems, actually producing major change is, at best, a very slow process.

No Need for God. Buddhism frees the individual to develop spiritually without having to submit to some Higher Power. However, treating God as extraneous or irrelevant presents its own risks. Shouldn't God be the natural source of strength on which people can draw in order to grow and change? Avoiding that source could well undermine any substantive efforts to improve as a person. Further, if a personal God exists who cares about people and desires to relate to them, then shunning such a God leaves one vulnerable to whatever responses God may have to those who ignore his existence and role in human affairs.

A Mind Trip. Buddhism appeals to highly intelligent, very disciplined people. However, the very elements that make it appealing to such people also make it inaccessible to those with normal attention spans and mental discipline. In this sense, it is a very narrow way.

Charting a Path. Buddhism gives the aspirant the opportunity to chart his or her own path. However, the path the aspirant chooses may not be a wise one. Also, it not unusual for self-made people to suffer from arrogance.

Liberation from Suffering. Buddhism seeks to liberate its aspirants from the misery caused by their desires and attachments. Yet, the antidote offered is to seek to destroy the notion that each person has a soul.

Self-Denial. Buddhism requires a commitment to practicing self-denial, and this can lead to greater happiness. On the other hand, the necessity of repeated periods of protracted deep meditation is daunting and difficult.

Reincarnation and Karma. These Eastern beliefs provide a ready explanation for why bad things happen to people: You did something bad in a prior life (or in this life) and now you are paying for it. This view does have the benefit of seeming just, and it encourages good behavior in people. On the downside, there is no escaping the negative consequences of past misdeeds. Mercy, grace, and forgiveness (either from a personal God or from other people) are not available as a way of breaking free from the consequences of past negative actions.

Truth Within. Buddhism teaches that real truth lies deep within, negating the need to seek outside counsel. The risk is that such a perspective leaves the aspirant quite vulnerable to self-delusion and the rationalization of moral choices that might be questionable, unwise, or immoral.

Compassion. Buddhism stresses the need to exhibit compassion toward others. However, since such efforts are primarily a means to self-improvement, the compassion expressed can seem shallow.

Adaptability. Buddhism facilitates and encourages getting enmeshed with different religions. In Asia Buddhists have incorporated elements of many indigenous religions, accepting a wide range of superstitions, occult beliefs, and practices. These practices include worship of idols, magic, sorcery, witchcraft, divination, animism, making sacrifices and offerings to various spirits, and occult sexual practices to accelerate progress toward enlightenment.

Christianity: Strengths and Weaknesses

Quick Conversion. In Christianity, conversion can be quite rapid and dramatic. Whether continued spiritual growth ensues is often less clear. When too much priority is given to conversion and too little to spiritual growth, superficiality and hypocrisy are not unusual.

Well-Defined Truths and a Clear Path. Christianity provides a well-defined set of doctrines based on the Bible. Truth is eternal, unchanging, and independent of every person. However, believing in that truth at the expense of valuing empathy and mutual understanding can easily result in intolerance toward people of other faiths.

Empowerment. Christianity provides access to the enabling power of the Holy Spirit in transforming one's life, radically shifting a person's focus from self to God and others. This enabling is a moment-to-moment thing. When the believer is submitted to God, love, power, and wisdom are infused into the believer. When the believer chooses to follow selfish desires instead, the Holy Spirit becomes dormant and ineffectual.

High Standards and Hypocrisy. Christianity holds up high standards for behavior and motivation, which can be maintained as long as the believer humbly submits to God's direction and empowerment. When the believer retreats back into selfishness, all manner of subtle as well as blatant sinful behavior is possible.

Quick Liberation. Christianity provides a way to be quickly liberated from the weight of all past negative karma (though the forgiven person may still have to face some inevitable consequences). The availability of the mercy, grace, and forgiveness of a personal God can be enormously freeing in leaving behind the effects of past misdeeds. The risk is that believers can develop a cavalier attitude about the need for moral purity by brashly presuming God's continued forgiveness for their ongoing sins.

Free Will and Resurrection. Without the pluses and minuses of different kinds of karma from past lives (because there weren't any), Christians are free to live and grow as they choose in their one life on earth. Though this also means that they don't have the benefit of good karma from good deeds during past lives, they do have the immediate empowerment by the Holy Spirit to live a righteous life of love and service to others.

Compassion and Tolerance. In Christianity, compassion toward others can be fueled by the believer's appreciation for God's love for them personally. On the other hand, when a believer does not appreciate God's love for all of mankind, and expects others to hold the same beliefs as their own, a judgmental attitude toward those with different beliefs is not unusual.

Returning to the Precautions of the Dalai Lama

This book began with an invitation to the reader to consider concerns expressed by the Dalai Lama:

> In the West, I do not think it advisable to follow Buddhism. Changing religions is not like changing professions. Excitement lessens over the years, and soon you are not excited, and then where are you? Homeless inside yourself.[2]

We saw that westerners are at first attracted by the parts of Buddhism that are common to Western religion, but later hesitate when they encounter some elements that are uncomfortably Eastern. We would do well to recap each of these.

Common Elements

- Altruism.
- The ethics of Judaism.
- As one sows, so shall one reap.
- Some meditative practices, such as guided meditation.

Potentially Uncomfortable Eastern Elements

- Intense, prolonged, extremely repetitive meditation to tune out of this world.
- Withdrawal from society, the lonely pursuit of personal growth.
- Eradication of one's own soul.
- Belief that you may reincarnate as a rat, a snake, or a mosquito.
- Reincarnation intertwined with karma, coupled with the extreme difficulty of working off negative karma, which is thought to often haunt a person into several future lives.
- An absence of mercy, grace, and forgiveness.
- Imperceptibly slow spiritual progress.
- Spiritual elitism (only one in a million, or less, will attain enlightenment).
- Buddhism in Asia has incorporated much from the religions of the indigenous people, accepting a wide range of superstitions and occult beliefs and practices. These practices include worship of idols, magic, sorcery, witchcraft, divination, animism, making sacrifices and offerings to various spirits, and occult sexual practices to accelerate progress toward enlightenment.
- A serious bias against women is deeply embedded in Asian Buddhism.

These ten Eastern aspects of Buddhism head the list of things that westerners are most likely to feel uncomfortable adopting.

Considering the Precautions of Jesus

I would like to leave you with one final challenge. Imagine Jesus citing precautions similar to those of the Dalai Lama. His words might be something like this: "In the West, I do not think it advisable to mix the core of Western culture with Christianity. The result is grotesque and bears no resemblance to authentic Christianity. 'If anyone wishes to come after Me, he must deny himself, and take up his cross and follow Me.'"[3]

Westerners have little concept of how to deny self. Our culture is saturated with "the pursuit of happiness" touted in the Declaration of Independence. Taking up a cross is also foreign to westerners, as is following the leadings of a personal God.

Could it be that Buddhists monks who renounce all material possessions and worldly desires, preach nonviolence and compassion, and meditate long and habitually are behaving in a way that is more consistent with the teachings of Jesus than are the great majority of those who call themselves Christians? Some would argue that this is true. Nevertheless, if the content of the minds of most of these Buddhists were compared with the God-consciousness that is so key to real Christianity, we would still have to say that there were critical differences that could not be discounted.

---

[1] Revelation 3:15–16 (NIV).

[2] Patrick French, Tibet, Tibet (New York: Alfred A. Knopf, 2003), 27.

[3] Mark 8:34 (NASB).

A Fictional Postscript:
How It Might Have Happened

When Buddha was a young man, he was a prince named Siddhartha. His father, a king, provided three palaces for Siddhartha to live in, but forbade him to leave the royal grounds. And so he was quite isolated from the suffering and challenges of the outside world and from religious teachings. When Siddhartha was twenty-nine years old, his father finally allowed him to tour the surrounding area to meet some of his future subjects. He came across an old man, a diseased man, a decaying corpse, and an ascetic. These encounters deeply disturbed and depressed him. This is Buddhist legend.

In this chapter we will imagine that Siddhartha has wandered into a throbbing marketplace. It is choked with poor folk foraging among the stalls in shabby rags, haggling over subtropical produce such as mangoes, loquats, tamarind, and breadfruit. Siddhartha happens upon a thickly bearded older man wearing an unusual robe and a skull cap. Curious, he strikes up a conversation.

SIDDHARTHA (*bowing with his hands touching, fingers pointed upward*):
Namaste! My name is Siddhartha. What is yours?

JEWISH MAN (*nodding cautiously*): Abram.

SIDDHARTHA: Excuse me, sir. May I ask why are you dressed so . . .
differently?

ABRAM: I am a Jew. My people immigrated to many places far and wide after hordes of Babylonian soldiers invaded our land and drove us out.

SIDDHARTHA (*gasping*): When did that happen?

ABRAM: I was a child of age six when my family fled our homeland. That was fifty-four years ago. We first migrated to eastern Persia, then to Afghanistan—a very harsh, forbidding land— and finally here, northeast India, a much more pleasant place. We settled here twenty-eight years ago.

SIDDHARTHA: So you arrived here a year after I was born . . .

ABRAM: I suppose so. You are young and handsome. Are you a nobleman?

SIDDHARTHA: I am a prince, though not a happy one. My father overprotects me. I am twenty-nine, yet only today has he allowed me to leave the royal grounds. I have been shocked by what I have encountered. *(He thrusts his hands into the air in bewilderment.)* First, a very old, miserable man. Then a man about my age using crutches. And a dead body left in a ditch by a field. Rats, flies, and maggots were feasting on it. Horrible! I also talked to a monk who told me he owned nothing but his robe and sandals. Such poverty! The real world is awful.

ABRAM: It is worse than that. You have not been run out of your country by invaders. Things are not quite so bad here. At least we can eke out a living as shopkeepers and laborers.

SIDDHARTHA: Good sir, I have heard many stories about the Jewish people. I would love to learn more about your rulers. Tell me about King Solomon. I have heard he was so wise that rulers from every nation sent their wise men with gifts, so they could learn from his great knowledge and understanding. Is this true?

ABRAM: Yes, it is. . . . How did you know that?

SIDDHARTHA: I have friends who practice the Jain religion. They have mentioned Solomon's writings in our discussions. They tell me their ancestors admired his rules of conduct, although their own rules are much stricter than his.

ABRAM: How did they get copies?

SIDDHARTHA: Many ships carried goods between the Middle East and India—olive oil, pomegranates, cedar wood, carved figurines, fabrics, and rolls of papyrus. Some of those scrolls included Solomon's writings.

ABRAM: There has been much trade between our lands for centuries past. What you say makes sense. To us Jews, Solomon was the wisest man ever. He assembled hundreds of sayings into a Book of Proverbs. He reigned during the height of Israel's glory. Oh, if only I had lived back then. It is a struggle to be refugees far from our homeland, with no hope of returning.

SIDDHARTHA: It must be quite difficult. Are there any of his sayings that have been especially comforting to you? I would like to know more about them. Could you recite some for your favorites?

ABRAM (*clearing his throat*): Not easily, but I do have them on papyrus scrolls.

SIDDHARTHA: Are they in Pali?

ABRAM: Not the oldest copies, but a Pali translation is now available. Your people keep asking for it. They are most curious about spiritual things from foreign lands.

SIDDHARTHA: If you had to cope with Hinduism and to appease its 3 million gods, you'd be looking for alternatives, too. How much would a copy be?

ABRAM: Ten silver coins.

SIDDHARTHA: That is no problem. I will pay it.

ABRAM: Come with me to my village, and I will get one for you.

They amble along, chatting, negotiating a muddy, pothole-infested road through groves of bodhi trees and amaranth bushes.

* * *

One week has passed, and Siddhartha has read most of the scroll. This morning he has cautiously left the palace and journeyed to Abram's village. As Siddhartha approaches Abram, they greet each other. Abram offers Siddhartha a cup of diluted chai. He accepts, and they sit on a fallen log in front of Abram's hovel to talk.

SIDDHARTHA: I didn't know Solomon lived in India!

ABRAM: He didn't. Why do you think he did?

SIDDHARTHA: Listen to this. He must have been in India to have written this:

Again I looked and saw all the oppression that was taking place under the sun: I saw the tears of the oppressed—and they have no comforter; power was on the side of their oppressors—and they have no comforter. And I declared that the dead, who had already died, are happier than the living, who are still alive. But better than both is he who has not yet been, who has not seen the evil that is done under the sun.[1]

(*Abram and Siddhartha stare at one another for a few seconds.*)

SIDDHARTHA: Solomon would not have allowed such misery and oppression in his own realm. It seems as if he is talking about someone like my father, who wants me to become like him. I could never be an oppressor.

ABRAM: But you do have to be a warrior, don't you?

SIDDHARTHA (*with a look of horror*): Never! Killing is never right. I would die or go to prison before I would strike someone with a sword. I would renounce whatever power had become mine.

ABRAM: I have heard that you take part in your father's war games.

SIDDHARTHA (*clearing his throat and wincing*): Those are just games. If we actually harm another combatant, we are punished.

ABRAM: So your father thinks you would fight in battle?

SIDDHARTHA (*grimacing*): Alas, he does. He would strike me down if I refused to go to war. I am most grieved. Fortunately, things have been peaceful for many years.

ABRAM: You could quickly become a great sorrow to your father!

SIDDHARTHA (*looking down and shaking his head*): He demands silence from me whenever I am near him. He suspects I disagree on many things, and he will not hear of it. I am heir to the throne, yet I cannot speak!

ABRAM (*with a look of amazement*): We Jews declare a boy to be a man when he turns thirteen. As a man, his opinions are heard.

SIDDHARTHA: How can one become a Jew?

ABRAM: It is not easy. You are better off as you are. Though life is hard, I try to be content. One of my favorite sayings of Solomon is this:

Better one handful with tranquility than two handfuls with toil and chasing after the wind. . . . Better a poor but wise youth than an old but foolish king who no longer knows how to take warning.[2]

SIDDHARTHA (*sighing*): I wish someone like you were my father. I would be better off as a poor but wise youth.

ABRAM: You do not know the sorrows of my people, or how good you have it.

SIDDHARTHA (*with a doubting look*): Life is suffering . . . for all people. If only there were a way to be freed from suffering. I must search for that way.

ABRAM: You have the leisure of doing that, do you not?

SIDDHARTHA: How? I must wait on my father . . . or his officials . . . or my wife. I am constantly pestered . . . harassed!

ABRAM: Yet you have rich food and splendid surroundings.

SIDDHARTHA: They are no real condolence. They leave me empty. My father, my wife, they drive me mad. Sometimes I think about fleeing the palace and going away to seek the truth.

ABRAM: You are too sensitive and tender-hearted to be a king. You must be tough!

SIDDHARTHA: Money and security are a trap, holding a man in until what is noble within him has been utterly stifled.

ABRAM: Ah! The facades of wealth and power! It reminds me of this proverb:

Whoever loves money never has money enough; whoever loves wealth is never satisfied with his income. This too is meaningless. As goods increase, so do those who consume them. And what benefit are they to the owner except to feast his eyes on them?[3]

SIDDHARTHA (*eyes moistening visibly*): I couldn't agree more. These sayings are most precious and powerful. They offer the secrets to happiness and great blessings. If I meditate on them daily, will that make me a Jew?

ABRAM (*raising his eyebrows*): Have you heard the story of the later years of Solomon's life?

SIDDHARTHA: Only fragments . . .

ABRAM: Before you consider becoming a Jew you should become acquainted with more of our writings. Besides his collection of proverbs, Solomon wrote another book when he was old. It is called Ecclesiastes. He was deeply depressed and disillusioned when he wrote it.

SIDDHARTHA (*a look of curiosity washing over his face*): Rich, deeply depressed, disillusioned. That would be me. Do you have a translation?

ABRAM: Only the first five chapters, so far. We are working on more chapters, but it is slow work.

SIDDHARTHA: Can I obtain a copy?

ABRAM: Yes. Another five silver coins.

Siddhartha hands him the coins. Abram fetches a copy from his hovel. They meet again a week later. Squatting outside of Abram's hut again, they survey part of a scroll that they have rolled open.

ABRAM: What did you think of this book, this Ecclesiastes?

SIDDHARTHA: I could have written it! It spoke straight to my aching heart and my empty soul. So eloquent . . . forceful.

ABRAM: So you agree with most of it?

SIDDHARTHA: There is one troubling thing. He mentions "God" here and there. I do not believe in God. My people have thousands upon thousands of gods. Gods bring people nothing but suffering, oppression, and despair. There are so many injustices in our society—Hinduism sanctifies them all! I cannot imagine how awful it would be if all these gods were compacted into one overwhelming, frightful deity . . . a ferocious, bloated Brahma!

ABRAM (*shaking his head in sorrow and humiliation*): Most Jews here don't believe in God either. God abandoned us, letting Babylonians destroy our land, driving us out of our beloved country. Why should we believe in such a feeble, indifferent god?

SIDDHARTHA: You shouldn't. We see things much the same way!

ABRAM: It seems so. We Jews couldn't handle one god. How your people willingly suffer under thousands of gods, I do not understand.

SIDDHARTHA (*clearing his throat*): I am not a Hindu. Never have been. I was raised by my mother's younger sister, Maha Pajapati, without belief in any gods.

ABRAM: You have been blessed in that.

SIDDHARTHA: If only we could have a religion that leaves gods out, and just focuses on how to live right . . . as Solomon taught. The Jains do that. The only thing is they go to extremes in protesting Hinduism. They totally isolate themselves from everyday society and starve themselves so they can meditate and seek inner truth.

ABRAM: They are fanatics who accomplish nothing! On the other hand, we have found much value, insight, and cultural richness in Solomon's sayings, so we try to live by them . . . at least much of the time. I mean . . . we live by them when they are helpful, and quietly ignore them when they are not.

SIDDHARTHA (*with an odd smile*): You equivocate . . . beautifully!

ABRAM (*smiling*): There is much hope for you.

SIDDHARTHA: Is there? If the great Solomon became disillusioned and depressed when he became old, even though he had all his wise sayings to counsel him, what is to stop that from happening to me?

ABRAM: Ah! Alas! The later years of Solomon's life . . . a very sad story. He made peace with all the kings of surrounding nations, marrying dozens upon dozens of their royal young women. Soon he had a hundred of them. Then several hundred.

SIDDHARTHA: Say nothing more! That is enough to undo any man! Very sad . . .

ABRAM: Many of them begged him to build altars to their gods and to offer sacrifices. He refused at first. He held out for quite a while, but then he gave in to the most alluring and persuasive ones. Ah, women!

SIDDHARTHA: And so, what is so bad about that? What kinds of food or plants did Solomon's foreign wives offer up? Hashish? Opium? Was every one getting . . . high? (*He swirls his hands into the air in a artful frenzy.*)

ABRAM: Alas! If only it had been so. Usually, a lamb or pig or cow was butchered and burned on the altar. But then it got much worse. First-born children were killed and sacrificed.

SIDDHARTHA (*gasping in horror, covering his face with his hands*): That is . . . utterly unthinkable. (*He begins to weep, shaking.*) No one should follow such perverted gods. Even the Hindu gods only demand sacrifices of food or plants. And Solomon went along with this?

ABRAM: Tragically, he did. It became routine, as it had been in the lands of Solomon's foreign wives.

SIDDHARTHA (*with a look of shock*): Why? How could a man with so much wisdom allow such vicious practices?

ABRAM: I suppose he got to the point where he felt he was above it all. You know, the rules didn't apply to him. Wealth, power, and fame went to his head. He hoarded women, horses, and gold. Our own sacred texts forbade him to do that, but he ignored these prohibitions, and even his own proverbs.

SIDDHARTHA: If I remain in my father's palaces, some day I will succeed my father as a rich, powerful king. Then I will also do terrible things, like my father. My armies will wound and kill. I will exact heavy taxes, increasing the poverty and misery of my subjects . . . so my palaces can become more grand. It is all so sick!

ABRAM: I can't picture you doing that.

SIDDHARTHA: I can't imagine Solomon casting newborn babies on flaming altars, either. I just can't.

ABRAM: Yet it happened. He allowed it, to appease his pagan wives.

SIDDHARTHA: So you have told me. Power and wealth corrupt . . . everyone! The only way to avoid corruption is for me to abandon everything my father set up for me and to flee from his wicked stronghold. If I do that, I can seek truth and find a way to bring an end to the pervasive suffering that is life. I could study Solomon's sayings and live by them, in poverty and solitude. I will meditate on his sayings, and write them "on the tablet of my heart," as he urged people to do.

ABRAM: I am surprised that you feel that way after I just told you about what Solomon did during his later years.

SIDDHARTHA: There is nothing wrong with his sayings. The fault was his increasing lack of objectivity. You cannot see yourself clearly when you are entangled with women, horses, and gold!

ABRAM: Amen. As great as Solomon's sayings are, it is even more important to observe one's self with real impartiality. We must stay true to what we believe.

SIDDHARTHA: Solomon should have completely renounced his throne, riches, women, and wealth. Then he could have withdrawn into the wilderness to rekindle his own search for deeper wisdom. And he would have stayed pure and devoted to his sayings.

ABRAM: You make it sound so simple! Yet, if we are honest, it would be extremely difficult to do. How can you walk away from everything you have worked hard for?

SIDDHARTHA: I have never had to work hard for anything, so giving it all up is much easier to do. I do agree with you, though. Once you get to a certain point, the core of your being becomes sold out to corrupting things, and there is no turning back to purity. I must act now.

ABRAM: The later years of Solomon's life should be enough to scare us into purity. He became like a Hindu, worshipping dozens of gods and trying to appease them to get favors from them for his wives. That never has worked in India and I'm sure it didn't work in Israel.

SIDDHARTHA: Rather than helping people to cope with the hardships of life, Hinduism solidifies the rule of the rich and powerful. It commits common people to a hopeless resignation to a life of suffering and despair. Some way of escape must be found. Thanks to Solomon I can see how critical it is to be serious in pursuing righteousness.

ABRAM: Oddly enough, Solomon agreed with you. One of his proverbs says, "He who follows righteousness and mercy finds life, righteousness, and honor."[4] I guess he felt that he had already practiced enough righteousness in his life that he didn't need to continue to do so to reap the benefits of a good past.

SIDDHARTHA: He abandoned his ethical moorings.

ABRAM: Yes, those instilled by his father, King David. Clearly, we all need to take every precaution in observing ourselves ruthlessly and impartially.

SIDDHARTHA: I don't think keen observation is nearly enough. One must *completely* shun the illusory pleasures of this life. Freed from worldly attachments . . . one can find peace, contentment, and true happiness.

ABRAM (*sighing*): So simple, yet so hard. How do you intend to attain real detachment?

SIDDHARTHA: Solomon himself said it. He wrote, "The path of the righteous is like the first gleam of dawn, shining ever brighter till the full light of day."[5] If I do nothing else in this life, I want to shine brightly, to become enlightened, like this verse says. The key is following the right path. I want that more than anything else in life.

ABRAM: I think you are on to something.

SIDDHARTHA: I want to build an impenetrable moral fortress all around me . . . to avoid my own demise.

ABRAM: And how?

SIDDHARTHA: Take Solomon. He should have divorced all his foreign wives and concubines and sent them and their children back to their homelands.

ABRAM: He should have given away all his gold and horses so that everyone could share in them?

SIDDHARTHA: Yes. He should have.

ABRAM: Not only that, I think Solomon should have rejected God and founded a truly humanistic religion—based on his rules of wise living. After all, his proverbs were not only his, but those of many sages who preceded him. They were distillations of many prior centuries of wisdom.

SIDDHARTHA: Perhaps we do not really need the old sages. These are deep inner truths. Every person could know them if they strove very hard for understanding and looked within themselves. After all, the self is the master of the self. Who else can that master be? With the self fully subdued, one could obtain the sublime refuge.[6]

ABRAM: There is no need for god. Just like the Jains, one can abandon all gods and embark on a Shramana venture of rejecting all beliefs and all dependence on any deities.

SIDDHARTHA: I couldn't agree more. This is how to do it. . . . First, I will organize all of Solomon's proverbs into categories. Certain themes come up again and again in his writings, like threads in a tapestry. There are eight that I have observed: right view, right intention, right speech, right action, right livelihood, right effort, right mindfulness, and right concentration. His collection is much more comprehensive than those of the Jains or of any Hindus. The path is clear.

ABRAM: I think you will become a great man. Perhaps you could change India, and other parts of Asia as well. The need is very great. This country is infested with money-grubbing priests and the petty gods and kings they serve.

SIDDHARTHA (*looking quite distressed*): I don't want greatness, if that is defined by how highly other people think of me. Desiring that would be a real trap. Greatness must be defined only in reference to being true to what is deep within. Solomon put it well when he wrote,

He who is slow to anger is better than the mighty, and he who rules his spirit than he who takes a city.[7]

ABRAM: From what I have been able to tell, the rules of conduct Solomon set forth in his proverbs are a stronger foundation than those of Hinduism, the Shramanas, and the Jains. And if you proclaimed a path of moderation—choosing righteous living as a middle ground between appeasing gods and renouncing everything—then you would have a secular religion that would really guide and help people.

SIDDHARTHA: That there is much need is without question. All the sects of India are so riddled with weaknesses and excesses. I fear that the greatness of Solomon's wisdom isn't enough to banish those shortcomings. And then there are my own failings. How can someone like myself, who has been so sheltered, be able to master such a corrupted world?

ABRAM: Siddhartha, if you can stake out a middle ground between a Hinduism that can justify almost anything by choosing a god that caters to that thing, and the extreme asceticism and isolationism of the Shramanas and the Jains, you could come up with something profoundly reasonable and effective as a religion. I think that is what Solomon espoused.

SIDDHARTHA: You are profound, and very optimistic! For my part, I believe this world is so twisted that the best thing to do is to withdraw from it and begin to focus on purifying myself. That must happen before anything else takes place.

ABRAM: That is where we all must begin.

SIDDHARTHA: I agree. May I ask a favor of you?

ABRAM: If you wish. How could I refuse you? I live in your father's realm!

SIDDHARTHA: I must not take these scrolls back to my palace again. If my father discovers them, he will destroy them. And worse, he will never let me out of the palace grounds again. Will you keep them until I escape from my palace?

ABRAM: Certainly. I will do that for you. I sense that some day you will become a great man who will liberate many people from Hinduism! Your people need this more than another king.

SIDDHARTHA: I am indebted to you! You have given me hope, and
you may have pointed the way to my future. May you live in
peace and happiness here in your village!

ABRAM: Shalom!

SIDDHARTHA: Namaste!

* * *

The above dialogue is fictional, but it does suggest a plausible way
in which Buddha could have learned about the writings of
Solomon. We do not know whether Pali and Sanskrit existed as
written languages during Siddhartha's lifetime. What is more likely
is that the colonies of Jews that settled in India around the time of
Buddha's birth brought written Hebrew scrolls of portions of the
Bible with them. To survive in India, some of these Jews would
have had to learn the prevailing language. They could have been
fluent in Pali or Sanskrit while also being fluent in their native
tongue, Hebrew.

Instead of receiving written translations of Solomon's writings
into Pali or Sanskrit, perhaps Siddhartha met frequently with one or
more bilingual Jews who orally translated some of Solomon's
writings for him. This may have happened either before or after he
fled the palace. In any case, Siddhartha may have meditated on
these writings during his travels. He would then have been well on
his way to becoming the great master who forever changed the
course of Asian religion and culture.

---

[1] Ecclesiastes 4:1–3 (NIV).

[2] Ecclesiastes 4:6, 13 (NIV).

[3] Ecclesiastes 5:10–11 (NIV).

[4] Proverbs 21:21 (NKJV).

[5] Proverbs 4:18 (NIV).

[6] Dhammapada 160.

[7] Proverbs 16:32 (NKJV).

Appendix
Solomon's Precursors to Buddha's "Right" Steps

The Noble Eightfold Path is a central part of Buddhism. It consists of the eight steps of Right View, Right Intention, Right Speech, Right Action, Right Livelihood, Right Effort, Right Mindfulness, and Right Concentration. All of these steps of Buddhism, however, were described as *right* by King Solomon of Israel hundreds of years before Buddha lived. And the goal of enlightenment was also alluded to by Solomon:

> The path of the righteous is like the morning sun, shining ever brighter till the full light of day.[1]

> The light of the righteous rejoices, but the lamp of the wicked will be put out.[2]

In this chapter, we will look at the tight parallels between Solomon's proverbs about the righteous and the steps of Buddha's Eightfold Path by categorizing Solomon's proverbs by topic. Every one of these verses refers to the *righteous*, the *upright*, or the *wicked*, or perhaps to two or more of them in the same verse. Within each step, the verses of Solomon are presented in order by chapter and verse. In a few cases I have also included verses written by others, such as King David, Solomon's father. Verses that are not by Solomon are so noted.

Right View

> Wealth is worthless in the day of wrath, but righteousness delivers from death.[3]

> He who trusts in his riches will fall, but the righteous will flourish like the green leaf.[4]

Better is a little with righteousness, than vast revenues without justice.[5]

Right Intention

The integrity of the upright shall guide them, but the willful contrariness and crookedness of the treacherous shall destroy them.[6]

The righteousness of the upright delivers them, but the unfaithful are trapped by evil desires.[7]

The desire of the [consistently] righteous brings only good, but the expectation of the wicked brings wrath.[8]

The thoughts of the righteous are right: but the counsels of the wicked are deceit.[9]

A wicked messenger falls into trouble, but a trustworthy envoy brings healing.[10]

Fools mock at making amends for sin, but goodwill is found among the upright.[11]

The thoughts of the wicked are an abomination to the LORD, but the words of the pure are pleasant.[12]

The wicked man craves evil; his neighbor gets no mercy from him.[13]

Fervent lips with a wicked heart are like earthenware covered with silver dross.[14]

The righteous is concerned for the rights of the poor, the wicked does not understand such concern.[15]

Right Speech

Blessings are on the head of the righteous, but the mouth of the wicked conceals violence.[16]

The tongue of the righteous is choice silver, but the heart of the wicked is of little value.[17]

The lips of the righteous nourish many, but fools die for lack of judgment.[18]

The lips of the righteous know what is acceptable, but the mouth of the wicked what is perverse.[19]

Through the blessing of the upright a city is exalted, but by the mouth of the wicked it is destroyed.[20]

The words of the wicked lie in wait for blood, but the speech of the upright rescues them.[21]

An evil man is ensnared by the transgression of his lips, but the righteous will escape from trouble.[22]

Right Action

Do not envy a violent man or choose any of his ways, for the Lord detests a perverse man but takes the upright into his confidence.[23]

The fruit of the righteous is a tree of life, and he who is wise wins souls.[24]

The righteous man walks in his integrity; blessed (happy, fortunate, enviable) are his children after him.[25]

To do righteousness and justice is more acceptable to the Lord than sacrifice.[26]

The violence of the wicked will destroy them, because they refuse to do justice.[27]

The sluggard's craving will be the death of him, because his hands refuse to work. All day long he craves for more, but the righteous give without sparing.[28]

Right Livelihood

Ill-gotten gains do not profit, but righteousness delivers from death.[29]

A righteous man cares for the needs of his animal, but the kindest acts of the wicked are cruel.[30]

Right Effort

He who pursues righteousness and love finds life, prosperity and honor.[31]

Right Mindfulness

The tongue of the righteous is as choice silver, the heart of the wicked is worth little.[32]

The lips of the righteous know what is fitting, but the mouth of the wicked only knows what is perverse.[33]

The righteousness of the blameless will direct his way aright, but the wicked will fall by his own wickedness.[34]

The righteous should choose his friends carefully, for the way of the wicked leads them astray.[35]

The mind of the [uncompromisingly] righteous studies how to answer, but the mouth of the wicked pours out evil things.[36]

A wicked man puts up a bold front, but an upright man gives thought to his ways.[37]

Solomon's father, David, wrote this:

I said, "I will watch my ways and keep my tongue from sin; I will put a muzzle on my mouth as long as the wicked are in my presence."[38]

Right Concentration

The Lord detests the thoughts of the wicked, but those of the pure are pleasing to him.[39]

In psalms written around the time of Solomon, we read the following verses:

Blessed is the man who does not walk in the counsel of the *wicked* or stand in the way of sinners or sit in the seat of mockers. But his delight is in the law of the Lord and on His law he *meditates* day and night.[40]

Behold, I long for Your precepts; in Your righteousness give me renewed life.[41]

May my tongue sing of your word, for all your commands are righteous.[42]

As the above compilation shows, for six of the eight steps there were several verses from Solomon's Proverbs or the Psalms that were evident precursors of each step. There were only two verses for the step of Right Livelihood, but then very few of Buddha's own proverbs relate to this step. Only one proverb of Solomon's dealt with Right Effort, yet Buddha devoted many of his proverbs to this step, noting four different types of Right Effort, as detailed in the second half of Chapter Six.

For a more detailed analysis of these parallels, see Chapters Four through Eight.

---

[1] Proverbs 4:18 (NIV).

[2] Proverbs 13:9 (NKJV).

[3] Proverbs 11:4 (NIV).

[4] Proverbs 11:28 (NASB).

[5] Proverbs 16:8 (NKJV).

[6] Proverbs 11:3 (AMP).

[7] Proverbs 11:6 (NIV).

[8] Proverbs 11:23 (AMP).

[9] Proverbs 12:5 (KJV).

[10] Proverbs 13:17 (NIV).

[11] Proverbs 14:9 (NIV).

[12] Proverbs 15:26 (NKJV).

[13] Proverbs 21:10 (NIV).

[14] Proverbs 26:23 (NKJV).

[15] Proverbs 29:7 (NASB).

[16] Proverbs 10:6 (NASB).

[17] Proverbs 10:20 (NIV).

[18] Proverbs 10:21 (NIV).

[19] Proverbs 10:32 (NKJV).

[20] Proverbs 11:11 (NIV).

[21] Proverbs 12:6 (NIV).

[22] Proverbs 12:13 (NASB).

[23] Proverbs 3:31–32 (NIV).

[24] Proverbs 11:30 (NASB).

[25] Proverbs 20:7 (AMP).

[26] Proverbs 21:3 (NKJV).

[27] Proverbs 21:7 (NKJV).

[28] Proverbs 21:25–26 (NIV).

[29] Proverbs 10:2 (NASB).

[30] Proverbs 12:10 (NIV).

[31] Proverbs 21:21 (NIV).

[32] Proverbs 10:20 (NASB).

[33] Proverbs 10:32 (NIV).

[34] Proverbs 11:5 (NKJV).

[35] Proverbs 12:26 (NKJV).

[36] Proverbs 15:28 (AMP).

[37] Proverbs 21:29 (NIV).

[38] Psalm 39:1 (NIV).

[39] Proverbs 15:26 (NIV).

[40] Psalm 1:1–3 (NIV) (emphasis added).

[41] Psalm 119:40 (AMP).

[42] Psalm 119:172 (NIV).

Bibliography

Abhedananda, Swami. *Journey into Kashmir and Tibet*. Translated by Kashmiri 0. Tibbate. Calcutta: Ramakrishna Vivekananda Math, 1987.

Avari, Burjor. *India: The Ancient Past*. London: Routledge, 2007.

Bodhi, Bhikkhu, ed. *In the Buddha's Words: An Anthology of Discourses from the Pali Canon*. Boston: Wisdom Publications, 2005.

Borg, Marcus, ed., with coeditor Ray Riegert and an Introduction by Jack Kornfield. *Jesus and Buddha: The Parallel Sayings*. Berkeley: Ulysses Press, 1997.

Brockman, John, ed. "The Politics of Christianity: A Talk with Elaine Pagels." July 17, 2003. Edge Foundation, www.edge.org/3rd_culture/pagels03/pagels_index.html, retrieved April 27, 2010.

Chang, Lit-Sen. *Asia's Religions: Christianity's Momentous Encounter with Paganism*. Vancouver, Canada: China Horizon, 1999.

Cioccolanti, Steve. *From Buddha to Jesus: An Insider's View of Buddhism and Christianity*. Oxford: Lion Hudson, Monarch, 2007.

Crim, Keith, ed. *The Perennial Dictionary of World Religions*. New York: Harper and Row, 1989.

Dalai Lama. See "His Holiness the Dalai Lama."

Dhammapada. See "Muller, Friedrich Max, trans.," and "Kaviratna, Harischandra, trans."

Durant, Will. *The Story of Civilization, Part I: Our Oriental Heritage*. New York: Simon and Schuster, 1963.

Elwell, Walter A., ed. *Baker Encyclopedia of the Bible*. Grand Rapids, MI: Baker Book House, 1988.

Fisher, Mary Pat. *Living Religions: An Encyclopaedia of the World's Faiths*. London: I. B. Tauris, 1997.

French, Patrick. *Tibet, Tibet*. New York: Alfred A. Knopf, 2003.

Gard, Richard A. *Buddhism*. New York: George Braziller, 1961.

Garden, Mary. "Can Meditation Be Bad for You?" *Humanist*,
    September/October 2007,
    www.thehumanist.org/humanist/MaryGarden.html, retrieved
    November 22, 2010.

Gethin, Rupert. *The Foundations of Buddhism*. Oxford: Oxford
    University Press, 1998.

Hanh, Thich Nhat. *Living Buddha, Living Christ*. New York: Penguin
    Putnam, 1995.

His Holiness the Dalai Lama. *Becoming Enlightened*. Translated by
    Jeffrey Hopkins. New York: Simon and Schuster, Atria Books,
    2009.

Hopkins, E. Washburn. *History of Religions*. New York: Macmillan,
    1918.

Kaviratna, Harischandra, trans. *Dhammapada, Wisdom of the Buddha*.
    Theosophical University Press Online, 1980,
    www.theosociety.org/pasadena/dhamma/dham-hp.htm.

Landaw, Jonathan, and Stephan Bodian. *Buddhism for Dummies*.
    Indianapolis: Wiley, 2003.

Lewis, C. S. *A Year with C. S. Lewis: Daily Readings from His Classic
    Works*. Edited by Patricia S. Klein. San Francisco:
    HarperSanFrancisco, 2003.

Muller, Friedrich Max, trans. *The Dhammapada: A Collection of Verses,
    Being One of the Canonical Works of the Buddhists*. Vol. 10, Part 1,
    of *The Sacred Books of the East*, translated by Various Oriental
    Scholars, edited by F. Max Muller, at "Dhammapada (Muller),"
    Wikisource,
    http://en.wikisource.org/wiki/Dhammapada_(Muller).

Olson, Carl E., and Anthony E. Clark. "Are Jesus and Buddha
    Brothers?" *This Rock* 16, no 5 (May-June 2005),
    www.catholic.com/thisrock/2005/0505fea1.asp, retrieved
    February 17, 2011.

Overy, Richard, and Geoffrey Barraclough, eds. *The Times Complete
    History of the World*, 7th ed. New York: Metro Books, 2008.

Prothero, Stephen. *God Is Not One: The Eight Rival Religions That Run
    the World—and Why Their Differences Matter*. New York:
    HarperOne, 2010.

Rawlinson, H. G. *Intercourse Between India and the Western World.* London: Cambridge University Press, 1916, available at www.columbia.edu/cu/lweb/digital/collections/cul/texts/ldpd_5 949061_000/index.html, retrieved April 12, 2010.

Roche, Lorin. "The Dangers of Meditation," www.lorinroche.com/page8/page8.html, retrieved September 18, 2010.

Smith, Huston. *The Religions of Man.* New York: Harper and Row, 1965.

Thirumalai, Madasamy. *Sharing Your Faith with a Buddhist.* Grand Rapids, MI: Baker Book House, 2003.

Thompson, John A. "India." In *Baker Encyclopedia of the Bible,* edited by Walter A. Elwell. Grand Rapids, MI: Baker Book House, 1988.

Valea, Ernest. *The Buddha and the Christ: Reciprocal Views.* Seattle: BookSurge, 2008.

Walton, John H., Victor H. Matthews, and Mark W. Chavalas. *The IVP Bible Background Commentary: Old Testament.* Downers Grove, IL: InterVarsity Press, 2000.

Scripture References

About the Author
R. E. Sherman, FCAS, MAAA

R. E. Sherman has been a highly successful management consultant for nearly forty years. From 1984 to 1991, he was a principal at PriceWaterhouseCoopers, the world's largest accounting and consulting firm. He has written several professional papers, two of which won national prizes. He has written seventy articles since 1986 in a major trade magazine.

For the past decade Mr. Sherman has worked with an Israeli physicist in examining claims about codes in the Hebrew Bible. He authored a book on their findings, *Bible Code Bombshell* (2005), which has sold 10,000 copies. He lives in a vibrant, eclectic college town, which is home to a large number of Buddhists, Jews, and Christians. He is a follower of Christ who respects and appreciates sincere followers of other major religions. He has many Buddhist and Jewish friends. He has been a serious student of the Bible for the past thirty-nine years. In this book he has tried to present each religion objectively and (whenever possible) positively, honoring the literal claims of its followers.

Mr. Sherman has been married for thirty-five years. He and his wife have two adult children who share his beliefs and seek to practice their faith. His daughter has been actively engaged in helping homeless children in a major U.S. city.

He graduated from the University of California at San Diego with a B.A. and an M.A. in Mathematics. He also passed three qualifying exams for a Ph.D. in Mathematics before deciding to pursue a career as an actuary. He is a Member of the American Academy of Actuaries and a Fellow of the Casualty Actuarial Society. He has served as an expert witness in numerous major lawsuits. That experience helped him to improve his skills in assessing the quality of evidence presented in support of different positions.

8796543R0

Made in the USA
Charleston, SC
15 July 2011